Home on the Canal

The Maryland Paperback Bookshelf

Publisher's Note

Works published as part of the Maryland Paperback Bookshelf are, we like to think, books that are classics of a kind. While some social attitudes have changed and knowledge of our surroundings has increased, we believe that the value of these books as literature, as history, and as timeless perspectives on our region remains undiminished.

HOME ON THE CANAL

Elizabeth Kytle

The Johns Hopkins University Press
Baltimore and London

Originally published by Seven Locks Press, 1983
Maryland Paperback Bookshelf edition, 1996
05 04 03 02 01 00 99 98 97 96   5 4 3 2 1

The Johns Hopkins University Press
2715 North Charles Street
Baltimore, Maryland 21218-4319
The Johns Hopkins Press Ltd., London

Library of Congress Cataloging-in-Publication Data will be found
at the end of this book.

A catalog record for this book is available from the British Library.

ISBN 0-8018-5328-1 (pbk.)

To the memory of the unsung:
the laborers, mostly Irish, who dug and blasted the canal;
the masons who glorified it with their stonework;
and the horses and mules
without which it could not have
been built or operated.

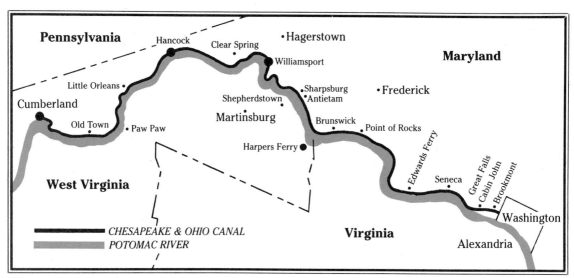

Chesapeake & Ohio Canal,
184.5 miles.

Contents

PART II.

THE HARD GOOD LIFE

Recalled by

Acknowledgments

Among the works I consulted in preparing the history, *The Great National Project* by Walter Sanderlin must have special mention because it is the only one that was indispensable. I cannot conceive of a short history of the canal written at this time that would not draw heavily on Sanderlin's one-of-its-kind, carefully documented, comprehensive account. I avoided publications that were undocumented or lacked lists of sources.

My warm and particular thanks go to William E. Davies for his generosity in reading the manuscript and for giving help in the form of technical interpretation. A recognized authority on the canal and the canal company, Mr. Davies is preparing definitive histories of both.

Mr. Melvin I. Kaplan made a substantial and much appreciated contribution by putting me in touch with three of the men featured in the reminiscences and by furnishing some material.

The men and women whose recollections comprise the second part of the book gave freely of their time and thought as they "took a right good stare," as one put it, back at their years on the canal. Among these canal veterans I especially thank Mr. J. P. Mose, who took a keen interest in this project from its early beginning. He sustained this interest as time passed; he referred me to other canal people for interview; he voluntarily brought me authenticated material; and, as afterthoughts, enlivening details on the canal and the lives that were lived on it. He and his brother, Mr. Lester M. Mose, Sr., had the idea of contributing the list they made from memory of canal boats and their captains. The names on this list are names to be remembered by any who are interested in the canal and the life on it. Mr. Lester Mose is the only surviving captain.

Mr. Robert Greenberg, whose interest in the canal far predates my own, has my thanks—because when we imagined a book something like this one and I said, "*Some*body *ought* to do it!", he said, "Would you?"

E.K.

NOTE: Places in this text described as being in West Virginia—for example, Harpers Ferry—were, of course, in Virginia prior to 1862.

Author's Note

I have used no reminiscences except those I collected. Purists may regard them (Part Two) as tainted because they have been extensively edited. I feel that they are valid and improved (and so do the respondents who had opportunity to comment before publication) because, while I did not consider as sacred every syllable that fell from lips, I handled the spoken words with the highest respect.

I do not imagine that anyone, with the possible exception of Adlai Stevenson, ever spoke extemporaneously in such a way that every word was valuable and contributed to a readable whole. The reminiscences were delivered in a standing jump, so to speak, without preparation of any kind and by people not trained for or practiced in speaking for lengthy direct quotation. So, for the sake of our old friends unity, emphasis, and coherence, I have freely rearranged the long quotations that make up the recollections. To avoid excessive repetition from one to another with a common experience, I have taken out much; I have put in nothing. In short, I have transformed what came off the tapes and out of untaped conversations; but I have done this in such a way that everything attributed to the respondents is in their very words.

Elizabeth Kytle
Cabin John, Md.
September, 1982

Not failure, but low aim, is crime.
—James Russell Lowell

So in each action 'tis success
That gives it all its comeliness.
—William Somerville

Home on the Canal
Part One
An Informal History

Introduction

THE CHESAPEAKE and Ohio Canal has been described as one of this country's loveliest failures. Lovely it surely must have been. Too many who lived and worked on it remember it this way for that to be quirky or merely nostalgic, and objective observers have called it the country's prettiest. Failure it surely was, almost as if some bad fairy had been hovering about when President John Quincy Adams toilsomely turned the first spadeful of earth to begin its construction. For one thing, the Baltimore and Ohio Railroad, which was to harass and eventually take a big part in killing the canal, was begun on the same day. That day was July 4, 1828.

The canal's pastoral beauty rested, as does so much that is beautiful or pleasurable—rich glossy fur coats, white-columned ante-bellum houses with sweet rivers flowing past, the lingering quality of perfumes—on a matrix that was grim. The canal was dug and the masonry built largely by immigrants fetched for the purpose, and their lot was lamentable. Many were cheated of their wages by contractors; all performed pulverizingly hard labor, using man- and mule-power and outlandishly inadequate equipment; all endured intolerable living conditions; and there was mass death by cholera.

Out of this literal and figurative muck and mire there emerged a waterway that was goodlooking, functional, and exalted by stonework of conspicious excellence. That any part of the masonry is standing is at least a partial triumph over time, vandalism, weather, and the sure ravages of disuse and lack of maintenance. The meager remains illustrate the truism that even the ruins of beauty can be beautiful.

The
Shortest Route West:
George Washington dreamt here.

TO COMPLETE THE FATHERHOOD of his country by serving as its first president, George Washington set aside a major concern. This concern, to which he returned after his presidency, made him also the father of the Potomac Company, the direct ancestor of the Chesapeake and Ohio Canal Company.

In 1754, only 22 years old but already Virginia's hero,[1] Washington had pondered on the idea of a canal to skirt the tumultuous and impassable Great Falls of the Potomac. This was as bold an attitude as that of the man "who first eat [*sic*] an oyster," as at that time there was no such thing as a canal in America and the great canal age had not begun in the British Isles.

Canals had, however, captivated builders and traders since ages past. As far back as 600 B.C., the pharoah Necho undertook to connect the Nile with the Red Sea by a canal, a forerunner of the Suez. Darius of Persia continued work on this early effort and Ptolemy II eventually finished it.

The Romans promoted similar projects. While their vocabulary of canal terms has not been lent to the English language, one made the transition and is still in use. It is *piede liprando* or *aliprando,* the terms for the width of a canal at water level, which width is never allowed to be obstructed in any way or in any circumstances.

From their earliest history canals developed from river navigation when railroads were nonexistent and roads unequal to a felt need. Initial stirrings of what became the canal age in

America in the 19th century began in England with one Henry Briggs, who lived from 1561 to 1630. Looking at a map of his country one day, he took note of a place where the Rivers Thames and Avon were only about three miles apart. He "getts a horse and viewes it" and finds that there is "levell ground... easy to be digged," and that "a marriage between those Rivers would be of great consequence for cheape and safe carrying of goods between London and Bristow" even "though the boates goe slowly and with meanders."

Every one of the earliest canals ran on a "levell," for it was not until the invention of the lift lock, which moved boats between water levels, that inland navigation, such as Washington wanted, could be developed. The ordinary pound lock (for impounding water in an enclosure) is said to have been invented by the Chinese Chhiao Wei-Yo A.D. 983. It had vertically rising gates. Other locks with vertically rising gates are known to have been used in the Netherlands in the 11th century, in Flanders and Italy in the 12th, and near Bruges in the 14th. Around 1485 Leonardo da Vinci invented the simply designed swinging miter-gate. By 1600 this type of lock gate was in use all over Europe. It was used in the Chesapeake and Ohio Canal and is still used in small waterways.

IN COLONIAL AMERICA, tobacco planters turned their thoughts canalwards as they saw coming events casting their shadows before them. A chain of adverse circumstances was threatening to disrupt their entire design for living.[2]

For one thing, overproduction of their one cash crop, combined with the dwindling of European markets for the sot weed, began to deal them a heavy double blow. For another, there was the blighting effect of England's Navigation Acts. Smuggling and other elusive tactics neutralized the first and second of these, but the third, effective in 1673, weighed directly on the colonies and was more difficult to thwart. This one imposed on the colonists, right in their own backyards, a substantial number of English tax collectors, a development the Americans found pungently distasteful.

The pernicious factor system aggravated the planters' troubles. English agents of English commercial houses brought ships every year to each planter's very doorstep, his wharf. Through these factors, the planters did what those in colonies, including the colony that was the South after the Civil War, always have done: they sold raw materials cheap and bought manufactured goods dear. Wines, plate, fabrics, furniture were often bought on note, and this was not uncommonly as near-ruinous as today's charge account can be. The factors made a profit on every transaction, and they set both the prices at which the Virginians' tobacco was sold and the prices of goods charged to their accounts. The factors were on Easy Street, and, for all their London boots and silver and solid mahogany, many planters were bogged down in a white-collar version of owing their souls to the company store.

Besides all this, the transoceanic shipping business underwent changes that worked hardship on the planters. As vessels became larger, they followed organized routes and did their business at established ports of call. Stops at each and every planter's wharf were inconvenient and economically infeasible.

Tobacco seemed to be bound up with everything. In the early 1600s tobacco saved Virginia, but by the early 1700s it was destroying the plantations; two or three successive crops reduced the richest of soil from earth to dirt. During the same 1700s the European market deteriorated further. More than ever, Virginians longed for linkage with the West and its cornucopia of opportunities.

Exhaustion of the acres by tobacco and a passion for acquisition of land carried some colonists farther and farther west. Beyond the Alleghenies were both settlers and traders, markets for buyers and sellers. Roads were so bad, however, that it was less arduous to travel roundaboutly for several hundred miles by river and sea than overland for 50 miles. Unlike most American rivers, the Potomac is an east-west river. On the map it is the shortest route from tidewater to the West. To a degree, for much of the eighteenth century, it served as a two-way conduit for furs, textiles, firearms, agricultural produce, livestock,

7

and trinkets for Indian traders, but it was not sufficiently navigable to meet the needs of the East. As the transmontane trade increased, and as it was seen that it could be increased greatly, more and more thought was given to the problem of how to establish a fully efficient route to the West.

In 1748 eastern seaboard planters organized the Ohio Company to settle land and develop the potential for fur trade in and over the Allegheny Mountains. The Washington family, represented by Augustine and his sons Lawrence and 16-year-old George, owned shares in the new enterprise. Although the company became a casualty of the Revolution, it represented the first step on a path that eventually led to the construction of the waterway affectionately, sometimes crossly, spoken of by its friends as well as detractors as "the old ditch." In neither case was the term to be taken seriously. Nothing 184.5 miles long and six feet deep is a ditch.

It was a long time before the idea of a continuous canal took shape. In Washington's day the thought was in terms of river improvement. This included digging out the channel, removing boulders, and building short skirting canals around the river's worst obstacles to navigation. In 1774, as a member of the House of Burgesses, Washington had introduced a bill for improving navigation on the Potomac in primarily these ways. He was successful in getting approval of the Burgesses for a company to improve the river and charge tolls, its goal being the opening of a trade route to what was then called the Ohio country. An expert woodsman, Washington had made several journeys through the wilderness, had gone to the heads of the Potomac and the James Rivers, and his observations reinforced his earlier judgment that a water route to Ohio was well within the realm of possibility.

All this could come to naught, however, without the approval of Maryland, which also abutted on the Potomac. Fearing that their city would be left out in the cold, Baltimore businessmen set themselves against the plan and the state withheld its approval.

At the close of the Revolution in 1783, Washington went home to his beloved Mount Vernon and lost no time in resuming activities promoting river improvement by means of an inland waterway. He made river-study trips, accompanied on many of them by John Fitzgerald, who had been one of his aides during the Revolution. He also initiated a flourishing correspondence with many people, including Thomas Jefferson. It was Jefferson's view that if Virginia did not move quickly on the canal project New York might well build a canal and monopolize the western trade. In agreement, Washington concentrated on lobbying for legislation to open the way to the West. He wrote letters steadily and held forth with such enthusiasm that it was said he often continued long after his hearers had wearied of statistics about the proposed canal and would have welcomed a change of subject.

The Virginia legislature's approval of a stock company that would address itself to river improvement was a matter of record, but Maryland's necessary approval was still lacking. Times had changed, however, since the Baltimore merchants had been able to stick a spoke in Washington's wheel. The Revolution's hero was not eulogized as first-in-war first-in-peace until his death, but at the end of the war he held a commanding position in the public regard. This time the Baltimore opposition was overridden right handily. The Potomac Company was chartered by both states in 1784 and, not astonishingly, Washington was elected president.

The company began operating on May 17, 1785. Washington plunged into the venture with such vigor that James Madison said it was "hardly to be described, and shows that a mind like his, capable of great views and which has long been occupied with them, cannot bear a vacancy."

It was first thought, by Washington as well as others, that a European would have to be engaged to design the necessary locks for the canal to skirt the Great Falls. But then Washington thought of James Rumsey of Shepherdstown, West Virginia, who had kindled his imagination the year before with accounts of experiments in steam navigation. Rumsey was not specifically qualified to design and build canals, but neither was anybody else in the country and Rumsey had a fine reputation as inventor and engineer. The Potomac Company resigned itself to "local talent of doubtful quality" and put him in charge of its audacious undertaking.

Rumsey and the other "local talent of doubtful quality" succeeding him produced five skirting canals. All five canals worked and one was an extraordinary engineering feat. Things went sour for Rumsey in 1786, after rather a brief stint on what must have been a tremendously exciting project for him. He quarreled with his assistant, Richardson Stewart, and finally brought formal and grave charges against him. These ten counts included incapacity, want of truth and candor, cruelty to servants, and allowing his men to terrorize the country people. The charges were not proven, but Rumsey felt so strongly about them that he resigned. Following Rumsey in rapid succession were Stewart, James Smith, Captain Christopher Myers, Leonard Harbaugh, Thomas Leoffler, and in 1802 Harbaugh again. By good chance, George Gilpin, a company director, had some engineering skills and did considerable supervising as the work progressed. He also surveyed the river from end to end.

Despite all the chopping and changing, work proceeded apace. The company pushed forward at all five falls that had to be bypassed, and by 1792 three canals not requiring locks had been completed. These were the ones around the uppermost rapids: House's Falls near Harpers Ferry, West Virginia; Payne's Falls of the Shenandoah; and Seneca Falls, at Seneca, Maryland. Work at Little Falls was more difficult, and that at Great Falls formidable.

At Little Falls the main drawback was lack of adequate labor. To save time, wooden locks never meant to be permanent were built. They were finished in 1795.

At Great Falls the river drops 76 feet in 1,200 yards, and rocks and rapids make it impassable. In addition there are perfectly vertical stone cliffs just below the falls and on to the river's edge, rising to heights of 30 to 40 feet. Work had been well under way when it came as a nasty surprise to Rumsey that the place where the canal's return to the river would have to be cut through was solid gneiss, a metamorphosed rock corresponding in composition to granite. Company, engineers, and laborers showed their mettle in the fashion commented on later by the ubiquitous Mrs. Trollope.[3] "There is no point in the national character of the Americans," she wrote, "which commands so much respect as the boldness with which public works are undertaken and carried through. Nothing stops them if a profitable result can be fairly hoped for."

The cliffs at Great Falls made the return of the canal to the river expensive, tremendously difficult, and dangerous. With black powder—which, properly handled, does not produce the shattering action of later developed high explosives—the laborers blasted a 200-foot passage through the granite-hard bluff. The walls of the chasm produced by this ticklish blasting operation are smooth and straight. Iron hooks, which were aids to boatmen, and holes, drilled for blasting but not used when final-decision time came, can still be seen in one wall of the stone gorge.

Payroll of the Potomac Company, with the verifying signatures of George Washington, John Fitzgerald, and George Gilpin. Fitzgerald was one of Washington's aides during the Revolution and their association carried over into private life. Together, the two made a series of river-study trips before the company was formed. Gilpin, one of the company directors, had earlier made an end-to-end survey of the Potomac.

Of the five stone locks required for the Great Falls canal, Locks 4 and 5 were placed in the gorge, each lock 12 feet wide and 47 feet deep. Passing through the 200-foot gorge, boats moved up or down 36 feet. Lock 3 had a zigzag to allow boats to turn into and out of the gorge. Remains of these locks, including the unusual Lock 3, are still visible.

Before he took office as president, Washington's abiding interest in the canal drew him to the work site on frequent inspection tours, even in cold and foul weather. Sadly, he did not live to see his brainchild materialize into one of the engineering triumphs of the century. He died in 1799, three years before the five skirting canals were substantially completed. While hardly accomplishing what he had hoped for, the canals did make possible a certain amount of trade.[4] For 26 years gondolas and sharpers made the trip from western Maryland to Georgetown, carrying furs, grain, lumber, flour, and, less often, mountain whiskey.

Trips on gondolas and sharpers were not for the fainthearted or for unskilled rivermen. The craft were tossed and buffeted by a river of strong currents, menaced by rapids and whirlpools and concealed rocks, and many gondolas did not last long enough to reach Georgetown.

The gondolas were one-shot affairs at best. These log rafts, 60 by 10 feet, were themselves heavy and capable of supporting many tons of cargo; but they were so insecurely slapped together that they would have broken up like fragile cockleshells if subjected to the roughness of the river in attempts to pole them upstream on return trips. Their owners sold both cargo and rafts on arrival in Georgetown, where the logs were sawed into lumber, and made their trips home on foot.

Sharpers were boats about 60 feet long by 7 feet wide, flat-bottomed and pointed at the ends. They too were propelled by poles pushed against the bottom of the river. The sharpers saw little use, as they were unable to get through the shallows left when the spring floods slackened. It was thanks only to floods that navigation was possible ever and that for not more than 45 days a year. It was impossible to deliver cargoes on any kind of schedule, users lost business, and the company lost the tolls it had counted on.

Meanwhile, commercial and political interests were seeking to make overland travel to the Ohio territory a less formidable, less bone-shocking, undertaking. In 1806 Congress authorized construction of the National Road, which was to run from Cumberland up the Potomac westward over the mountains to Red Stone Creek on the Monongahela, following roughly the path carved out by the Ohio Company years earlier.[5] But to connect the prospering city of Baltimore with this potentially profitable artery, it was necessary to produce, by improvement and new construction, a network of pikes, the first 20 miles of which were opened to traffic as early as 1807. The National Road, begun in 1811, was finished in 1818 when it reached the Ohio border at Wheeling, West Virginia, 131 miles west of Cumberland. The connection of Baltimore to Cumberland, however, was not completed until 1821. A 40-mile tie-in to the National Road, from the west end of the Conococheague Creek Bridge to Cumberland, was begun but made only creeping progress, largely for lack of money. The work languished until the Maryland legislature concocted an inventive scheme to finance it, a scheme that could have made Maryland bankers feel a fresh sympathy for Canute Christians:* by act of the legislature, the state's banks could get their charters renewed only if they invested in the highway. The road was aptly called the Bank Road, and a marker was put up proclaiming that the banks of Maryland had paid for it by purchase of stock.

For some years the National Road and its connecting turnpikes promised to be one of the nineteenth century's more successful enterprises. The road itself was a marvel for its time—a cleared strip 66 feet wide with a leveled roadbed 30 feet wide. The brand-new macadamizing process[6] was used for part of its

*Canute Christians were those who, to save their lives, at least went through the motions of embracing their sovereign's religion. Canute (c. 995–1035), king of Norway, Denmark, and England, practiced "forcible conversion" to Christianity. He converted his subjects in droves when he offered them a choice between on-the-spot baptism or on-the-spot death. Or so the story goes.

surface, and its grades and curves were so beautifully moderate that many remained as the road was changed and improved over the years. It had a slight crown, a drainage ditch on each side, and other niceties. To any family venturing to load a few belongings onto a Conestoga wagon and head for the West, such a road was traveler's bliss. Freighters felt much the same way about it. It so increased western trade that there was a period during which Baltimore outclassed Philadelphia and was second only to New York. One local newspaper reported that "a gentleman traveling 35 miles on the road between Baltimore and Frederick met or passed 235 wagons. . . nearly seven for every mile."

At no time, however, did this heavy overland traffic present a threat to the Potomac Company. Even the splendid National Road could accommodate only wagons, and transportation of freight by wagons had already been shown to be more expensive than by water.* As late as 1822, the ratio of costs was estimated to be as high as 8 to 1 in favor of water transportation.

What *was* a threat, one that Potomac Company directors understandably failed to identify, was a cloud no larger than a man's hand. This was a newfangled thing called a locomotive engine, then in an experimental stage in Baltimore. In time, a railroad, together with the C&O Canal, would demote the Cumberland Road from the standing of national highway to ordinary country road, and a railroad would be the downfall of the C&O. But in the early 1800s locomotives had shown an ability to draw a string of cars on rails only if they ran on level ground. Noting the little there was of level ground between Cumberland and Baltimore, directors of the Potomac Company put their minds on more urgent matters.

The most urgent matter was money. The company had approached financial exhaustion while the canal at Great Falls was under construction, and had turned its attention to fund raising. By special permission from Maryland and Virginia, the company began to collect tolls on river use as if the locks at Great

*One reason was that even through dead water a horse could drag 50 times as much weight as on dry land.

14

Falls existed and were in use. Income from this irregular but legal measure fell pitifully short of what was needed. In 1799, when the company was at the point of failure, the State of Maryland bailed it out, enabling it to finish the Great Falls canal.

This completed the group of five canals and allowed the company to direct its efforts elsewhere. It began an ill-starred attempt to improve the major branches of the Potomac, which consumed the company's means and brought in no appreciable returns. Although the company strained every nerve to complete the proposed river improvements, its affairs took a downward turn from which they never recovered. It pled with Virginia and Maryland legislatures for more money, but, for all the good this did, it might as well have been pleading for a dragon to protect the river from droughts and floods. A new stock issue was offered for sale but found no takers. A joint commission representing Maryland and Virginia found the company deep in debt and "likely to remain so," counseled against further aid, and recommended "a more effectual means of improving the navigation of the Potomac." The company borrowed from banks and ran a lottery. Nothing worked.

The failure of the lottery dashed the company's hopes once and for all. Debts piled up until the profit from operation of the canals was not even enough to pay interest on them. By 1822 the company was moribund. Although it dragged on until 1828, its significance was a thing of the past.

[1] Washington was painfully aware that he had been thrust into a position far beyond his youthful abilities, and he made mistakes in the French and Indian War. He served bravely but he was not a brilliant success. Nonetheless, he came out of the war as Virginia's favorite son.

[2] When tobacco made its appearance in Jamestown, the colony was in "the last stage of wretchedness" and nothing was standing between the surviving settlers and failure but their stubborn refusal to give up. Ten years later the place was in bloom, comparatively speaking. Tobacco had met Virginia's need for a money-making crop and for a system of landholding that was inviting to immigrants. It was futile for King James to point out that "the black stinking fume

thereof" was "dangerous to the Lungs." Tobacco planting was a mad success and the colonials determinedly planted more and more of it—even when they weren't growing enough foodstuffs to maintain themselves—and Englishmen determinedly bought it.

It is a hard thing, and a queer thing too, that the product that saved America's first settlement has killed and is continuing to kill Americans. A contemporary resident of Virginia stood one day beside the pathetic remains of the foundations of a tiny Jamestown house and, perhaps to cover emotions evoked by the ambient air, said, "Just think. Here we gave lung cancer to the world!"

[3] Frances Milton Trollope, English novelist, spiritualist, bazaar keeper, travel writer, and mother of Anthony Trollope. She of the sharp eyes and sharper tongue is best known in the U.S. for the scalding commentary in her book *Domestic Manners of the Americans,* published in 1832.

[4] The Indian name for the present city of Washington and its environs was Potawomecke, meaning trading place. Lord Baltimore's settlers transferred this name to the river. It is also said to mean river of swans.

[5] This road was first called the Cumberland Road because it was at Cumberland that the federal government began work on this connection of the East to newly opened areas beyond the Ohio River. The road came to be called Union Pike and, most commonly, the National Road.

In connection with the road's origins, the cliché "old Indian path" comes trippingly off many tongues. George R. Stewart laid *this* ghost to rest nearly 30 years ago in his book *U.S. 40,* but it still is called back. One Indian, young or old, who blazed a trail does not produce an "old Indian path" any more than Jamestown Road is the road to Jamestown, as some motorists between Williamsburg and Jamestown have lost their way by assuming.

The National Road's earliest beginnings were with the Ohio Company in the middle 1700s. In order to get its royal grant of land, the company had promised to build a fort and settle 200 families within seven years, and it imperatively needed a pack-horse trail. To investigate the possibilities, it sent out Christopher Gist and Thomas Cresap, experienced frontiersmen; and with them as guide went one Indian, Nemacolin, a Delaware chief. A few years later, in 1752, Gist and Nemacolin returned and hacked out a passage from Wills Creek (where Cumberland came to be) to Red Stone Creek on the Monongahela. No doubt they incorporated into the path parts of traders' trails and antique Indian paths; but for the most part they created a new way, rightly called Nemacolin's Path.

A year or so later, during the French and Indian War, Washington widened this narrow road to accommodate the army's supply wagons. Then it was no longer called for Nemacolin but for Washington. In 1755 General Braddock reworked it so that he could get his artillery over it. His officers widened it to 12 feet, relocated it as need arose, and pretty much made another road, called Braddock's Road.

The route of the National Road as we think of it followed the general lines of Nemacolin's, Washington's, and Braddock's roads, after which there was a good deal of relocation, and, again, an essentially new road, part of the present Route 40. Certain adjustments to the road as proposed had to be made in Pennsylvania. That state had not been represented by a road commissioner when the line was laid out, it would have to pay heavily in taxes for the road, it ran a chance of losing heavily, and the road as originally designed bypassed both county seats that were near it. Raising what seems only a mild objection to such, Pennsylvania approved the road but with the proviso that any road built within its borders pass through Uniontown and Washington. This modest requirement added 20 miles to the

16

road, bringing it to its total of 131 miles.

The National Road was but one of many impressive projects labored on by gangs predominantly Irish. A Pennsylvania farmer watched it taking shape between Braddock's Grove and Uniontown, and was lost in admiration. He wrote of "that great contractor, Mordecai Cochran" and his "immortal Irish brigade, a thousand strong, with their carts, wheelbarrows, picks, shovels and blasting tools, grading the commons and climbing the mountainside . . . leaving behind them a roadway good enough for an emperor to travel over."

[6] Later, roads called macadam roads were kept in condition by periodic surface dressings of tar or asphalt and chippings. The original road designed by Scotland's John Loudon MacAdam, of which the National Road was an example, allowed of no binding material whatever, not even large stones or loose earth. The slight convexity of the National Road was a MacAdam shape and its drainage ditches were part of his design. His road was made of a one-foot-deep layer of small broken stones (in the National Road 12 to 18 inches deep), in shape as nearly cubical as possible, able to pass through a ring $2\frac{1}{2}$ inches in diameter but too large to pass through a 2-inch ring. Vehicle wheels ground the stones together and the dust this produced gradually filled the spaces between them. The great value of the macadam road was that it was not cut to pieces, as the oldtime roads had been, by the narrow, sharp wheels of wagons.

The Route West

Planning:
"A hundred miles in five years."

USUALLY THERE IS A BLURRING of demarcation lines where change has taken place, and there was a certain overlap in the decline and fall of the old Potomac Company and the emergence of the Chesapeake and Ohio Canal Company.

In 1822, with the Potomac Company tottery but existing, the Committee on the District of Columbia informed the Congress that it would be practical to connect Washington with the West by a canal. This report, made in response to numerous petitions for river improvement, can be considered the origin of the Chesapeake and Ohio Canal.

The report's release was both preceded and followed by efforts in Virginia, Maryland, and the District of Columbia to form a company. Canal conventions were held, with much surveying, estimating, inviting, accepting, and rejecting. It was at the Loudoun County, Virginia, convention, in the spring of 1823, that the proposed waterway was named the Chesapeake and Ohio, presumably because the State of Maryland had the authority to extend the work to the Chesapeake Bay. The preferred name was Union Canal, but it was discovered that this name had already been given to a short canal in Pennsylvania.

By this time it seemed clear that a canal would be the best way to move heavy freight to the West, even though Baltimore had been connected by highway to Wheeling on the Ohio since 1821. It was also clear that whatever happened with the canal project would depend on the United States government. One thing that happened was a plentiful loss of time. Construction was not begun until 1828, by which time the Erie Canal was acquitting itself more than creditably and the Pennsylvania Canal was under construction.

Much of the delay in forming the canal company came from differences of opinion on the legality of the federal government's sponsorship of internal improvements. President Monroe felt that a constitutional amendment would be necessary. Ironically, the contrary opinion was expressed by Secretary of War John C. Calhoun, then and now considered a strict constructionist. As had Albert Gallatin, secretary of the treasury under President Madison, Calhoun argued that no amendment was needed.*

There had been no cause for debate over the legality of the Cumberland Road, as a compact with Ohio when it entered the Union in 1803 obligated the federal government to build a road to her border. President Monroe did, however, veto a bill to collect tolls to furnish money for its repair, explaining that he could find nothing in the constitution to justify this. He favored a constitutional amendment that would allow the federal government to build major national works but assign jurisdiction and maintenance, as well as building of less ambitious improvements, to the states.

In November, 1823, the first Chesapeake and Ohio Canal convention was held in Washington. An impressive number of delegates, representing all the counties through which the proposed waterway was expected to pass, came from Virginia, Maryland, and Pennsylvania. Among them were Francis Scott Key and Bushrod Washington, George Washington's nephew.

By that time public opinion had risen in support of the Calhoun position on federal subsidization without necessity of constitu-

---

*Some of Calhoun's fellow Southerners regarded him as strict to the point of being hidebound. They still did in 1846 when he held that it would be unconstitutional for the federal government to accept a bequest from the English John Smithson for the establishment of what became the Smithsonian Institution in Washington. In the 1820s they complained that a federally sponsored canal and strict constitutional construction were two parallel lines that could never meet. Calhoun's position was that the constitution was not something to get cute or crafty with, but something to be construed with common sense.

tional amendment, and President Monroe had fallen in with it. In the month after the convention, he recommended that Congress approve the project if its members could reconcile federal funding with their view of the constitution. They could. The Chesapeake and Ohio Canal Company was chartered in a measure that the president signed on March 3, 1825, his last day in office.

The charter authorized the new company to accept subscriptions to finance a canal beginning at tidewater on the Potomac. The waterway was to run from the District of Columbia to Cumberland, Maryland, and from there across the Allegheny Mountains "to some convenient point of navigation on the waters of the Ohio or its tributary streams." The line of the canal was divided into two sections, the eastern, which was the tidewater-to-Cumberland one, and the western, which was to begin where the eastern ended and extend to the Ohio River.

The eastern section of the canal, Congress stipulated, had to be completed before the western section could be begun. The company was empowered to condemn whatever land it needed, and it was to be forever free from taxation. It was made obligatory, however, that within 5 years the company must have at least 100 miles of canal in use and in 12 years complete the entire project.

Early in 1825 the U.S. Board of Engineers, commissioned by Congress to survey the proposed route, stated in a preliminary report that such a canal would be practicable. But when the Engineers' full report came in the fall of the following year, it was unsettling. It repeated that the canal would be physically practicable, but estimated its cost at $22,000,000—nearly five times as much as the convention delegates had in mind. The large figure was the result of the federal government's insistence on a larger canal than originally proposed.

Delegates reassembled in Washington in December of 1826. It would have been pardonable for an onlooker to assume that they had come together again to seek solutions to the difficulties presented them. But he would have been wrong. This convention made it clear at once that it had reassembled to deny that difficulties existed and to show that the estimates of the U.S. Board of Internal Improvements were a tissue of errors.

Delegates scrutinized the Engineers' report, finding fault almost point by point, and delivered themselves of a thumping rejection. They claimed that "through a want of accurate local information" the U.S. Engineers "had been betrayed into great errors in their results, arising from the extravagance of the prices established as the basis of their estimates." They went into minute detail in what they considered proof that prices of labor, provisions, materials, excavations, embankments, masonry, "&c., &c." were all vastly overestimated and that the canal could be built for half as much as the Engineers had figured.* Shortly thereafter, the convention's estimates and those of the Engineers were considered and revised by experienced civil engineers James Geddes and Nathan S. Roberts. They estimated that the canal could be built from Georgetown to Cumberland for something close to $4,500,000.

This revived the sinking spirits of canal supporters, who had been crestfallen since the Engineers' report, and subscription books were opened. In May, 1828, Congress passed an act subscribing $1,000,000, bringing forth jubilant observations—a flag on City Hall in Washington, a "great illumination" and a banquet at Cumberland, and booming cannon in Washington and Georgetown. The City of Washington subscribed $1,000,000; Georgetown $250,000; Alexandria $250,000; Maryland $500,000. Tiny Shepherdstown, West Virginia, subscribed $20,000. Subscriptions by private citizens amounted to $600,000. Baltimore held itself huffily aloof—having found that its own dream of an arm of the canal from Point of Rocks to Baltimore, which would have put the main terminus of the canal in Baltimore, was out of the question for money reasons—and cast its lot with the railroad. Virginia cooled after learning that the canal would go up the Maryland side of the river all the way to Cumberland. In the end, Virginia

---

*Referring to this feat of denial and repression, James M. Coale, president of the canal company from August, 1843, to February, 1851, said to stockholders in 1851, "A body of men, however upright and intelligent, are easily satisfied of what they wish to believe."

backed out, contributed nothing, and itself built an aqueduct and canal to connect Alexandria with the Chesapeake and Ohio at Georgetown.

Meeting in Washington June 20–23, stockholders elected a board of six directors—two from Washington, one from Alexandria, one from Georgetown, and two from Maryland, representing collectively the three states that were parties to the charter, the three District cities, and the United States. It was the most illustrious board the company was ever to have. Elected president was the Hon. Charles Fenton Mercer, of Virginia, then a U.S. Representative. Mercer had been the moving spirit of the 1823 meeting in Leesburg (Loudoun County), at which the idea of a continuous canal to connect the Ohio and the Potomac was first advanced. Both in and out of Congress he had been unflagging in his efforts to get the company incorporated.

On the 25th of June, a three-man board of engineers was appointed to design and see to the construction of the canal. Benjamin Wright was named chief engineer, and the other two members of the board were Nathan S. Roberts and John Martineau. These three were specifically charged, "until their separate divisions shall be allotted to them," with examination of the route, location of the canal and its feeders, and preparation for construction by contract.

Wright had been chief engineer on the Erie Canal (completed in 1825) and from then throughout the canal mania he was everywhere. He was consulting engineer on the James River and Kanawha Canal and chief engineer on the Delaware and Hudson Canal. At the time of his appointment with the Chesapeake and Ohio, he was chief engineer of the Chesapeake and Delaware Canal. His associates were engineers of practical experience, the only kind in existence at the time."*

---

*Resident engineers (a residency was made up of a number of half-mile sections) appointed were Thomas F. Purcell, Virginia; Daniel Van Slyke, New York; Wilson M.C. Fairfax, Virginia; Erastus Hurd, Massachusetts; Alfred Cruger, New York. Some assistant engineers were H. Boye, Denmark; Charles Ellet, Jr., Pennsylvania; James Mears, Jr., New York; Charles Ward and R.G. Bowie, Maryland; Charles B. Fisk (later chief engineer), Connecticut.

Schools of engineering did not develop in the United States until the second half of the century. When Judge Wright became chief engineer of the Erie Canal project, his relevant qualifications consisted of having been a part-time surveyor. As for his fellow board members, Dr. John Martineau was a close associate of Wright's in New York, and Nathan S. Roberts, also of New York, was one of the makers of the survey of 1827. Their combined knowledge of hydraulics could have been blown away like a dandelion's spore ball.

But they were men of natural ability who were good at mathematics, had plenty of common sense and ingenuity, and that's what engineers were made of in those days. Learning by doing, these self-made practitioners produced impressive structures within a matter of only several years and gained richly deserved recognition as hydraulic engineers.

While Wright and James Geddes were accumulating their own store of competence and knowledge, they were attracting a group of young men who worked with them and learned from them. (One is too interesting to go altogether unmentioned, though the C&O was not one of his projects. Canvass White, working with Wright on the Erie Canal, solved so many problems that he stood out as an adept and was later considered a mechanical genius.) Roberts made a lasting and enviable reputation as designer-builder of the Erie's famous Lockport combines, the canal's most sensational component.* The combines, between Buffalo and Lockport, consist of a twin chain of five locks each, cut through the long and solid rock cliff of the Niagara River. These two sets of water terraces, standing as one, allowed boats to ascend and descend at the same time, passing side by side.

At the same time engineers were appointed, a system of rewards "for diligence and fidelity" was set up. Winning contractors were to receive prizes made of silver and decorated "with suitable devices" for best work of various categories completed on

---

*Engineers have rated other components superior to the combines, but the combines made up the flashiest integral part and for this reason are the most remembered.

time. For the best constructed lock on the first division of the canal, there would be a silver cup valued at $50; for the best constructed culvert, a silver medal, valued at $10; for the best portion of slope or vertical walling on a residency, "not less in quantity than 500 perches," a silver medal, valued at $20; for the neatest and best executed section on the first division, complete in all details of excavation, embankment, and walling, a silver medal, valued at $20; for the first section completed, a silver medal, valued at $20; for the greatest amount of common excavation done on any section in a month's time, a silver medal, valued at $10.

A contractor receiving a $50 silver cup would be getting a prize costing as much as two and a half months' pay for a stone mason who had helped build the award-winning lock. A $50 cup in 1828 was the equivalent of an over $5,000 prize in 1980, when the average rate of pay for a stone mason was $12.31 an hour or roughly $2,085 a month. For winners of medals who didn't fancy trophies in this form, the company offered to make equal-value substitution of silver articles of the contractors' choice.

The June, 1828, canal convention first decided on a canal 40 feet wide by 4 feet deep, the minimum size the charter allowed. After debate, the board of directors' final decision was for a canal measuring 60 feet wide at the surface of the water (the Roman *aliprando*), 6 feet deep, and 48 feet wide at the bottom.

The directors opted for the larger size, feeling that there would be advantages and very little additional cost. The most expensive part of the canal, the masonry, would remain unchanged by the increase in width and depth. The larger size would provide the company with saleable water power, although the water was not the company's to sell and this point was in dispute for a long time. The larger dimensions would also reduce water resistance to the equivalent of unimpeded sea navigation. These elements were important in the directors' thoughts of a future including steamboats, industries along the canal, and many years' use of the waterway.

"The dimensions of a canal, apart from considerations of water supply, are regulated by the size of the vessels which are to be its users." So the Encyclopedia Britannica tells us, and most would see this as only reasonable; but the dimensions of the Chesapeake and Ohio were set in a Never-Never-Landish fashion.[1] The dimensions were fixed arbitrarily and the size of the boats was ever after restricted by them. As it turned out, the canal was too small and its size proved to be a handicap. Had it been larger, it could have handled more tonnage and perhaps had some shadow of a chance to make a profit remotely proportionate to its cost.

The mules that powered the boats that carried the coal that made the canal go were not completely disregarded at the planning stage. The waterway was designed so that there was a two-mile-an-hour current going downstream. With the current, the mules had to pull no harder to move a loaded boat downstream than they did to pull an empty one back to Cumberland. Coming back, although moving against the current, the boats were "light" (empty) and the mules could pull them upstream without undue effort.

The downstream current, then, could have been a very fine thing for the mules. But it was too little too late. The mules needed consideration before the boats were ever in the canal. As it worked out, the worst abuse and damage suffered by the mules took place in Cumberland's loading basin where there was no current. It took brutal effort for mules to begin to even budge a more than 120-ton boat in still water. People were no different then from now, and there were drivers who were impatient and unfeeling. Overeager to get the trip behind them and the money in their pockets, they forced the animals into such violent straining at the starting point that spavined mules were a sad and too familiar sight on the canal. Much of this physical damage has been attributed to "bad handling." Some find it difficult to see how there could be such a thing as good handling when two large or three small mules had to move a many-tonned boat in still water in a confined space. Even so, there were some captains who managed and could take justifiable pride in the fact that their mules were not spavined.

It would seem both simple and easy enough to have kept plenty of starter mules at the basin to help the boats' teams get the boats into the canal. Teams made up of many mules could have moved the horrendous dead weights into the canal without suffering abuse or lifelong injury or both. No such method was ever used, however, and each boat was started by only its own team. The mules didn't die on the spot, and nobody in authority was moved to relieve their condition. And, like the Irish who dug the canal, the mules had no advocate and their fate did not loom large in the deliberations of company directors. As one latter day boatman pointed out, "Mules didn't cost much."

Planning included setting a date for groundbreaking: July 4, 1828. July 4 was a favorite date for important beginnings. The ceremonies were held at a U.S. powder magazine at the head

Mules made the Canal go. These were resting and savoring a bit of outdoor freedom and feeding at portable troughs while boats were unloaded at Cushwa's coal yard in Williamsport. Their plumpness suggests that they were (1) owned by the boatmen or (2) lucky in their off-season caretaker or (3) photographed in midsummer or later.

of the Little Falls, five miles west of Georgetown near the present day community of Brookmont, Md. This spot was chosen because of the charter's stipulation that the canal was to end at tidewater of the river in the District. The directors took this to mean the highest point of the tide, the foot of Little Falls.

Shortly after the groundbreaking, the company was to be torn with controversy as to the location of the eastern terminus of the canal. Although the directors had figured that Little Falls was the spot indicated by the charter, Washington City had another idea. It held that the canal should end where there were shipping facilities, and insisted that the city build a branch canal from the mouth of Tiber Creek, now Constitution Avenue, to the Eastern Branch (of the Potomac), now called Anacostia River. Washington City had a lot of weight to throw around if it chose to do so, and all concerned were sensitive to the fact that the company could not survive if Washington withheld payments on its large subscription to canal stock. Mr. Mercer proposed the mouth of the Tiber as a compromise between Little Falls and the Eastern Branch, and the stockholders agreed readily.

The main basin was to be at the mouth of Rock Creek, between Georgetown and Washington; but it was agreed that when Washington constructed a basin three feet above tide at the mouth of Tiber Creek the canal company would extend the canal to that point.

The groundbreaking proceeded as blithely as if all this dissension were not in the offing. As the canal was an early and great work of national improvement,* its beginning was a momentous occasion. Suitable plans were made for the ceremonies. Attending or taking part were the president of the United States, John Q. Adams; cabinet members; diplomats and other representatives of foreign countries present at the time in Washington. There was "a great concourse" of private citizens.

To the vivacious music of the Marine Band, dignitaries walked in procession through the streets of Georgetown to waiting river boats that carried them to Little Falls. At the powder magazine,

*The Erie Canal was a project of the State of New York.

27

the group formed a large circle in the center of which the groundbreaking took place.

President Adams, a longtime supporter of internal improvements in general and the canal in particular, made a speech, grasped the spade presented him by Mr. Mercer, and thrust it into the ground. The spade struck a root. Adams made two more tries, and succeeded after removing his coat. For this uncharacteristic informality he was roundly applauded by the crowd. The president allowed that the same sort of shirt-sleeved determination should mark the endeavors of the company to get the eastern section of the canal begun.

On that same bright July morning, 40 miles away in Baltimore, another prominent citizen was starring in another important ceremony. He was Charles Carroll, and the ceremony was the setting of the cornerstone for the Baltimore and Ohio Railroad. At the age of 90, Carroll was still an astute judge of business ventures. He was perceived by some as the richest man in the country, known by all as the sole surviving signer of the Declaration of Independence.

Laying of cornerstones was the prerogative of Masons, and Carroll was not a member of the order. But Carroll, who had emerged from retirement to become a director of the new railroad, did take spade in hand to turn the first clod of earth for the B&O Railroad. The ritual was taken up by members of Masonic lodges, and stonemasons completed it by setting the cornerstone, called The First Stone, that they and their fellows had given. However tiny the scraping given off by the setting of The First Stone, for the canal it was the sound of the axe.

The railroad began with a gaudy flourish. People had flocked to Baltimore from all around the countryside, and the city was teeming. Just those taking part in the parade made up a huge crowd. The parade included a swarm of floats, numerous bands, and companies of uniformed men. In what was frankly called a pretentious procession, there were, among others, representatives of the Society of the Cincinnati;[2] the president, directors, military and civil engineers of the railroad; a few veterans of the Revolutionary army; state legislators; countless visitors.

The floats were the contribution of the trade associations of Baltimore, and they were many—from the farmers and planters, gardeners, plough makers, millers, bakers, victuallers, brewers and distillers, tailors, blacksmiths and whitesmiths, weavers, dyers, stone cutters, glaziers, Windsor-chair makers, and more.

The concept of the railroad has been generally regarded as a sober, solid one, and the canal has been described as an almost romantic undertaking. This is too harsh an assessment of the canal and an overgenerous one of the railroad. H. Sinclair Drago observes in *Canal Days in America,* "Even when viewed from the advantage of hindsight, there does not appear to have been any reason to believe that in only a decade or two railroads would be offering a challenge that other forms of transportation could not meet." The railroad was a more adventurous undertaking than the canal. It was even reckless, and would be so remembered except that it succeeded.[3] The B&O began building its road without having the least assurance that its crude cars and engines would be able to maneuver on its crude tracks in the heavier snows and floods of the line's more northern reaches.

This respective success and failure was for the future to unfold, however, and the railroad's flamboyant groundbreaking did not mar the joyousness of the canal's more modest observation. After the ceremonies, President Adams and other dignitaries returned to the District, boating down the river in a festive atmosphere.

[1] When a newcomer joined Peter Pan and the lost boys, he was assigned to a tree that would be his personal connection between the boys' underground living quarters and the rest of Never-Never-Land. It was explained that when a tree didn't fit a new arrival, "Peter does some things to you" and then the *boy* fit the *tree.*

[2] Preparing to go home at the end of the Revolution, upset because unpaid, Washington's officers organized the Society of the Cincinnati, naming themselves for the early Roman hero who temporarily left his farm to go to war.

The Society was represented to Washington as a mutual aid association for the founding officers against the day when they might experience disabling financial reverses. Taking this at face value, he read the charter only superficially and readily agreed to be its president-general.

Later, a word from a friend who knew both Washington's proclivities and those of the new society prompted the General to scrutinize the charter. One wonders if as he read he was reminded that Lucius Quintius Cincinnatus had been not only a farmer-general but a confirmed enemy of the common people and had determinedly fought a proposed code of laws which would have been equally applicable to patricians and plebeians. Be that as it may, Washington disapproved of the passing on of membership by primogeniture, and he disapproved of the society's intent to enlarge itself by including civilians. He concluded that it was in reality a political society, a kind of organization he could not abide. He made his sentiments known and fell out with the group when it refused to be apolitical. He did not break with the Society, however, but retained membership and office throughout his life.

[3] Railroads were such an eye-widening novelty that there were jokes about the reception the unsophisticated gave them, such as:
"Why did you run so far right
    in front of that train?"
"I *knew* he'd catch me if I got over in
    that plowed-up field."
Around 1830 what is often thought of as the country's first railroad began running the 13 miles between Baltimore and Ellicott City. The first passenger train terminus, the Baltimore and Ohio Railroad Station at Ellicott City, is now a museum.

The Granite Railway of Quincy, Massachusetts, was actually the very first railroad in the country. It was an industrial railroad, carrying no passengers. The B&O early made use of mechanical innovations introduced by W. Gridley Brant of the Granite Railway.

Construction:
Twenty-two years and $14 million.

DURING JULY AND AUGUST, 1828, contracts were let for the 17 miles of the canal from Little Falls to Seneca and for the 34 sections above Little Falls which, despite many hindrances, engineers had laid out. Almost throughout the canal's construction, many small contracts were let simultaneously and work was going on at various sites up and down the line. It was only at the last minute that the finishing of the canal was put into the hands of one contractor.

The canal company had enormous difficulty getting together enough laborers. The Potomac Valley was almost entirely agricultural, and there was no labor pool of a size to draw from. Further, and probably more significant, canal-building jobs were spurned by birthright Americans. The *Boston Pilot* and other Irish-American newspapers cautioned Irish immigrants over and over not to take the hard and dangerous canal or railroad jobs, as this toil was "the ruin of thousands of our poor people" who were treated "like slaves."

Many immigrants, however, had no chance to receive these local warnings, as companies sent agents abroad to import their work forces. Agents operated mostly in Great Britain, and the laborers they drew in were, so to speak, signed, sealed, and delivered when they arrived on these shores. Casting a wide net, agents reached out beyond the laborers who were readily available, advertising in city newspapers and in the Catholic press in Ireland. It was not unusual for them to advertise for many more workers then they had any need of, as a means of attracting an excess of applicants and thus keeping wages low.

Immediately after the groundbreaking, Mercer placed advertisements in publications in Dublin, Cork, Belfast, and in Holland. Prospective employees were offered meat three times a day, plenty of bread and vegetables, "a reasonable allowance of whiskey," and from $8 to $12 a month in wages, $20 for masons.

The canal company's representative in Great Britain was Henry Richards, who had worked on the Erie and the Chesapeake and Delaware Canals. Himself a Welshman, he recruited suffering and restless Welsh, English, and Irish workers who had undergone the rigors of heightened cost of living combined with a deeply troubling degree of unemployment. As ever, a depressed economy held the opportunity for bargains for some segment of society. The way Mr. Mercer put it, writing to the American consul in Liverpool, the company's advertisements might have a powerful attraction "to those who, narrowed down in the circle of their enjoyments, have at this moment a year of scarcity presented to them."

Those who came could not have found their circle of enjoyments perceptibly broadened. The immigrants were indentured,* as they were required to sign very tough contracts in return for coming to the United States at what the company called its expense. The truth was that they came at their own expense. In effect, the company advanced them the price of their passage, and got from each of them four months' hard, not to say cruel and unusual, labor to pay back the cost.

In August, 1829, the first group of around 320 began its journey on the *Pioneer,* the *Julian,* and the *Boston.* Another group came later on the *Nimrod,* and the last, in October, on the *Shenandoah.*

Nobody can now say with how much or little hope the uprooted foreigners set out for America and the canal; but their illusions, if any, were tarnished and knocked to flinders on the

---

*The legal term indenture came from the format of a deed executed between two or more parties (two in the instance of an immigrant brought over by the canal company), a copy of which was provided to each party. The contract was written twice on the same sheet of paper divided by a toothed line called an indent. Copies were separated by cutting along this line.

ships that brought them. These people had undoubtedly become all too well accustomed to very plain fare at best, and could hardly have been picky eaters. Even so, they often found the daily rations of bread and meat, handed out once a day by overseers, too revolting to choke down. Ships' captains refused direct involvement, but many times suggested to the immigrants that they "take matters into [their] own hands." Whatever may have been meant by that, the overseers suffered nothing worse from the immigrants than outpourings of oral abuse.

When the foreigners reached this country, no lamp was lifted beside a golden door.[1] The company insisted that they be brought to Alexandria and Georgetown, as in other ports they might have been enticed away by other employers. And once here, there were mutual disaffections from the outset.

Some of the immigrants had refused to acknowledge indentures, and almost the first thing they saw in the new world was the inside of a jailhouse. Of those who went straight to work, their employers were pleased with some; they considered others worthless. Some laborers soon had grievances against individual contractors. Of that group, some sought redress in orderly ways. Others simply took French leave. Not that they had any place to go; they just went. Some of these were captured and imprisoned; others were taken back to the canal where many were racked by sickness. Still others streamed into Georgetown.

The importation of laborers had begun in August, 1829. By October many were starving on the streets of Georgetown and had to be taken in at the city poor house. During an influx of Puerto Ricans into the city of New York in the 1970s, the mayor pointed out that the resultant distress was not primarily a city problem but a national problem. Georgetown officials made such a statement in 1829. They held that the plight of immigrant indigents was not essentially a Georgetown problem but a condition the canal company had brought about and should take care of. Private citizens had their sensibilities outraged, both by what they saw with their own eyes and by what the immigrants reported, and they made vehement attacks on the canal company.

In that same October the company announced that it would no longer import indentured laborers. The reason given was that too many had run away without putting in the four months' labor to pay the company back for their crossing. The company said it would still hire men who could raise the price of their passage.

The vulnerable, displaced laborers performed back-breaking toil under spirit-breaking conditions, using the primitive tools available: axes, stump-pullers, plows and scrapers (drawn by horses), wagons, wheelbarrows. Their employers and supervisors had little regard for them, often referring to them as "the plagues."

"The newcomers were often idle and quarrelsome," wrote George Washington Ward, "and the laws of free America were found ill adapted to such conditions." The laws of free America did nothing to protect these defenseless men, free in name only, from unprincipled contractors. And, although much has been made of the excessive drinking and the general disorder the laborers generated, a writer for a Department of Interior publication, the *C&O Canal,* published when Harold Ickes was secretary, had the grace to imply that the generous allowance of whiskey may not have brought on so much brawling if there had been better living and working conditions.

Of the first group that came over, Richards wrote to his employers that he had carefully chosen them and that the Irish among them had "worked some time in England and amongst Englishmen and are good workmen and peacable [*sic*]." Masons and quarrymen came from England and Wales. Some of the immigrants were "small and young," but not so much so as to be thrown back. Richards felt that matters could be evened up by requiring them to serve longer than the others to buy their way out of indenture. He was at pains to send as few women and children as possible, and those few only from the families of workmen of exceptionally good reputation.

The main part of the labor force was made up of Irish and Germans. There was so much tension and antagonism between these groups that they were never assigned to the same crews,[2] and the Irish fought among themselves. There was such bad blood between Corkmen and Longfordmen, carrying over from longstanding animosity at home, that every pay day, with extra drinking and its loosening of inhibitions, saw serious fights. It is only fair to bear in mind that before whiskey became the precipitating factor, there had been constantly gnawing at the men the major causes of frustration and frayed tempers—the miseries of low pay (average, $10 a month), long hours, bad housing and worse food. As an old expression has it, the company's promises had been like pie crust: easily made and easily broken.

Lest the offer of a whiskey allowance,[3] one promise not immediately broken, be mistaken for a kindness or an indulgence, hear Mrs. Frances Trollope on the subject. Commenting on the "miserable lodgings" of these Irish workers, she went on to point out that the large allowance of whiskey was given "to stimulate them to harder, longer tasks and to enable them to stand the boiling heat." As Washington used to be officially designated a hardship post for foreign diplomats and their associates because of the enervating humid heat, it was a jolting change of climate for the Irish who came from a place where a week at a temperature of 82 is considered a debilitating heat wave.

Many of the contractors were Irish-American, but this didn't hold them back, any more than compatriotism had held back Henry Richards or the greedy anywhere in any time, in the exploitation of their fellows. And "Poor Paddy" was viciously exploited.

Some contractors deliberately sowed discord among their crews and then, when the laborers were fighting one another, used this as an excuse, of which the logic is not immediately discernible, for not paying their wages. Other predators legally fleeced them in the company stores. The diggers were often working knee-deep in water, and, aside from the wholesale slaughter of a cholera epidemic, there was much incapacitation and death from dysentary, tuberculosis, and accidents, all up and down the route the canal followed.

Somehow the 20 miles of canal between Seneca and Georgetown were completed in the summer of 1831. In addition to the troubles with the much-censured laborers, the canal company had had frequent difficulty in getting hydraulic lime for cement. Often the only lime to be had was of poor quality and insufficient at that. Work on the masonry was held up time after time.

THE C&O WAS TO BE a lateral canal, i.e., an artifical waterway built beside an unnavigable river from which it received its water. Countless times in the years to come there would be loud lamentations brought on by the closeness of the canal to the river. In accord with the plan for all sections, the Seneca-to-Georgetown section was put into use as soon as it was completed. Water was supplied first to the Seneca-to-Little Falls section by the feeder at Seneca. When the Little Falls-to-Georgetown segment was finished, it was watered by Dam No. 1 at Little Falls. Sections in the canal above the Seneca feeder could not be used until the next feeder was reached at Harpers Ferry, 12 miles above Point of Rocks.

But at Point of Rocks, 48 miles from Georgetown, work on the canal was brought to a halt, not to be resumed for almost four years. The Baltimore and Ohio Railroad, claiming right-of-way along the narrows, had got an injunction prohibiting canal construction in that area. So fully had the C&O believed this to be its rightful sphere, by inheritance from the old Potomac Company and by its own charter, that it had not seen any necessity to reinforce its claim but had simply gone about its business of building. The railroad, however, perhaps because it was consciously and deliberately in the wrong, had been extremely self-assertive. It had aggressively gathered land waivers in the narrowed valley where it knew very well that usurpation would provoke a head-on collision with the canal company. Its grab did indeed precipitate showdown time, and the canal and the railroad fought it out in the courts for four years.

The Potomac Valley narrows so much in this part of the disputed area that, as the canal and the railroad were following

the same path, they slammed into each other at Point of Rocks.*
Here the river and the bulging lower slope of Catoctin Mountain were separated by only a narrow strip of land. This strip
was not wide enough to allow presence of both canal and railroad. While each company clamorously claimed precedence,
the railroad, having positioned itself at the disputed spot, de-
manded something like squatters' rights.

The canal company was chartered earlier than the railroad
company, and it contended that its prior right was assured by
the location of the canal by the U.S. Board of Internal Improvements in 1826 and again by another survey and location in 1827.
The canal company felt morally certain that it had abundant
valid grounds for protest and accusation of wrongful encroach-
ment; but the legal question was whether the canal company's
rights, received from the Potomac Company, were still sound
or whether the B&O had acquired rights when it was chartered
by the State of Maryland.

The chancery court decided for the B&O, but in January, 1832,
the court of appeals in Annapolis ruled for the canal company.
The railroad was ordered not to take possession of or make use
of the land on the Maryland side of the river between Point of
Rocks and Harpers Ferry until the canal had been built along
this stretch. The loss of time, however, had been almost enough
to wreck the canal company. It did survive this wounding en-
counter and move ahead, thanks to courts of law; but in the
final outcome, as George Washington Ward wrote, "that higher
court of great natural and economic forces which must ever
determine the direction of material progress [had] answered in
favor of the railroad."

That answer was for eventually. Although the canal won a
technical victory, a tangled skein of circumstances had the train
and the boats running along cheek by jowl. The railroad was
not a neighborly neighbor. The engineers vented on the non-

*The entire disputed area was the 12 miles between Point of Rocks and Harpers
Ferry. In this space there were two other sites like that of Point of Rocks: Miller's
Narrows, between Weverton and Sandy Hook, and Maryland Heights, across from
Harpers Ferry.

Shrieking steam whistle was anti-C&O trainmen's habitual and displaced spiteful assault on the nerves of the non-combatant mules. Making its own comment of a vastly different nature, this excuse-my-dust picture was used for years by the B&O in its publicity. The extravagant jet of steam, which gives the train such speed and swagger and strut, appears to some photographers to have been airbrushed in.

combatant mules their animosity toward the boatmen, and habitually terrified the animals with earsplitting shrieks of their whistles. The nearness of the train was in itself quite terrifying enough, and it had been stipulated by the court that the B&O must build a tight board fence between the two works.

This "concern" of the canal company for the mules appears quite self-serving, as terrified mules might react in ways disruptive to the work and as the company was not noticeably concerned when the animals were not even half fed during the non-working winters. Nonetheless, there was this stipulation. The railroad found the fence "impractical" and, rather than comply with this requirement, it used horses for a time to pull its cars between Point of Rocks and Harpers Ferry. Late in 1836 this was renegotiated and the canal gave in to the railroad's steam operation. As ever, the mules had to tough it out as best they could.

By February, 1832, at which time the canal company was legally free to get on with its construction, it was bankrupt. Funds had to be raised before the slightest degree of further work could be begun. Before it got into quite such dire straits, the company had tried to persuade the federal government to keep up its support. This was vital, as it was this support that brought the canal as far as Point of Rocks. Continuation of support was denied, and the company pinned its hopes on the State of Maryland.

Maryland, interested in developing her western counties, had always had a keen interest in internal improvements. The state was not enthusiastic, however, about singlehandedly taking on the completion of the canal to Cumberland. When Maryland realized that there was no longer any hope of the federal government's continuing support, the state set about raising money to protect its earlier investment. In 1834 the General Assembly authorized a loan of $2,000,000 to the canal company.

Back in January, 1832, immediately after the court's favorable decision on the canal company's right-of-way from Point of Rocks to Cumberland, the company had asked for bids on contracts for the waterway as far as Williamsport. The winter was so harsh, however, that all work above Harpers Ferry had to be postponed.

As shown in the company's annual report, proceedings of the directors, and correspondence among members of the board, renewed construction was accompanied by the same tribulations as those of earlier years. Supplies of rock and cement were insufficient and work on masonry lagged; some contractors absconded; cost of land continued to be high and difficult to meet.

One owner of land needed by the canal happened to be an implacable enemy of the project, and he doggedly hung on to his property. When it was condemned he was awarded high damages, which set a precedent. Other landowners sat up and took notice and promptly raised their prices. Even former friends of the canal leaped to cash in on this situation. Things got so bad that the directors even considered approaching Virginia landowners in order to shift the canal to their side of the river. This idea was entertained in the vain hope that to do so would bring down prices of Maryland land that they really wanted.

The B&O, continuing to fight after its defeat in the courts, kept up its agitation in the Maryland legislature and simultaneously carried on a harassing campaign of nuisance activities to hold back canal construction. Petitions, some only endorsed by the railroad company and some originating with it, were circulated to force the canal company to build wharves at Point of Rocks as transfer facilities for the Baltimore trade. Other such petitions were aimed at forcing the canal company to build bridges over the waterway—and it was well known that cross-canal bridges were an abomination to the company—for the convenience of Maryland farmers in gaining access to the river. It is not to be believed that the railroad was an innocent bystander in the singular performance of one Caspar Wever when he journeyed to Annapolis to try to halt canal construction on his land until he was paid to the last penny. There were additional instances of the railroad's sniping.

It was soon painfully obvious that Maryland's $2,000,000 would fall far short of what was needed to get the canal to Cumberland, and the company appealed to the state again. And again Maryland came to its aid. The state subscribed $125,000 in 1834, made the already appropriated $2,000,000 loan the next year, and bought $3,000,000 worth of stock in 1836. All this put the state in tacit control of the company.

THE YEAR 1832 was catastrophic. It began with what later dwindled into nothing but at the time seemed important. This was an ill-considered experiment with prohibition, as unsuccessful as that enacted into national law in the 1920s.

The wildly mistaken notion was that a dry work force would make use of time formerly lost by drinking and disorderly conduct. The laborers' contracts included provisions against distribution of whiskey—which hardly squared with labor recruiting ads that had promised "a reasonable allowance of whiskey"—but these provisions had not been previously invoked. The rule banning liquor was difficult to enforce and, as prohibition only increased drunkenness, it was soon rescinded.

Drunkenness was not to be wondered at. Along with Hardy's Tess, the toiling canal laborers, with a pitiless present and a future promising nothing, still had "the irresistible, universal, automatic tendency to find sweet pleasure *some*where [italics mine], which pervades all life, from the meanest to the highest. . . ." It seems glaringly obvious that whiskey was their sole source of even fleeting relief from the wretched circumstances in which they existed.

One engineer reported that when the men were denied liquor during the working day they drank at night. In his opinion, the same amount of whiskey that they drank at night, had it been stretched out over the day in nips, would have had but small undesirable effect. Gulped at night, however, by men who must have been tired to the marrow of their bones, it quickly made them either fighting drunk or falling-down drunk. Many a morning found some of them lying where they had dropped in their tracks, unable to do a lick of work. The company discarded the attempt at prohibition and gave out that it was doing so because alcohol would be beneficial as a preventive in the approaching sickly season.

In the Potomac Valley there was every year a genuine sickly season, with ailments thought later to have been air-borne and water-borne, lasting July through September. At its approach, many contractors and company officials as well as laborers customarily decamped, regarding absence as the best preventive. In 1832 the canal company hired a doctor to recommend health practices for all at work sites and to prescribe for those who were sick.

Ordinary sickly-season fears disappeared, engulfed by a larger fear, when the country was menaced by Asiatic cholera coming down from Montreal.[4] The Hagerstown *Mail* reported that, "among the timid and superstitious," alarm at this intelligence was heightened by expectation of the appearance of Halley's comet. They "looked forward with absolute dread of its baleful light," as in the public mind it had long been connected with coming disaster. This was not necessarily an overreaction by a few people who were timid. Since ancient times, there had been the belief that the movements of celestial bodies influenced the affairs of man on earth, and comets had come to be associated with plague, famine, and war.[5] (Halley's comet did appear in 1835, for the first time since 1759.)

"Timid and superstitious" to one side, it was unlikely that anybody on the eastern seaboard was not realistically aghast at the prospect of a cholera epidemic. From the U.S. Senate, Henry Clay asked that President Andrew Jackson designate a day to be observed as a day of prayer that God would "avert from our country the Asiatic scourge" or to "ameliorate the infliction as to render its effects less disastrous among us." That year's Fourth of July in Hagerstown, near the work site of the canal, was far from a typical Independence Day. Businesses were closed and, instead of inclining towards lively demonstrations, the general frame of mind was subdued to the point of somberness. A large gathering, including 500 children, walked in procession to the Lutheran Church for anxious prayer services.

At this time, William D. Bell, moderator of Hagerstown, informed the townspeople that the cholera would soon appear in their midst. The pestilence was then raging in New York. It reached Baltimore the first week in August. By the first of September it had come to Washington County, appearing first among Irish laborers on the canal site opposite Harpers Ferry.

Four laborers died during that first week in September. As they had been Roman Catholics and the only Catholic cemetery in the county was in Hagerstown, their bodies were brought there for burial. This so intensified the fear of the townspeople that local officials decided they could not let it become common practice. Father Ryan, priest of St. Mary's Church in Hagerstown, worked with Alfred Cruger, chief engineer of the canal company, to establish a Catholic cemetery near the canal. This made for a necessary but cruel and gruesome circumstance in which laborers not yet stricken had to be aware that almost before their very eyes there was being prepared a place which would likely receive their own remains and that right soon.

Within the next week one canal laborer died in Hagerstown and there were several cholera deaths in Sharpsburg, 12 miles away. There were others in Boonsboro and in the southern part of Washington County.

For unknowable reasons, the Board of Health assured the citizens of Hagerstown and the county that the cholera was not contagious and that, if treated in early stages, it would not be fatal in more than one case in a hundred.

The spread of the disease gathered momentum and deaths added up. In October there were 17 in seven days in Hagerstown, and more out in the county.[6] The next week brought more deaths in town and county, including that of canal workers and the secretary of the Hagerstown Board of Health. There were deaths at the poor house, and a traveler from Pennsylvania, planning to pass through Hagerstown, suddenly came down and died in the Globe Tavern there.

Letters told of victims who turned black and died within 24 hours of the onset of the disease, of the cholera's being fatal in nearly every case, and of appalling cruelty brought on by uncontrollable fear. The cholera having been demonstrated to be both highly contagious and lethal, laborers fled the canal in terror.

For most of them it was too late and they managed to get only 5 to 15 miles from the canal before death overtook them. One engineer, Thomas Purcell, wrote, "Humanity is outraged by some of the scenes presented; men deserted by their friends and comrades, having been left to die in the fields, the highways, or in neighboring barns and stables."

He went on to tell that citizens of Sharpsburg went to victims and tried at least to ease their last moments a bit, but this nobility was fruitless. It did let the mortally sick know that some measure of compassion remained, but it saved nobody and it cost the good Samaritans their lives. Nearly everybody who came in contact with the suffering or the dead contracted the plague and died. On a small scale and with a different disease, it was history repeating itself. The time came when hardly any could be found who would dare to bury the dead. Many were buried in common graves in order to get it over as quickly as possible and with the minimum of exposure.

The canal company was quick to do what it could, which was negligible, to help the victims. A hospital was built in Hagerstown near the present site of the Catholic cemetery, and makeshift hospitals were set up west of Harpers Ferry. Given the nature of the disease, it is extremely unlikely that it was possible to accomplish anything substantial. The scourge can be prevented, but its victims can only rarely be saved. The preventive is a high standard of cleanliness, chiefly a sanitary sewage system and clean drinking water. Under the conditions of their existence, canal laborers probably had neither and were as easy prey as cholera ever had. By winter of that year the epidemic had run its grisly course. This too is the nature of the disease. When an outbreak occurs in a nonendemic location, cholera rains death and then vanishes.

Canal laborers were buried in Roby Cemetery near Lock 60, about five miles below the tunnel, and in another about a mile above the tunnel at Sulphur Springs. In 1833 "a great many" died near Williamsport and were buried on the hill in the northeast section of the Friend estate, along the Clear Spring road. This spot has been called Hospital Hill ever since. Memorial stones were erected there, but none remains.*

After the summer of the epidemic, construction went along with a fair degree of steadiness until 1834 when a cluster of riots stopped everything. These began in January, 1834, and recurred over the next two years.

"Riots" is the term that has been latched onto, but many of these eruptions were actually unorganized and non-productive strikes. It was as true then as it was 130 or so years later when Martin Luther King, Jr., said it: "Violence is the voice of the unheard."

When the Irish canal laborer was cheated by his employer, he had no higher authority to whom to appeal; and inevitably he fell back on the strike and the boycott and the secret society as he had learned to do when victimized in Ireland. Short of unconditional surrender to intolerable treatment, there was no other course to take here either. The American labor movement was just barely coming into being. It had only a tiny membership and this was a house divided. Some held to political ac-

*Otho Swain (page 130) remembered that such stones were once at Great Falls, but only one still stood during his lifetime.

44

tion as the preferred method of fighting, and others clung to the old-country practices of strike and boycott. Mercifully, there appears to be no record of canal workers' stooping to one old-country practice, that of maiming and killing their oppressors' animals in misplaced revenge and violent persuasion. It is true that the secret societies often committed violence; but some of them did have some of the goals of the then undeveloped labor unions, and they fought with the primitive weapons at their disposal to improve contracts and repel competitors.

On January 20, 1834, came a clash between Corkmen, working on the dam above Williamsport, and Longfordmen, working on the dam below the town. According to the Hagerstown *Mail*, the cause was the fatal beating of John Irons, a Longfordman, by one of the Corkmen. In the resultant brawl several men were killed. The militia arrested 34 men and jailed them in Hagerstown, but the Irish had no intention of dropping the matter. They began getting weapons together. Williamsport citizens stood guard at both ends of the aqueduct to keep the belligerent factions separated.

On Thursday the 24th violence broke out again. Armed with guns, clubs, and axe handles, at least 600 Longfordmen fought 300 Corkmen and overwhelmed them. The Fardowners, as the Longfordmen were called, claimed that they had intended only to march to the upper dam and make a show of strength, not to attack. After the Williamsport people had allowed them to cross the aqueduct on these terms, their original 300 were joined by three or four hundred more. The Longfordmen said later that they had found 300 Corkmen in a field near the upper dam, armed and drawn up in battle formation. They also claimed that the Corkmen's force of 300 had attacked their force of 600 to 700.

Whoever attacked, the fight didn't last long. An indeterminate number were killed in short order, and the Corkmen took flight from the vastly superior force. They were pursued relentlessly and many were overtaken and killed in the woods to which they had fled. The Hagerstown *Mail* reported that five Corkmen were found dead in one spot, bullets through their heads, and that wounded were strewn all about the woods. It was not until around ten that night that the Longfordmen "marched quietly" through Williamsport and back to their quarters below the town.

The next day the county sheriff, Colonel William H. Fitzhugh, arrived with two Hagerstown companies of volunteers, and they arrested one ringleader. A schoolteacher, Captain Isaac H. Allen, organized the Williamsport Riflemen. The Clear Spring Riflemen were also on hand. Leaders of the Irish factions, together with their deputies, invested by their men with authority to make a settlement, returned to Williamsport. They met with representatives of the local militia at Lyle's Tavern. There they were presented with a formal peace treaty which they signed. The deputations were then warned that if either side violated the treaty the citizens of Williamsport, the militia, and the other Irish faction would unite to drive the offending group from the county.

Not knowing of the peace talks, about 100 Corkmen from farther up the line started out to join their friends and do battle. After they had passed Harpers Ferry they met the militia who explained to them the treaty and its provisions. These laborers handed over their arms and returned to work. The men who had been jailed in Hagerstown were released.

While all this was going on, a feeling was growing among the citizens of Williamsport that the presence of hundreds of armed and angry and desperate men constituted a danger that could not be met by local militia. They sought help from their state delegate, in the form of a request for help from the federal government. President Andrew Jackson sent regular army units (two companies from Fort McHenry), which remained along the canal for some time. Jackson's action marked the first time in this country's history that the U.S. military intervened in what was termed a labor disturbance.

Another conflict erupted in the winter of 1835, less furious than the first. In January, 1836, there was another battle between Irish factions in which two shanties were burned and several men wounded. It had seemed that outbursts were more likely to occur during winter months of enforced idleness, but they soon spread to other seasons.

In April, 1836, a work force made up largely of Dutch was

attacked by some Irish workers and its members beaten and scattered. The Irish went on to the tunnel at Paw Paw, West Virginia, where work was in progress, and found the contractor there highly resistant to intrusion. Lee Montgomery managed to keep his crew together, his men refusing to be coerced into leaving the job. He said later that his group was largely made up of hand-picked men and that they had "some guns and a few Little Sticks" had they felt called on to use them. It was said of Montgomery himself that he would be able to use a "little stick" as efficiently as any and better than some, but the parson-contractor said he would pray not to be obliged to "hold them uneasy."

The following year, a time of economic depression for the nation, there was more trouble at the tunnel. Montgomery had added English laborers to his crew to strengthen his work force and to enable it to repel the strikers when they should come again. The Irish succeeded in driving off 38 of the 40 new laborers, however, and work at the tunnel was halted.

LABORERS WANTED.—I want 500 able bodied men to work on the Chesapeake and Ohio Canal near Clear spring, Washington county, Maryland. Rate of wages, from $1, to $1 25, per day. Rate of board, from $2 to $2 25 per week. JAMES O'REILLY.
Georgetown, July 21, 1837.
The Baltimore Chronicle, Philadelphia Pennsylvanian, and New York Courier, will please copy the above, once a week three weeks. and forward their accounts to this office.

Wages higher in 1837 than in 1829 when the first laborers were fetched from the British Isles. Workers were promised $8 to $12 a month ($20 for masons), plus "meat three times a day, plenty of bread and vegetables, and a reasonable allowance of whiskey." Disillusionment began on the ship and was completed shortly after arrival. Clear Spring is above Dam No. 5, which is eight miles north of Williamsport.

Friction continued throughout that summer. Contractors and workmen who failed to cooperate with the desperate rioters were threatened, property was destroyed, and men were beaten. A pall of fear hung over the workers, and those who were beaten did not dare to bear witness against their assailants.

Every year bred its crop of outbreaks. The insurgent workers burned shanties, partly to make trouble for the contractors and partly to drive away German laborers whose presence reduced the number of jobs for the barely surviving Irish and ran down the already low wages. The canal company had hazarded a guess that this violence was largely instigated by "a terrorist society" based in New York. Walter Sanderlin's guess, made after study of the evidence of history, was that this society was likely to have been an early labor union or an Irish fraternal organization.

Beginning on the first day of the year, troubles piled up in 1838. In mid-May another revolt took place among Irish laborers, provoked by contractors' failure to pay them for work done. The contractors were strapped for money; but the Irish, who scratched out an irreducibly meager existence even when wages were paid, were not of a mind to work for nothing at all or to accept excuses. They destroyed work they had done and for which they were plainly told they would not be paid.[7]

The canal company called on the local militia for help, but found it loath to respond. For one reason, both the company and the state had refused to pay the militia the last time their services had been engaged. Further, members of the militia maintained that the canal company was to blame because it had withheld money from contractors at critical times. Officers of the militia reported that some of their men had bluntly warned that they would not move against the laborers and some had even said that if they did turn out it would be to "fight for the Irish."

These officers pointed out that the laborers and their families were in dire straits, living in deeply deplorable conditions, but that even so they were resolute in their determination to keep interlopers from working until they themselves had been paid for work done. Suffering though they were, the Irish refused an offer of 25 cents on the dollar and continued to stand firm. They were then offered nothing. Merchants in Hagerstown sided with the Irish against the company and let them have provisions on credit to tide them over until at least surface harmony could be achieved.

Three companies of state militia finally and grudgingly did turn out—two Hagerstown companies under Captain Artz and Captain Robertson, and the Smithburg Company under Captain Hollingsworth—but nothing significant took place. A new uproar at the tunnel brought action from the company directors. They suspended work at the tunnel, firing some rebelling laborers and blacklisting others. On the first of August some 130 men were discharged. Most had been working at the cut and inside the tunnel.

Matters rocked along for an entire year. Then came August 11, 1839, when the pressure-cooker situation overheated and blew up again. This shameful episode began with atrocities and ended with brutal repression and everybody but the victims showed up in a lurid light.

About 100 Irish laborers burst into violence at two spots at Little Orleans, between Hancock and Cumberland, parts of the canal that were under construction by their old enemies the German contractors and laborers. They attacked the Germans, stole whatever was worth stealing, razed their living quarters, and beat up any who resisted. Apparently this behavior fed on itself until some of the Irish ran amok. They killed a German laborer by throwing him into a fire. A man named Hughes was so brutally beaten that he died of injuries.

Later in the month Colonel C.M. Thurston of Cumberland, acting on directions from a representative of Governor William Grason, raised two companies of militia. It was not until August 22 that he sent agents to the riot area with instructions to get information substantial enough to warrant the use of troops to quell "the insurrection." The agents reported unfavorably on the Irish, but their recommendation was not that the ready and waiting militia be called out. They felt that a detachment of civilians would not be sufficiently intimidating to the Irish, and they considered federal troops more suitable. The Governor, however, held that use of federal troops would be illegal. (Illegal or no, President Jackson had used federal troops in a like situation five years before.)

While this was being worked through, sufficient evidence came from an unexpected source. A Catholic priest, Father Guth, who worked in Old Town among Germans, handed in a list said to be the names of those who took part in the August 11 riot. Carrying this list and his orders, Colonel Thurston descended upon the disordered area on August 27. He had been joined by two troops of Washington County cavalry, which brought his force to 150 men.

According to newspaper reporters, the troops adopted "very decisive measures" and their "proceedings seemed harsh." Colonel Thurston's report was that his men had behaved with restraint. They had shot eight to ten of those fingered by Father Guth, destroyed some $700 worth of confiscated firearms, and wrecked about 50 shanties and stores, allegedly because the owners refused search. The assault slackened briefly, as after the initial stunning surprise the Irish leaders took what cover they could and were in somewhat less of a sitting duck position. Then along came Charles B. Fisk and the cavalry. Fisk, the canal company's chief engineer, was described later as having been "very active and useful in . . . pointing out the guilty" and directing destruction. The militia reported that not one of the 40 to 50 demolished shanties had been touched except by specific order of Fisk.

There were three more such "active" days. More shanties were torn down, more weapons destroyed, and one man arrested was accidentally shot and killed by a private citizen assisting the militia. Evidence was collected that satisfied the militia and the canal company that the Irish were part of a secret organization that directed their movements. Thurston and the militia arrived back in Cumberland on the evening of August 31 with 26 prisoners.

Before the trial of these prisoners, the company hired one

James Finney to take on the dubious distinction of being one of this country's earliest labor spies. For $100 he energetically carried out his assignment, and in five days 19 prisoners were bound over for trial on an assortment of charges. Their trial took up the second half of October. The exertions of Fisk and Finney, plus a general feeling against the Irish, brought conviction for 14 men. Two were given penitentiary sentences of 17⅔ years, seven of 15⅔ years, three of 9⅔ years, one of 6⅔ years, and one of 4⅔ years. Four were acquitted, and one was sent to Washington County for trial.

Another riot at the same place some weeks later brought the same kind of ferocious retaliation. The following period saw the Irish quiet in the fashion sometimes described with shameless euphemism as "pacified." They were not in the least pacified in any reasonable sense of the word; they were crushed.

A number of Allegany County citizens raised their voices against the cossack-like behavior of the troops that Thurston considered so restrained. According to the protesters, many of the shanties and shops that were made firewood of, at the specific order of an officer of the canal company, had belonged to Irish who had had nothing to do with the riots, and the "riotous and unlicensed houses" that were torn down were legally operated wayside inns. These morally indignant citizens caused suit to be brought against Thurston, Hollingsworth (who had led a small group of cavalry), and Fisk. The court decided against all three. They appealed to the legislature but were brusquely brushed aside. This public shame did not faze the canal company. It had still won, in that it had done what it wanted to do, and this was irreversible.

The Irish continued to keep body and soul together under intolerable conditions. No longer could they drive away company-encouraged laborers trying to get their jobs, and, as a natural result, wages fell from $1.25 to $.87½ a day. What had been meted out was not justice for a guilty few but revenge on all; but any whose makeup allowed them to take pride or comfort in it could hug to their mean-spirited bosoms the fact that the forces of law and order had prevailed. The harm did not end there. This compound incident set a precedent in American enterprise, and, as W. David Baird was to write many years later, its social significance was that "law and order would come to have more relevance to economic and social repression than to domestic peace and tranquillity."

In 1834, the year the riots began, the canal was finished between Point of Rocks and Harpers Ferry, a 12-mile section begun the year before. Also finished in 1834, the section from Harpers Ferry to Dam No. 4 below Williamsport made 86 miles of completed canal. At this date the canal was considered unequalled; by comparison, the Erie was said to be as a mill race. (The *original* Erie drew only 4 feet of water and was only 40 feet wide. To become the great Erie, it was rebuilt in 1850 and again in the early 1900s.)

At the lower end of the canal, Alexandria was doing its all to keep a hold on its thriving business. Back when the canal company began operation, Alexandria had subscribed $250,000 worth of stock. The town's interest in the C&O lay in its anxious conviction that it needed to be reached by the canal if it were to continue to flourish. Alexandria had long been an important port, and it didn't intend to lose its position by default.

The town requested that the canal company build an aqueduct across the Potomac at Georgetown and an extension of the C&O along the southern edge of the river. This request was not granted, as the cost would have been more than the canal company could bear. Reports of the prospering Erie Canal so threatened and therefore emboldened Alexandria, as they had done the men who began the C&O, that the town chartered a corporation and built an aqueduct and a seven- to eight-mile canal itself.

Work had begun on July 4, 1831, and in December, 1843, after persevering in the usual obstacle course of engineering problems, the corporation finished a wooden aqueduct resting on stone pillars. Wooden piers had been planned originally; but the builders soon realized that a wooden trunk on wooden piers would not be strong enough to bear the weight of the canal water in the tumultuous current of the river and they were obliged to switch to stone piers. The aqueduct was 40 feet above the river, and the builders went down through some 30 feet of mud and water to reach bedrock to anchor the piers. Naturally, this feat was accomplished without benefit of compressed air tools or any sophisticated equipment, and it was something of an engineering victory.

The given name of the structure was the Potomac Aqueduct, but boatmen commonly called it the Alexandria Aqueduct or, more often in the canal's later days, "the aqueduct bridge."[8] The aqueduct was placed at a spot where the Potomac was half a mile wide, between Georgetown and Rosslyn. For a long time it was an important outlet for C&O trade, the only link between the river's Maryland and Virginia shores. One of the original eight stone piers remains, having been successfully pled for as a historic artifact when all eight were scheduled for demolition.

CANAL CONSTRUCTION had been slowed by riots, rising construction costs, dearth of building stone in the upper valley, land damages, and the Paw Paw tunnel.

The tunnel, outstandingly the most imposing of the canal's structures, was built in preference to taking on a struggle with terrain that was not only forbidding but across the river in West Virginia.* Added to the disinclination for crossing, there was an inhibiting agreement the canal company had with the railroad. This was that the railroad was to stay on the south side of the river and the canal company would be allowed to cross only if absolutely necessary *and* the B&O didn't need the space.

The tunnel site is one of the necks of land inside huge loops in the river called the Paw Paw bends. Because of the contour of the Potomac here, the builders made an exception to their rule of following the river closely. Had they not done so, they would have had to build five miles of canal and towpath from cliffs and a twisting turning river bed, crossing to West Virginia and returning. There were cliffs on both sides of the site and

---

*Although none of the canal is on the Virginia side of the river, the tunnel was given its name for its proximity to Paw Paw, West Virginia.

the level next to it. This was truly to be on the horns of a dilemma: two options, both unsatisfactory. The dismaying choices were weighed and the decision was for the tunnel, largely in response to the exertions of the company's chief engineer, Charles B. Fisk.

It is C.B. Fisk whose name is over the south portal of the tunnel—put there by the company despite his vociferous objection—but Ellwood Morris was the designer and the engineer in charge of construction of this work.* Morris had a valuable assistant in Henry M. Dungan. The name of James M. Coale, president of the canal company from August, 1843, to February, 1851, is over the north portal.

The site of the tunnel was chosen in December, 1835, and in June, 1836, Lee Montgomery, its carefully selected contractor, got his carefully selected crew to work. It was a tribute to Montgomery that he was entrusted with this monumental undertaking. He was a Methodist preacher as well as a contractor (as well as by reputation a rather rough-hewn fellow and a hard drinker), and the board of directors held him in high regard both as a person and as a contractor known for his intense press-forward way of working through a project. If he was a hard drinker, he was far from alone. Oceans of liquor were consumed as the canal was built, and by no means all by "wild Irish" laborers.

The tunnel was shaped by blasting out large spaces with black powder and reaming them with sledges and picks. The workers were not experts at blasting, and there was a great deal of overbreakage; the excavation was 40 percent larger than needed. At this place in the mountain the rocks were crumpled together; and every time a blast hit a place where they formed an arch, it tore right up to the top. All this surplus space was dealt with

---

*Engineers reported specifications for principal parts of the tunnel as follows. "The tunnel arched throughout with brick except for 25 feet at each end which will be of stone. The arch will be a semicircle of 24 feet diameter; the width of the waterway 19 feet, and towpath five feet. Depth of water through the tunnel will be seven feet; the height of the tunnel, in the clear, above canal water surface, 17 feet. The sides of the tunnel and face of the rock bench, left for the towpath, are also to be lined with brick."

Certificate of stock issued to Washington's nephew, George Corbin Washington, and signed by him as president of the company. Issued in the month before construction of the tunnel was begun and in the year before one of the country's periodic depressions. Engraving is of a scene at Harpers Ferry.

by lining and filling. First a brick lining was built for what would be the tunnel's arched ceiling. Behind this lining, which varies in thickness from one spot to another but in most places is 13 layers of brick deep, in some as much as 33 layers, excavated material was packed in, put back more or less where it came from. As with the construction of the whole tunnel, this involved an appalling amount of hand work. Steam drills were on the market by then, but Montgomery lacked the money to make use of them.

Work gang followed on the heels of work gang as construction proceeded. The upper half of the tunnel, the arch, was built first. As it began to take shape, other crews followed along to cut the platform. Always, there were many crews working simultaneously in different areas of the structure.

As the tunnel carried the canal through a rock mountain, it would have taken forever and a day to finish if bored through in end-to-end fashion. At the beginning, work was done from both ends at once. The slaty rock was reasonably hard, but loose enough to make frequent trouble by caving in. It was dangerous work and it went at a snail's pace.

South Portal of the tunnel near Paw Paw, West Virginia. The canal established the level of the tunnel, and at this end it was possible for the waterway to proceed straight into the passage through the rock mountain. The tunnel is the most interesting structure on the canal, and the company's finest achievement. It was designed by Ellwood Morris.

The company engineers addressed themselves to the problem of slowness, and proposed two shafts reaching from the mountain top to the level of the canal. Montgomery figured that if the men could be working simultaneously from the four additional cutting faces which would be exposed by the sinking of these shafts, the work could be speeded up by 80 percent. Ellwood Morris drew up the specifications for these shafts.

Each shaft was actually a set of two: one for removal of excavated material and one for ventilation. The northernmost set was 122 feet deep and the more southerly was 188 feet deep. The ventilation shafts worked well and provided good circulation of air for men working near them.

As the gangs of laborers proceeded, they were reaming out three segments of the tunnel. When these completed segments met neatly, the body of the tunnel stretched out for its length of 3,118 feet, almost two-thirds of a mile. The tunnel is not visually beautiful as are the stone aqueducts; but it is a beautifully realized stucture and the supreme engineering accomplishment of the canal.

Helpful as they were, the shafts have been considered badly

placed. Rather close together at the north end of the tunnel, they did nothing for the work going on at the south end. Still, the immense need was at the north, where the approach was by way of a cut that required a larger volume of excavation than the tunnel itself. The old creek valley the canal builders were following rose so steeply at that place that the floor of the valley was 70 feet higher than the floor of the tunnel.

The south end of the tunnel had determined its level. On that side no cut was required and tunnel and canal could head straight into the mountain. Workers had only to clean the face of the mountain in order to provide a vertical place to begin excavating for the tunnel.

It was a daunting prospect though, to make the tremendous volume of excavation for the 890-foot cut at the north end and, worst of all, it had to be done by hand. Work at the cut caused additional stress and complication by blocking removal of excavated material. The shafts, being near the north end, were useful in removing this. There was also, of course, the mass of material dug out to make the deep cut, and this too had to be relocated. It caused no end of trouble. Much of this material was

North portal of the tunnel. At this end of the nearly mile-long vault, a mammoth cut had to be made to effect continuation of the canal into the mountain. The cut required a greater volume of excavation than the tunnel itself and a backbreaking amount of hand digging. The entire project was staggering, with towering obstacles to construction, grave financial troubles for all, and ruin for the first of several contractors.

stuffed into little side valleys in the mountain. The cut, an awfully deep one for its day, caused immeasurable toil and frustration and put everybody on the site through a harrowing ordeal.

When the tunnel was finished, the shafts were plugged with clay, concrete, and rubble, in an effort to make these areas watertight. There was, however, a small amount of leakage, and the shafts' locations can be identified by damp spots on the tunnel's ceiling. These spots are less noticeable now than they used to be, as considerable repair work has been done by the National Park Service.

All along the length of the tunnel wall on both sides, narrow wood fenders were placed for protection of the masonry from boats. Every 20 feet along the brick-lined walls there is a weep hole, a small cavity made by leaving out bricks. These holes provided drainage from the inevitable wetness of the walls. Along the towpath, which is a part of the tunnel in the same way a stone continuation towpath is an integral part of a stone aqueduct, an oak railing protected mules from falling into the canal. The railing bears grooves worn by towlines, coated with abrasive sand and grit, scraping across it as the mules drew the boat along. Going through the pitch black dark of the tunnel, boatmen kept their bow lights burning and mule drivers carried lanterns.

Completion date had been set for July, 1838, but it was not to be. Not only were the tunnel and the cut more exacting and burdensome and costly than they had been taken to be, but the company's money and labor troubles hampered all endeavors and often brought things to a halt. In 1846, financially ruined, Montgomery quit the scene and his crews scattered.

Before it was all over, the tunnel had been too much for several contractors. In 1849 Hunter, Harris and Company[9] contracted to finish both tunnel and canal, and the canal company pressed them to go full tilt and wind up things as quickly as possible. The contractors did all they could to comply. They enlarged the labor force and even built nine miles of railroad to expedite delivery of construction materials. They consistently and valiantly strove to fulfill their burdensome commitment, and in the course of these efforts made heavy sacrifices in the sale of bonds. They continued the work after they had abandoned all hope of making any profit on the job, but finally added one more corporate name to the list of those who went bankrupt working on the canal.

In the spring of 1850, only a stone's throw from their goal, the sadly familiar situation overpowered them. There had been too few workers, melting-away funds, and the possibility of violence from unpaid workers. Hunter, Harris retreated. It assigned its interest in the contract to two of its agents and attorneys, for the benefit of its creditors. Work was begun again, and the completion date pushed forward to July 1 and then to August 1; but by mid-July the agents and assignees announced their lack of funds and consequent inability to fulfill the contract.

The canal company formally declared the Hunter, Harris contract dissolved, and on the next day, July 10, 1850, entered into a new agreement. This was with Michael Byrne, of Frederick County, Maryland, who committed himself to complete the remaining undone bit of work for $3,000 plus $21,000 worth of bonds. Byrne sublet the contract to former employees of Hunter, Harris.

The work was small in quantity but tedious and troublesome. It consisted of finishing parts of the canal at a number of places between Dam No. 6 and Cumberland. By the fall of the year, 11 sections just west of Dam No. 6 had been completed and one lock touched up. The C&O Canal was finished.[10]

Its completion was some species of triumph over unrelieved hardship. Planned to go all the way to Ohio and to be built in 12 years, it got no farther than the eastern shed of the Alleghenies and it took 22 years to get there. It had cost $14 million, not counting repairs and interest—nine and a half million more than estimated. As a proportion of Gross National Product, this was as much as the country would spend 150 years later to put a man on the moon.

[1] The canal Irish would have fared no better had they landed at New York without jobs. At New York immigrants were pounced on at the gangplank by runners who fought one another over the newcomers' bundles of belongings so that they could whisk them off to their own employers at dirty, overcrowded boarding houses. That the runners and the boarding-house operators were often Irish-American made no difference in the fate of the newly arrived immigrants. New arrivals also suffered the calamitous attentions of brokers who sold them fake tickets if they wanted to go elsewhere in the U.S., and their baggage was stolen. Many were so thoroughly robbed on disembarkation that they had no chance of going to any other area, and New York had large numbers of indigent Irish.

[2] In the early 1900s this mutual detestation did a U-turn. A pseudoscientific notion sprang up that what was perceived as the imaginative but volatile Celtic blood should make a good mix with what was perceived as the stolid and pompous Teutonic blood, and marriage between Irish- and German-Americans became common on all social strata.

[3] It could hardly have escaped the company's attention as it composed its recruiting advertisements that, as Charles Hadfield writes in *The Canal Age*, "when the Irish built the Erie a tot of whiskey was doled out to them every two hours—to keep them going."

[4] The second of two pandemic waves of cholera began in India in 1826 and spread by land and sea. By sea it was carried to China, Ceylon, East Africa, the Philippines; by land, to Persia and Arabia and then to Russia through Astrakan. It reached European Russia by way of China, Manchuria, and Mongolia, and through Astrakan. It arrived in Moscow in 1830, spread into Germany and to Scotland and was carried to North America. It reached Canada in 1832 and spread south.

[5] People in Manhattan didn't feel any less terrified by the apparition in 1910 when it had the city "alarmingly bright" by May 4 and progressively brighter until May 10. That was the date on which the earth was due to pass through the comet's luminous 46-million-mile-long train. Enormous crowds of New Yorkers reportedly spent the 19th on their knees, imploring rescue by divine intervention. Eugene O'Neill, Jr., was born during this trying time and he came to regard the comet as a sign of his misfortunes, which were grievous enough to bring him to suicide. It was in 1910 that King Edward VII of England died, and many laid his death at the door of the comet.

Latter-day dread of this most spectacular of comets is the mixture as before. It has been spreading terror before it ever since its first documented appearance in the third century B.C. In 1066 astrologers gave out that the coming of the comet was an evil omen for England's King Harold. That year was, as is well remembered, the year in which Harold was killed in the Battle of Hastings; and the comet is stitched into the Bayeux Tapestry, which represents in embroidery on linen the events of William the Conqueror's invasion of England. In the 12th century it was widely believed to be a symbol and possibly an instrument of God's anger, and Calixtus II, Pope from 1119 to 1124, gave orders for a special prayer: "Lord, save us from the Devil, the Turk, and the Comet."

The comet is due to make its dazzling display visible again in 1986, but much of its splendor will probably be spoiled by neutralizing street lights.

[6] Despite the Hagerstown deaths, the *Mail* reported that the town had got off lightly compared with others in like situations. Credit went to the town moderator. Before the mass prayer meeting, Bell had urged all citizens to clean the town— streets, alleys, gutters, cellars, vacant lots, everything. Later, inspection teams said that the city was clean.

[7] If any feel tempted to look down on this as brutish behavior of a lesser breed without the law, let them dwell for a time on a scene presented the American public on television in early March of 1981. Angry and careridden auto workers, laid off because of the industry's falling behind Japanese sales in this country, demonstrated in protest. Typical of today's show-biz world, their demonstration was planned and staged for TV cameras. It took the form of demolishing a brand-new Toyota. (Whose brand-new Toyota was not explained.) They pounded the car with baseball bats and sledgehammers, and in a matter of a few short moments they had battered it into a crumpled wad of scrap metal.

[8] This aqueduct, or aqueduct-bridge as it came to be, is more interesting as American history than canal history. Eighteen years after the aqueduct was finished, the country was at war with itself. Right at the beginning of the war the Union commandeered the aqueduct, drained it, and made it into a five-foot trough that was used as a bridge for foot and wagon traffic. Over this improvised bridge Union soldiers passed to and from defeat at First Manassas. Later, a bridge was built on top of the aqueduct and this two-layer structure served both wagons and boats at the same time.

In 1887 Congress appropriated money to buy the aqueduct and convert it to a bridge. After this was done it had no connection with the C&O Canal—trade with Georgetown and Washington had declined anyhow because of Georgetown's low bridges—and the Alexandria Canal passed out of existence. The aqueduct-bridge was an important crossing until the (Francis Scott) Key Bridge was finished in 1933.

[9] James Hunter of Virginia; William B. Thompson, of the District of Columbia; Thomas G. Harris, of Washington County, Maryland.

[10] Finished in the sense that Cumberland was as far as the canal ever went. After the waterway reached that point there was little talk of the original plan to end it at Pittsburgh on the Ohio. It had long since been realized that the mountains would make such an attempt wildly unrealistic.

Construction

The Works:
Seventy-four lift locks,
11 stone aqueducts,
and a 3,118-foot tunnel
through solid rock.

THE FIRST SHIPMENT of coal was carried to Georgetown by a boat named Cumberland (or No. 1) shortly before the formal opening of the whole canal on October 10, 1850.

The opening was a momentous occasion and it was celebrated in Cumberland with appropriate, but not grandiose, ceremony. Festivities began early in the morning, which was customary in those days. By 8:30 a large crowd had gathered in the street in front of Barnum's and the United States hotels. Given pride of place were officers of the canal company, Maryland's former Governor Sprigg, and the mayor of Georgetown.

For half an hour the gathering was entertained by military evolutions smartly performed by the Eckhart Artillery, a local unit that, according to the Cumberland *Civilian,* arrived with "a battery of two handsome pieces." At 9 o'clock all present formed a procession: first the Eckhart Artillery, the Baltimore Blues, distinguished visitors and officers of the canal company, and state agents; behind them, the Mayor and Council of Cumberland, followed by a large number of county citizens escorted by the Mechanics' Band of Cumberland. The procession made its way to the canal, attracting more people as it went until there was "an immense assemblage of all ages and sexes."

The celebration began with the passing of five coal-heavy canal boats from the basin through the inlet lock and into the canal proper to the accompaniment of band music and artillery salvos.

There were speeches, beginning with a welcome from William

Price, Esq., on behalf of the people of Cumberland. From the deck of one of the canal boats Mr. Price commented that many of those present were young when construction on the canal was begun "and we have lived to see its completion only because Providence has prolonged our lives until our heads are grey." He spoke of those who had gone bankrupt by their involvement with the canal and ventured the hope that "those whose losses have been gains of the company should not in the hour of its prosperity be forgotten." He observed that, although the canal had been greatly decried and misunderstood, it was a magnificent work. He cautioned that achievement of full trade would not be the work of a day but, perhaps carried away by the exhilarating occasion, declared that the opening of the canal marked the beginning of a happy period in Maryland's financial life. Doubtless Mr. Price made errors of judgment before and after that October 10th, but probably not another so sizable; what with the canal and the railroad, the State of Maryland all but beggared itself.

On that day, however, the air was heady with hope and everybody's glasses were rose-colored. In his own speech, James M. Coale, president of the canal company, paid tribute to the State of Maryland, which had been a stalwart and steadfast benefactor from the beginning. He expressed the hope that the federal government would "redeem its early pledges" and enable the canal to be carried on to the Ohio River as first planned.

After the speeches, the canal company officials and distinguished guests, together with numerous Cumberland citizens, began a short ride down the canal in the packet boat *Jenny Lind* and in an especially fitted canal boat, the *C.B. Fisk*. Then came a small flotilla made up of the five coal boats—*Southhampton, Elizabeth, Ohio, Delaware,* and *Freeman Rawdon*—and one boat bearing the artillery unit. Bands made music for the celebrators' enjoyment during their brief excursion, and there were occasional booms from cannon. At a spring ten miles east of Cumberland, the *Jenny Lind* and the *C.B. Fisk* stopped for a banquet that included "a copious supply of the finest and choicest wines."

The coal boats, with their combined load of 491 tons, got on with their trip to the East. This carried down the C&O Canal on its first day in business more coal than was carried on the Lehigh Canal (on which the anthracite coal trade of Pennsylvania was begun) during the first full year of its operation in 1820.*

The party returned to Cumberland, arriving after nightfall, and rounded off the day with a banquet at Barnum's Hotel given by Cumberland citizens. Banqueters drank to the following toast: "The Chesapeake and Ohio Canal and the Baltimore and Ohio Railroad. The former has happily reached its ebony harvests amid the coal fields of the Alleghenies; may the latter journey vigorously on westward until it rejoices amidst the golden plains of the far Californias." After the feast there was music and dancing.

ALTHOUGH BENJAMIN WRIGHT was the principal among the participants, no single person can be named the architect of the canal. Nor were there any comprehensive blueprints. Using the surveys made between 1824 and 1828, Wright and other engineers established the need for aqueducts, the positions of locks, and elevation changes. Measurements, materials, and methods of construction for locks, culverts, dams, aqueducts, and waste weirs were gradually formalized into specifications between 1829 and 1832.

There were plans for some of the canal's structures, but in general there were only these specifications and the canal was designed freehand, so to speak. Where an aqueduct, for example, was to be placed, stakes were put down to indicate the centerline of the structure, the flanks, and the wings. All these points were determined in the field by the engineers. Height of aqueducts and length of their spans had been set, and this automatically defined the general shape of the arches.

*Two of the boats were stuck above Dam No. 6 because they had a draft of four feet, six inches too much for the canal's water level. One boat completed its trip to Williamsport, the other two to Alexandria.

The same was true of the route of the canal.* There was some sort of plan but it was not as if cast in bronze. As Alfred Cruger explained in answer to inquiries from stockholders, it was not astonishing that deviations from the plan occurred, "particularly on ground presenting so many difficulties." He continued, "Changes are always made. . .changes have been made, even after the work has been commenced, when the operations have sufficiently advanced on the ground (which was before doubtful in its character) to satisfy the Engineer that a change would be expedient."

He went on to tell how one section was changed by being placed "further on the hill, which presents the appearance of much rock, but which exhibited, upon being opened, a much larger portion of good clay than could have been anticipated; the effect of which will be to produce a saving of several thousand dollars in the construction: for the amount of wall is diminished; no embankment but what will be furnished from the Canal excavation, will be required; and there will even be a surplus quantity of earth to go to the adjoining section, thereby producing a similar effect, so far as that quantity goes, on that section, in reducing its estimated cost."

The finished canal was 185.7 miles from the guard lock at Cumberland to tidewater at Washington (184.5 to Georgetown), and for the most part 60 feet wide at the top and 6 feet deep. Its outstanding features were 74 lift locks; more than 150 culverts; 7 dams; a tunnel; 11 stone aqueducts; a miscellany of waste weirs, bridges, stop locks, river locks, guard locks; and a towpath 12 feet wide.**

The eastern end of the canal was the basin at the mouth of

*In laying out a canal, an engineer works within inflexible limitations, far more confining than those that apply in the shaping of a highway or a railroad. The canal must remain on one level or conform to the topography of its locale. The canal proper consists of level reaches at various heights, each enclosable by locks that enable vessels to proceed from level to level. The reaches must follow bases of hills and the curves of valleys, else heavy earthworks are required.

**By the time surviving boatmen were on the canal, lack of sufficient maintenance had shrunk the towpath to approximately 7 feet.

Rock Creek where the creek enters the river, between George-town and Washington. This basin was formed by damming the creek with a wide mole placed across its mouth. A tidal (or river, or outlet) lock made it possible for boats to enter and leave the basin to and from the river. At the confluence of river and creek, boats could enter by the tidal lock and go about five times the length of a football field to Lift Lock 1 in Georgetown, from where they could enter the canal proper. The canal ran west as far as Little Falls, and then up, always on the Maryland side of the river, with the locks functioning as stepping stones up the miles and a difference of 605 feet in elevation between Georgetown and Cumberland.

The artificial waterway devoured water and was insatiable. It had to have its supply replenished without interruption. One estimate had it that the canal would have dried up in eight days if its water supply had been cut off.

Furthermore, the water had to be moving. When water is con-fined and crowded into by a boat, as in basin or lock or aqueduct, it offers stiff resistance; and the smaller the space the more the resistance. Worst of all for the mules was to start moving a hor-rendously heavy boat in the still water of a loading basin. It was hard for them to pull a boat through an aqueduct, as this was a tight fit and the water had no room to be moving around the boat. It was less difficult for them on the main part of the canal, and least difficult in the slack waters. Boatmen now living men-tion the feeling they had of the boats "moving easier" the minute they got into the river with the water flowing all about the craft. They point out that this benefit was accompanied by the danger of going over a dam.

In addition to the canal's ravenous need for a constant in-pouring of water, it leaked continuously from bottom and banks and it occasionally lost water at locks. When there was a lift from an empty to a full lock, no water was lost; but loss did occur when draining a lock caused excess flow into the flume and this water went, by way of a waste weir, back into the river. Level walkers covered 20 to 24 miles of canal a day, keeping sharp eyes out for leaks. They themselves repaired small leaks on discovery, and reported larger ones to superintendents who called on section gangs to attend to them.

Leakage often took the form of piping. Once the tiniest trickle of water begins to go through an earthen structure, it must be stopped immediately or it becomes a major leak. An original wee bit of a puncture causes some material to wash out and then it continuously enlarges.

Boatmen said that crabs moving over from the river sometimes caused leaks in this way, as did muskrats. An anonymous New Englander, making one round trip on the canal in 1859 and then writing of his experience, noted that this "seemingly harmless animal the muskrat often causes thousands of dollars damage by boring their channels through the banks starting a leak that will sometimes make a break rods in width. On some canals they employ hunters and give bounties for all that are caught within a certain distance of it." The C&O gave a reward of 25 cents for each muskrat killed on the line of the canal.

Management of the canal as a physical entity was a matter of a fairly complicated system of frequent adjustments to maintain the proper water level. While the canal did have an unrelenting need for prodigious quantities of water, there came times when it got an oversupply. Waste weirs, usually built above locks, dealt with some of this, removing water surges created when locks were emptied. Weirs were equipped with horizontal planks of differing widths. By dropping the planks down into slots or by removing planks, the level of water could be regulated. When there was too much water in the canal, the lock would be protected by removing a plank or two, which eased surplus water into the river. For a simple rainy season or a moderately intense storm, the weirs were adequate.

For most of its 184.5 miles the canal's level was above that of the river, which afforded minimal protection against flooding. Wherever it dropped below river level, a dam was built. The dam raised the level of the river, water was diverted into the canal by gravity, and this fed the canal as far as the next dam. Wherever there was a dam there was a river lock and a crossover bridge for mules.

The dams that watered the canal were No. 1, at the head of Little Falls; No. 2, at the head of Seneca Falls; No. 3, at the head of Harpers Ferry Falls; Nos. 4 and 5, below and above Williamsport; No. 6, at Great Cacapon; and No. 8, at Cumberland. No No. 7 was ever built; it had been planned for a spot not far from the Paw Paw bends.

Dam No. 3, known as the government dam, was at Harpers Ferry before the canal was, operating water wheels for the arsenal. When the canal reached that point on the Maryland side of the river, this dam began to serve the canal too. The others were built as the canal was built.

To all practical purposes, Dams No. 1, 2, and 6 are gone, nothing remaining but rubbishy scraps. No. 3 has not produced power for several years. Dams No. 4 and 5 are still in operation. They have produced power all along, water power until 1913, hydroelectricity since. Between April, 1953, and June, 1954, No. 8 was blown up and the debris removed by the U.S. Corps of Engineers as part of a flood control project.

Lock measurements were fairly constant. With some irregularities, locks were 100 feet long by 16 feet deep and the lifts ranged from 6 to 10 feet with an average of 8. In general, aqueducts and locks were made of stone quarried reasonably nearby. In the upper Potomac Valley, with its lack of good stone, material had to be brought from long distances. When frugality dictated, rubble was used (with timber facing).

The Georgetown locks were made chiefly of the expensive but easy-to-cut Aquia Creek sandstone from Stafford County, Virginia, and some country (i.e., local) rock. Indigenous gabbro and mica schist were also used in the walls of the canal in Georgetown. It was necessary to blast out part of the canal there, and some of the gabbro and schist thus displaced was used in locks and walls.

This treatment of canal walls is a special instance; usually they were earthen banks. Georgetown's four closely spaced locks brought the canal up a steep 35 feet. This gave the banks a high way to go, and they required heavy reinforcement. The Georgetown locks now show many spots of patchwork, where repairs

have been made with bricks or slabs of granite. The log walls below Great Falls, remains of which were swept away by tropical storm Agnes in 1972, were another special case.

The quarry at Seneca was the source of material for a number of structures.[1] This rosy sandstone, known locally as Seneca stone, was a natural choice. It was known to be durable if care were taken in choosing pieces, and quarries and a stonecutting mill were practically on the site of the Seneca Creek Aqueduct and what came to be known as Riley's Lock. Lock and aqueduct were interestingly constructed as one unit, made of the reddest of this red sandstone.

In 1968, Paul H. Douglas and William K. Jones, referring to the Seneca Aqueduct, wrote in the *Smithsonian Journal of History,* "After more than 135 years, this aqueduct remains firm and straight and would need little repair if the canal were once

Unique on the canal, aqueduct and lock at Seneca Creek are built as one structure. Loaded boat has just entered aqueduct and will proceed directly into lock. White wait house on left; next to it John Riley seated on balance beam. Across from him is Fred Allnutt's general merchandise store.

69

Mason's marks in wall of Lock 24, Riley's Lock at Seneca. In a rather small area of this one lock, at least a dozen different masons' marks can easily be found. Although some are doubtless authentic (but made for personal reasons not connected with identification for pay as was the old European tradition), old canal hands caution that others are likely to be false and frivolous.

again filled with water." It was not until September 11, 1971, when a local storm went roaring through the area, that one of this aqueduct's three arches came tumbling down.

On the walls of the Seneca Aqueduct and Lock 24 there is a scattering of masons' marks, but it would be unwise to accept them all as authentic.[2] Some are, but, because of the ease with which the original marks could have been imitated, some cautious geologists consider it impossible to be sure which of this particular batch are and which aren't. Sandstone is soft enough that such marks could have been made by almost anyone on a canal boat while it was at a lock—or almost anyone else later.

Seneca stone was also used in Lock 20 at Great Falls (repaired over the years with limestone and brick); Lock 21, Swain's Lock; 22, Pennyfield's Lock; and 23, Violette's Lock.

The Brunswick lock, 34, is of granite. At one time it was doubled in length by a wooden extension, but extensions on all such remodeled locks were later removed and boatmen now living never saw them.

The Williamsport lock, 44, is made of limestone. This stone is widely used and is highly desirable as building material because it occurs in great masses, because it is a freestone, and because, as stone goes, it is soft. Soft is not to be confused with perishable. It is true that exposure to weather will eventually dissolve minute quantities of the surface of limestone. The degree is so infinitesimal, however, and the time it takes is so very long that this characteristic is not a consideration. David Gardner reports that he has "walked along the east end of the National Cathedral, built in 1908. . . .You can run your hand over it and feel little fossils sticking out. It has weathered maybe two millimeters. An eighth of an inch in 74 years is no big deal when blocks of stone are so thick."*

Lock 66 is one of the canal's composite locks, being made of a combination of masonry and wood. Its masonry was coarse, consisting of rubble and undressed, inferior stone. It was double-

*David Gardner is a professor of geology and physics at Montgomery College, Rockville, Md. He also teaches a course called Natural and Cultural History of the C&O Canal.

Remains of composite lock (Lock 64⅔) showing how such locks were built. Wall of inferior stone (all available in the upper Potomac Valley) covered with two layers of treated wood, the inner layer horizontal and the outer layer vertical. Wood sheath was not to add strength but to protect boats from damage by roughness of undressed stones.

Not a lock wall, but the kind of stone that made composite locks necessary and that formed their bases. (This is a part of one of the two supports for a crossover bridge.) An engineer in the field, at the upper end of the canal, wrote to the company that he had never before seen an area so "destitute of good building stone." With stones so shaped and textured, and with the cement dissolved and gone, such walls now have the appearance of dry masonry and great age and hold considerable charm for many.

faced with timber. The planking was not added to increase the strength of the walls but to give them a smooth surface. The roughness of undressed stone would have been too damaging to boats when there were occasional inevitable bumps.

Composite locks were all built in the upper part of the valley where the native stone is not good, or as Thomas Purcell, canal company engineer, put it, the region is "destitute of good building stone." In 1848 the company, on the recommendation of the chief engineer, changed the plan for the four locks at or near Old Town (68, 69, 70, 71) from cut stone to composite. It was too costly in time to haul stone to the sites, and too costly in money to use the better stone anyhow. That left the inferior stone locally available, and the engineer considered good composite locks far preferable to bad masonry ones. The austerity measure of composite construction was not a satisfactory solution, however, as the wood sheaths bulged and decayed. Most of this wooden facing rotted away long ago.

The locks just below the tunnel are additionally noteworthy in that they each have a ten-foot, rather than the regulation eight-foot, lift. This arrangement of fewer locks with higher lifts reflects

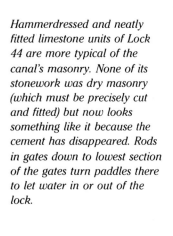

Hammerdressed and neatly fitted limestone units of Lock 44 are more typical of the canal's masonry. None of its stonework was dry masonry (which must be precisely cut and fitted) but now looks something like it because the cement has disappeared. Rods in gates down to lowest section of the gates turn paddles there to let water in or out of the lock.

a change in plans and accounts for some rather curious numbering. All locks from the tunnel to Cumberland were numbered while the tunnel was still unfinished. The original plan had been for four eight-foot locks immediately below the tunnel, but, to economize, three ten-foot locks were built instead. (The two-foot difference in rise was not critical.) This made it necessary to meddle with regularity and to number the locks this way: Lock 62, Lock 63⅓, Lock 64⅔, Lock 66. (There is no Lock 65.) This arbitrary arrangement brings these locks up to the earlier numbered ones, with 75 as the last of the canal's 74 lift locks.

Near Hancock the river takes on a shape similar to that at the tunnel. The canal crosses Prather's Neck, the land area between lengths of a loop in the river. For boats to negotiate the 32-foot rise from one side of the loop to the other, four closely spaced locks—47, 48, 49, and 50, known as Four Locks—were built in this one-mile segment of the canal. This saved four miles of canal construction which would have been necessary had the waterway followed its usual riverside course.

Enough room was left on the berm side of each of the canal's locks for an additional lock if trade ever warranted. These great expectations never materialized, but there were for a time more than a dozen double locks. Doubled locks, actually. These were

"That's Poppa," said Raymond Riley when he saw this shot of John Riley turning paddles to let water pour into Lock 24 at Seneca. The elder Riley tended lock here from 1892 until the canal closed in 1924. In background, behind balance beam, Sidney (Sid) Connell, section boss when this picture was made. Connell ran the repair scow from Seneca to Edwards Ferry.

73

simply locks made twice their original length by addition of wooden extensions, this in order to allow two boats to pass at a time.

Assiduous practice got the time for filling and emptying an ordinary lock down to three minutes. This was to set a record. Living boatmen agree that in normal work situations locking through took about ten minutes.

Lock gates were of wood and liable to early degeneration. Iron gates were tried in early sections of the canal, but were unsatisfactory. In an attempt to give longer life to the wooden

Skeleton of Lock 72's gates. Gate in foreground shows its halves meeting at an obtuse angle to form a watertight joint, pointing toward the higher reach of the canal so as to withstand pressure of the water from upstream. Gates were opened wide only to let boats pass; water was let into locks by use of moveable paddles at the bottoms of gates.

gates, paint was tried but discontinued—most likely because the expense wasn't demonstrably justified.

Some of the canal's masonry had a bedrock base, but most of it rested on timbers. Oak was popular, but there were also walnut, cherry, and whatever else was economical at any given spot. Such timbers can be seen today at the bases of ruined culverts, still sound because they have remained completely submerged in water and thus protected from air-breathing organisms that cause decay.

Many lock houses were of stone. They were attractive and

serviceable but, for good and obvious reasons, they were not built with the same care as were the best of the locks and aqueducts. Often they were done in random rubble, the roughest kind of masonry. Even so. These stones, irregular in shape and size and put together with a good deal of mortar in proportion to stone, have been made into particularly attractive houses.

In the upper Potomac Valley, with its dearth of stone, lock houses were frame buildings and, possibly built at a time when the canal company's finances were at particularly low ebb, at least two were made of logs.

For most of the length of the canal the towpath was on the river side. In Georgetown, however, because this was such a busy port and cargo was so often being handled, the towpath was much in the way. It was changed over to the berm side for the better part of a mile, and at 34th Street there was a cross-over bridge for mules. From there all the way to Dam No. 4 below Williamsport, the path was on the river side. Immediately above Dam No. 5 above Williamsport there is no canal, but slack water; so the towpath there is necessarily on the berm side.

Culverts carried creeks and other small streams under the

First aqueduct on the canal to be completed, the Seneca Creek Aqueduct saw use from 1831. Waste weir, at right, is removing surplus water from canal and discharging it in the creek. In 1971 a local storm crumbled one of the aqueduct's three arches (the one next to the waste weir).

Stone flower of the flock, the aqueduct over the Monocacy River, designed by Robert Leakie, was the longest and loveliest of the 11 on the canal. Made of pink and white quartzite from Sugar Loaf Mountain less than four miles away, its seven segmental spans stretch 433 feet.

canal. When streams were too big for culverts, aqueducts were built to carry the canal over them.

Each aqueduct was one of a kind, designed for the stream it bridged. The one that carried the canal over the Monocacy River was a great beauty, the most admired of the 11 on the canal. With seven 54-foot segmental arches, it is the longest of the lot. Most of its stone came from the Nelson Quarry, the main one of three then on Sugar Loaf Mountain.* It was hauled three and a half to four miles to the building site by horse-drawn carts on wooden rails. It is both pink and white quartzite, a stone similar to granite in its hardness but porous and therefore vulnerable. The pink gave trouble from the very beginning—in 1828 and 1829 frost action split much of it—and it long ago went rotten. Piers sank and the entire aqueduct gradually weakened until now its beauty is heavily obscured by closely spaced steel supports.

On this aqueduct there stands a memorial marker, an upright stone slab bearing the names of many involved in its construction.[3] It seems a shame, and an error as well, that the name of Robert Leakie is missing. It was Leakie who designed the

---

*Sugar Loaf is a monadnock, a mountain made of erosion-resistant rock, in this case quartzite, which stands alone in a formerly mountainous area that has been eroded to the condition of a plain. Sugar Loaf is isolated, well east of the Blue Ridge Mountains and not a part of that chain. It is an uncommon formation in that its origin is a mystery.

Handcrafted iron railings on the Monocacy Aqueduct. The beauty is still there, but now heavily obscured by closely spaced steel supports over the entire structure. Sinking piers and gradual weakening brought the aqueduct to this pass, but there is some hope that it will one day be returned to its pristine state in which it was extravagantly admired.

One beautiful arch forms the Town Creek Aqueduct, one of six single-span aqueducts in the upper Valley. It is 60 feet long. The one over Licking Creek is longest, at 90 feet; the one over Fifteen Mile Creek is shortest, at 50 feet.

aqueduct and was superintendent of masonry from 1828 to 1832 or throughout most of its construction. When he was compelled to resign because of illness, A.B. McFarlan(d), whose name does appear, succeeded him.

The tablet, which was not set up until after completion of the canal in 1850, includes the name "M. Byrne." Michael Byrne was the contractor for the aqueduct and for the section of the canal that included it. This was the same Michael Byrne who was the contractor for the short bit of the canal remaining undone when Hunter, Harris went bankrupt in 1850.

The Catoctin Creek Aqueduct is a sad case. It is the inanimate analogue of a dog, produced by a breeder who bred for questionable reasons, so big and heavy that its hipbones are unequal to the burden inflicted on them. Faulty design made this aqueduct unable to hold itself up. It was made of granite hauled by the B&O Railroad from Ellicott's Mills in Baltimore County and, with its 40-foot center arch flanked by 20-foot arches, it was a pretty thing. The long center arch was almost an ellipse, and the small arches at the ends were Roman. Elliptical and Roman arches make a better mix than oil and water, but that's about all. Even a segmental arch, let alone an elliptical, cannot be successfully placed against a semicircular arch unless there will be the most scrupulous maintenance. All the weight of a Roman arch pushes down, the segmental or elliptical arch pushes sideways, and the Roman can offer the segmental nothing to counter its side thrust.

In addition to its essential instability, the Catoctin Aqueduct was one of the worst built structures on the canal. During construction its west pier was rejected. It was torn down and rebuilt, but was never quite right. Moreover, this aqueduct leaked from the day water was let into it. Leakage became serious in 1859, and from then on its history was one of patch, patch, patch. Those most knowledgeable believe that it began sagging badly around 1926, with its piers cracking and settling. This worsened as years passed. Damaged as it was, it managed to withstand hurricane Agnes in 1972, but, after enduring torrential rain without letup for two consecutive days in October, 1973, most of the structure fell in a heap. The only part that still stands is the small arch on the east end.

Little remains of the Great Tonoloway Creek Aqueduct, but in its day it was interesting because its single arch stopped before it could complete the downward curve which would have made it a Roman arch. The west abutment was only 4 feet above the creek's surface, the east one on a rock ledge 16 feet above the water. The arch was abruptly ended, 12 feet short of a perfect form, when it came up against a limestone cliff.

The limestone aqueduct over Antietam Creek has three elliptical arches, the center span 40 feet and the two side spans 28 feet each. A well-built structure, it was finished in 1834 and was one of the prettiest and largest aqueducts on the waterway. The spot where it stands has a tragic significance, as this is the creek that literally ran red with blood on the worst single day of slaughter in the Civil War. The aqueduct is now in excellent condition, restored by the National Park Service.

Made of local limestone, the Conococheague Creek Aqueduct—three segmental arches of 60 feet each—was also one of the canal's larger structures and unique for its decorative pilasters. Completed in 1834, it saw many hard times. In 1851 it sprang serious leaks. In 1863 and again in 1864 it was blasted by Confederates and damaged in the northwest corner. It was repaired, of course—and the spot can be easily identified today because the stones used for patching were larger than the original ones. In 1865, ruinously weakened by war damage plus the old leakage problem, 155 feet of the aqueduct shattered and 115 feet of this stretch fell to pieces. A wooden trunk was installed and the stonework rebuilt between 1869 and 1871. The masonry wall on the lower end of the berm side toppled (again) in 1887 and was rebuilt. When the entire upstream wall "went out," as the boatmen say, in 1920—and small wonder that it finally did—that was the aqueduct's third fall.

One aqueduct, roughly 30 miles from Georgetown, was made of wood. It was listed in the company's engineering records as a culvert, but it carried the canal over Broad Run Creek, for which reason there are those who think of it as an aqueduct.

Underside of single-arch aqueduct over Great Tonoloway Creek. This aqueduct is an incomplete Roman arch. Cause of the irregularity was that the east abutment had to be on a rock ledge 16 feet above the stream. The intended semicircle was stopped, 12 feet short of completion, when it came up against a limestone cliff.

Another rather irritating anomaly is that the structure never had a whole number of its own but was called Culvert 44½.

Broad Run Creek was first dealt with by a red sandstone culvert of two 16-foot arches. This was washed out in 1846. The canal company then put in a timber trunk over the stream, making it an aqueduct but never changing its designation as a culvert in company records. When the wooden trunk was built, it was made shorter than the stone culvert that it replaced. The builders used what was left of one of the culvert's stone arches as an abutment and narrowed the creek at that point by placing the opposite abutment farther into the stream. The wooden trunk was positioned from abutment to abutment. Wood was not good in this context, and the trunk used to rot and fall apart and be replaced, and rot and fall apart and be replaced, over and over. Its remnants are now in utterly ramshackle condition, consisting of a wrecked floor of large and once stout timbers reinforced with iron rods that ran crossways the trough. Some of the bleached timbers of this small aqueduct are now snapped in half, and the broken and rusted reinforcements stick off every whichway.

The masonry was the glory of the canal. It still is something of an unofficial national treasure, even though a rickety and tumbledown treasure. The aqueducts exemplify an art which, if not lost, has long been in disuse. Excluding the oddly designated Broad Run structure, they were masonry arch bridges, the most graceful of all bridge types.

Stone is the best of all materials for arched spans up to 200 feet, and the C&O builders produced strong and visually pleasing masonry arch aqueducts.[4]

Properly built, supported, planted, and maintained, masonry arch bridges will last for a very long time. The water supply for 20th century Italians in the cathedral city of Spoleto arrives by way of an aqueduct built in 1364, and substantial stretches of the miles-long Roman aqueducts still remain.

The shapely little aqueducts of the C&O, however, were not built for the ages, nor was that ever their builders' vaulting ambition. Made with the inferior cementing agents available at that time, inescapably standing in water, these aqueducts never had a tremendous life expectancy.

The creeks in which they stood, flowing continuously and in one direction, eroded the undersides of the piers and, by degrees, dislodged them. As the piers sank, the aqueduct walls moved outward. This outward leaning was the first lurch toward collapse.

Although it was the undermining of piers and not the proximity of the river and its floods that did the most damage to the canal's structures, the river did its bit. Sturdy as they were, the aqueducts progressively weakened under the brutal buffeting of floods. For almost its entire length, the canal hugged the river's bank closely. In many places not much more than the towpath separated the canal from the river. There were stretches where cliffs had prevented the river from forming itself a bed that was more than a narrow gorge, and the canal had to run along the very rim of the river. This put the waterway in a position of naked exposure to the violence of every flood that came along, and there were many.

Weighty as water is, it was not the water of floods that did the most harm. It was the assortment of extremely heavy objects swept along by the rampaging river—tree trunks, boats, houses, barns—that were crashed against the walls of the aqueducts with the force and effect of so many battering rams. Much flood damage occurred when creeks rose faster than the river. At those times, water piled up against the upstream walls of the aqueducts, making them into dams. Aqueduct walls, and real dams as well, were repeatedly pounded and partially carried off but were promptly repaired. Since the closing of the canal, however, flood damage and lack of maintenance and repair have reduced all the aqueducts to various stages of disintegration.

The canal's masonry made nice ruins. To Americans sated with BIG, the remnants of the canal and its structures are appealing in their smallness, and the stonework makes a good show in those spots where the surroundings have been tidied up. (In unkempt spots it is pathetic.) The stone locks and aqueducts had undeniable beauty in their prime; and in ruins, because their cement is dissolved and gone, they appear to be dry masonry and they have something of the look of ancient walls.

HOME ON THE CANAL

[1] In 1847 when the first of the Smithsonian buildings was to be built, Seneca stone was chosen. Precedent would have dictated stone from Aquia Creek, as the White House and most other government buildings in Washington then were of that Virginia stone. After a survey of quarries, however, the Seneca stone was judged the pick of the Potomac freestones. Freestones are neither too hard nor too soft, and can be cut in any direction without splitting. The main ones are sandstone and limestone.

The Seneca stone had other desirable qualities including uniformity of color, which meant that it would be minimally liable to uglification by buildups of city smoke and dust. As to its durability and beauty, there was no question. When sandstone is bad, it's horrid; but when it's good, it's very, very good. There was wide variation in quality of the stone at the Seneca quarries, but that used in the Smithsonian's "castle" and in the canal's locks was the pick of the lot. There still is stone in the quarry at Seneca, but it is all leavings.

[2] Masons' marks of some description have appeared on building stones since time out of mind. Among comparatively modern European masons it was a tradition, handed down the generations, to cut their marks on "their" stones, perhaps for identification purposes at pay time. (Such marks have been found by the hundreds in the original walls of the White House.) The stonecutters on the canal were paid monthly wages. Had there been a need for identification of stones at pay time, all the masonry on the canal would be peppered with the marks. It is probably true that some few stonecutters, acting out a harking back to the longstanding tradition, made their marks on randomly chosen stones.

David Gardner, a geologist who describes himself as a canal freak, reports that on the Virginia side of the river, on the old canal that bypassed Great Falls, he has found marks "which are almost exactly like some I've found in the columns of the Capitol—[in the part that] was built after the British burned it. So I figure it's either the same mason or the same family." The Capitol was under construction all the time the canal was, and during the latter part of the time the old Potomac Company was building its skirting canals on the river's Virginia side.

[3] Inscription on the Monocacy Aqueduct marker:

Monocacy Aqueduct
Finished 1833

Chesapeake & Ohio Canal Co.

Engineers	Contractors
Alfred Cruger	M. Byrne
Principal	W. Byrne
C.B. Fisk	S. Lothrop
Assistant	
A.B. McFarlan	
Inspector of masonry	

C. Mercer (pres.)

J.H. Albert	
W. Smith	
P. Jarney	Directors
A. Stewart	
P. Lenox	
W. Price	

J.P. Ingle, Clerk
Clement Smith, Treas.

82

4 At the height of their development and popularity, such bridges were suddenly struck obsolete. In 1909 the first mile of concrete road in the U.S. was laid in Michigan, and the day of the masonry arch bridge was over. When portland cement became available, this ingredient made possible an excellent grade of concrete, and concrete quickly became *the* structural material. In comparison with stone it was cheap, and it was also easier to shape and to place. As with much progress, there was built-in retrogression; in the instance of concrete bridges, beauty of a high natural order was sacrificed.

In some form, concrete has been in use for 5,000 years. Ages ago in the Near East it was used, almost entirely for fortifications. The innovative Romans developed it to the point of its being the backbone of their construction methods.

To those who think of concrete mainly in terms of city pavements, it seems a prosaic and unimpressive material; but it has been a wonder-working power in architecture. The grandeur that was Rome rested on this cheap, strong, versatile product that lent itself so well to production of monolithic forms.

With concrete, Rome's engineers and architects were able to contrive gigantic interiors—so important to them for vainglorious parade of war trophies—and all the city's massive structures including sewers and aqueducts. These great construction artists made temples with cut stone doors, window frames, and columns, and concrete walls faced with small flat pieces of stone. They veneered concrete podia with thin slices of marble. They made the mammoth Colosseum—lacking concrete, its outlandish size would have been out of the question—with a concrete core and an exterior of cut stone. For their splendid Pantheon they made a great concrete dome and covered it with gilded bronze.

Concrete had released the Romans to thoroughly indulge their passion for the huge and the ostentatious. Such structures gave high visibility to their might, and pride-and-power was the name of their game. After they had the good concrete, they never had to design one other building of modest size or boxy shape. And they had the good concrete because it was they who discovered hydraulic cement. They made this by mixing lime paste with volcanic ash, *pozzolana,* from Mount Vesuvius.

The process for making this type of cement was lost when the Roman empire fell A.D. 476, and hydraulic cement did not reappear until past the middle of the 18th century. It was then that the English civil engineer John Smeaton devised a system by which he built the famous Eddystone light, a lighthouse that endured on a spot where none before it had survived the full force of the sea. For this lighthouse Smeaton made a binding agent and foundations from a mixture that amounted to our present-day concrete. This was the first known use of concrete since the days of imperial Rome.

In 1824, portland cement was invented by Joseph Aspdin, an English brickmason. He made it by burning limestone and clay together, and he so named it because its color was similar to that of limestone found on the Isle of Portland, a peninsula in the English Channel.

In Operation:
Winning isn't always not losing.

AS A RULE, each section of the canal was used as completed. In November, 1830, the first section, between Little Falls and Seneca, was opened, and in the summer of 1831 the Seneca-to-Georgetown section was ready. There followed a fruitless passage of time while the Point of Rocks controversy seethed. The canal was finished from Seneca to Harpers Ferry in 1834, to Williamsport in 1835, and to Dam No. 6, seven miles west of Hancock, in 1839. This point, approximately 135 miles from Georgetown, was the end of the canal until its completion in 1850.

When, in later years, the boats became uniform in size, they were 90 to 92 feet long and 14 feet wide, the largest the canal's locks could accommodate. The stable was at the bow, the hay house in the middle, and the cabin at the stern. Between stable and hay house and between hay house and cabin, 14 hatches covered space for 120 tons of cargo. A race plank about a foot wide wrapped around the outer edge of the entire deck, providing a path from one part of the boat to another.

Because the boat was designed for cargo, the families and hands had to content themselves with the smallest of accommodations. The approximately 12- by 12-foot cabin had an entry at the foot of a short flight of stairs. Counterclockwise, there was the galley, and rubbing elbows with the galley a tiny stateroom for the captain (and his wife if she were aboard). In the next corner a built-in bunk, or sometimes two bunks with one atop the other, provided sleeping space for children. (If there was a hand, he slept in the hay house.) Next came the dining table, placed in front of a window. (Canal boat terminology was semi-nautical. The bedroom was a stateroom, but a window was not a porthole and a bumper was a bumper.) In the fourth corner was a cupboard or a set of shelves. The facility was the same as it would have been in many homes in many towns in those days—a lidded china jar.

Outsiders marvel at the high threshold of irritability and the forbearance of people who lived in peace on such a small craft for long periods of time. Surviving members of boating families, however, took the living arrangements for granted and did not feel overly cramped. To outsiders, the idea of canal boat life suggests solid, oppressive togetherness. To those on the boat, it could often feel lonely.

Even though there was minute living space on these cargo carriers, crew members were separated by their jobs much of the time. The one who was steering had to stay put and steer; the one who was driving the mules had to stay out on the towpath and drive the mules; the one who was cooking had to stay in the galley and cook. Whoever was caring for off-duty mules stayed in the stable and sponged and curried. And this accounted for every worker on the boat.

Captains named their boats for reasons of patriotism or personal fondness, sometimes for admired abstractions. There were *Andrew Jackson No. 1* and *Andrew Jackson No. 2, Tip and Tyler, A. Lincoln,* and *Old Zack.* During the years shortly before the Civil War there were *Union, Yankee, American Flag, Liberty, Constitution,* and a scow named *Uncle Sam.* There were the *Ant,* the *May Fly, Cock Robin,* the *Reindeer,* and a scow called *Lion.* There were *Enterprise, Advance, Rough and Ready, Morning Star,* and the affectionately titled *Katie Darling* and *Granpa.*

For all the toilsome man hours that went into the construction of the waterway, it was mules that made the canal go. Two to three made a team, depending on their size, and while one team pulled the boat another was in the stable. Theoretically a team worked a six-hour trick, as a shift was called, and then rested before working again. Boatmen from the canal's later years recall that this plan was generally observed, but point out that each mule's fate depended on the captain of his boat. Some captains regularly ran day and night, making for longer hours or more tricks or both than the ordinary run.

As quoted in a Washington area newspaper some years back, a boatman told how a mule of his absolutely hated to go down into the stable, afraid because, the boatman supposed, it was mostly below deck and dark. Without embarrassment he reported that once he had driven the animal such an inhuman number of hours that the figure will not be repeated here. Even on this occasion, he said—when the mule could not have been other than nearly out on his feet and the stable meant rest to him—the mule tried to avoid going down into the dark stable. Other mules had the gratitude and sometimes the fondness of their captains and families, and many canal children learned to curry and care for mules and almost made pets of them.*

From the time the boats began using the first section of completed canal, the company had to direct operation as well as construction. It promptly provided users with an extensive set of rules and regulations, among the first of which was that all boats had to be moved by a towing line drawn by men or horses. (Later on, horses were almost entirely replaced by mules.) Other instructions called for the utmost care to avoid damage or injury to the canal or its users. For example, iron-tipped poles were forbidden, as were pointed boats and boats with ironclad corners, because of the harm they would have done to the masonry.

Craft were to pass on the right, with these priorities: boats had right-of-way over rafts, downstream (loaded) boats over upstream (light) boats, packets over freight boats, and mail packets over any and all other craft. Boats were to show lights on their bows when traveling at night. Locktenders were to be given sufficient notice to open the gates for approaching boats. (Many boatmen used bugles or horns, others simply shouted.)

*The way the mules meshed with the rest of the canal operation is covered in the second part of this book, in the recollections of surviving canallers.

Unless the locktender failed them completely, boatmen were not to lock themselves through; and when they did so, they were to handle the company's property with care. Boats were to be on the berm side of the canal when tied up, as on the towpath side they would impede traffic.

The canal was divided into long stretches, each of which had its superintendent. Superintendents were held responsible for all that took place in their territory, and it was generally agreed that their responsibility exceeded their authority. A repair gang was assigned to each section.

Application of rules was not wholly successful, and it didn't make things any better that superintendents were frequently changed. This rapid changing began with the earliest completed section of the canal and continued after it was finished.

Freight and toll rates were to be perennially sore subjects. In 1849, James M. Coale, president of the C&O at that time, differentiated between the two in a report to stockholders. He defined tolls as payment by shippers "for the privilege of carrying the tonnage on the canal," and freight fees as what the boatman charged "for conveying it to its destination." Coale said that the charge for conveyance was a matter of contract between the boatman and his employer and would vary with varying circumstances.

Such rates may have been, as Coale said, a matter between the boatman and his employer, but that never kept the company from putting pressure on the boatmen to lower them whenever the company felt a need to economize. In the canal's late years, when the towage company was in authority, it set freight rates as well as tolls. Not amazingly, this brought on frequent and rancorous clashes between company and boatmen.

A locktender, on 24-hour call, was given a rent-free house, an acre of land for a kitchen garden, and $150 a year. If he tended more than one lock, he was paid $50 for each extra one and he could take on as many as three altogether. Three brought in $250 a year, but to help him tend the extra locks he had to furnish his own assistants. For this reason, married men with large families were favored in the hiring. There were some few women locktenders, usually hired because they were widows of former locktenders. In the spring of 1835 the company decided to fire all women locktenders, with the idea that an all-male staff would make for more efficiency. (At least four of the widows were rehired.) It was explained that this was not meant to reflect poorly on the women's competence, but that the job did call for a good deal of physical strength and was considered usually more suitable employment for men. Doubtless the men were stronger, but they too had their little failings. Many were discharged for negligence, for being absent without a substitute, and for being drunk. Many a complaint was made about locktenders selling whiskey to boatmen and members of section gangs, and about the disturbances that resulted. The board of directors repeated over and over again its emphatic rule against

Lock tender and family at Lock 25 at Edward's Ferry.

selling whiskey, but it might as well have saved its corporate breath to cool its corporate soup.

For all the carefully detailed regulations, there was much abuse of both rules and property. The company's tools were broken by careless handling and were often lost or stolen; and the towpaths and aqueducts were invasively used by waggoners and horseback riders.

Canallers formed something of a subculture, forging friendships and marrying within the group. Children grew up on boats and boating was the life they knew. The first boatmen were a rough and a raffish lot. There was much jockeying for position at the locks, and jockeying for position easily passed into fisticuffs. The routine of boatmen's lives varied with the individual captains' temperaments, some proceeding at a reasonable pace to complete a run, some pushing on day and night.

The company did its best to rid the canal of many undesirable boats and to encourage the use of larger ones. Growing trade brought larger boats, and finally the average canal boat was as much as the locks could accommodate. By heavily increasing rates on rafts, the company sought to get them off the canal altogether, but this was difficult. Many farmers threw together expendable rafts which were sold for lumber at the same time their cargo was sold in Georgetown, the same as traders had done in their trips to Georgetown by way of the skirting canals of the old Potomac Company. And, like the early traders, these made their way home on foot.

At first the cargo was agricultural produce almost entirely, mainly flour, wheat, and corn. There was also some shipment of lumber, lime, stone, and some coal. Trade was slow-growing, partly because at this time the canal company did not make vigorous efforts to increase it. The directors often mentioned the value of the Erie Canal to New York in terms of how much trade it brought about, but they seemed to feel that the C&O would naturally attract business and they did little to do this themselves.

Also working against development of trade were halts caused by floods and breaks in the towpath. There was the continued opposition of the B&O Railroad. Maintenance of the canal was itself a job without end, as it had been even with the almost imperishable aqueducts of Rome, and many times in the early years trade had to be suspended for weeks at a time while breaks were repaired. While both canal and railroad were being built between Point of Rocks and Harpers Ferry, boatmen complained that rocks were falling or being thrown into the canal from the building site of the railroad higher up the slope, and that these rocks were piling up in the canal to the danger of the boats and making quick remedy imperative.

During this period, Charles Carroll, who said he considered his roles as founder of the B&O and the USA of equal importance, personally did his bit to add to the canal company's woes. He cold-shouldered all the company's offers for his acreage in the Potomac Valley. Explaining his unalterable refusals to sell, he wrote to Charles F. Mercer, president of the canal company, expressing a concern, touching if true, for his tenants. He made much of the hardship that canal construction would bring down upon them, and pointed out that they would benefit from it not at all. He wrote that the only result would be higher value of his land once the canal was finished—if it was ever finished, which he doubted.

There were other disputes as time went by, with the railroad, true to form, indulging in all sorts of harassing maneuvers. During their rivalry for the flour trade, the railroad had raised its rates and its directors urged the canal company to do likewise. When the canal company responded to this gambit by doing so, the railroad put its rates even lower than before and within a few months the canal company's flour trade was in sorry condition. The railroad kept up its efforts to wrest from the canal the remnants of its flour trade, with most of its ploys in violation of agreements with the company.

It was the fight for the Cumberland coal trade, however, that hit the canal hardest. Earlier, the railroad had operated behind a studiedly visible but flimsy scrim of concern for the canal's welfare. During the flour contention it came out in the open, later making an all-out attack on the canal company's coal trade.

As a matter of policy, the railroad devised all the troublesome predicaments it could for the C&O and continued with what was by then a custom of making agreements only to break them.

The canal company's best chance to make money was its sale of water. It carefully informed itself on the procedures used by other canals in water matters and took their rules as guides. It granted water rights at Williamsport, Weverton, Georgetown, and other places. Georgetown offered industrialists a fine combination of inducements including available labor, nearness to markets, and unrestricted water supply; and its millers, founders, and textile manufacturers were the canal company's main customers.

All that came after a battle. While the waterway was being built there were mills and factories along the path that it would follow, and there was the hope that others would be established as more of the canal was completed. The canal did stimulate industry in Georgetown. By 1851 the town had five flour mills, a grist mill, a cotton mill, a soap factory, an iron foundry, two bakeries, and a lime kiln. The four Georgetown locks furnished a 32-foot head of water, giving a good supply for industry. Baltimore, in competition with the Georgetown millers, was implacably opposed to the canal company's sale of water. Influential with the Maryland legislature, Baltimore succeeded in having a limit set on the number of mills in Georgetown that could use C&O-furnished water.

When this sale of water was first considered, the water was not actually the canal company's to sell. By 1837, however, the company had obtained all necessary approvals, including that of the Congress, and had legal authority to sell surplus river water. Until then, however, the company had undergone much maltreatment from numerous sources. One litigant hauled the company into court time after time. Time after time the canal won, but the company was put to extra and doubtless painful expense in terms of time and money, and the plaintiff was always ready with an appeal or another case. If canal company officials didn't already know it theoretically, they learned from this experience that winning isn't always not losing.

The
First Twenty Years:
Floods, war,
and politics.

AS SOON AS THE WHOLE CANAL was completed, the company began revising toll rates, a new permanent schedule going into effect in June, 1851. This placed commodities shipped on the canal into six classes. Classes I and II had the highest rates and included general merchandise, spirits, and agricultural produce. One commodity, salt, made up Class III. Classes IV and V consisted of heavy freight, mainly lumber, bricks, cement, and manufactured iron. The most important and most competitive freight was in Class VI, on which the lowest tolls were charged. In this group were coal, limestone, and iron ore. Coal was the principal commodity involved in the life of the canal, and its main source of revenue.

The Cumberland coal field was approximately 25 miles long and 5 wide. Not much more than half of it was mined, most of the coal being taken from a 14-foot seam known as the big vein. Most of the mining was done in George's Creek Basin, west of Cumberland, and the boatmen spoke of their cargo as George's Creek coal.

The canal company foresaw a rosy future for the coal field. The bituminous field nearest to the North Atlantic seaboard, it yielded an excellent grade of steam-producing coal. Government tests showed that pound for pound the Cumberland coal bulked up smaller and produced more heat than any other soft coal known in the country. Expectations soared. The field was regarded as perhaps not inexhaustible like that mill that is grind-

The Potomac and the Canal at Williamsport. One of Williamsport's claims to fame is that it was second only to Sharpsburg in the number of its citizens on the canal.

Loading coal at Cumberland. Boats waiting their turns to pull under a coal car standing over chute that emptied coal into holds. Otho Swain recalled, "When they'd get that first 30 tons on the back, the boat would raise up. Then they'd have to back the boat back, and they'd put another load on the front. That would even it up. Then they'd put on the rest of the load. It would generally take four box cars to fill a boat."

ing salt at the bottom of the sea, but certainly good for at least several hundred years. As for the railroad, nobody then expected it to carry heavy cargo. The president of the B&O was reported by the Hagerstown *Mail* to have said before Congress that the railroad was for transportation of passengers "and such light freight as we now send by express," and the canal company looked to the future with abounding confidence.

There were changes in the 1851 schedule as the years went by, with some commodities shifted from one class to another. Trade improved intermittently. In the first year of operation of the whole canal, tonnage doubled, going to 203,893 tons. This achievement was followed by ups and downs, and the amount of coal on the canal did not increase as expected.

The company then did its best to encourage trade. For example, it asked the Alexandria Canal Company to keep its locks open until 8 p.m., later than was usual. To bring delays to a minimum, it rescinded the right-of-way of packets over loaded boats. It also entertained ideas for improvement of the canal, such as the raising of the Georgetown bridges, a project that, originally proposed in the early fifties, did not materialize until 1867.

The disheartening fact was that the canal was an unreliable carrier. The river flooded regularly, and the political factor was just as troublemaking. In the spring of 1852, with the completed canal's business just well under way, the worst flood up to that time savaged the whole length of the canal. The company had taken the precaution of raising the canal's embankments at what seemed to be the most imperiled spots above the level of the hitherto worst floods in the records of the valley. In the flood of 1852, however, the river rose in some places 6 feet higher than ever before. At Great Falls the water reached a new high of 64 feet. The saddest thing was that, even with this worst-so-far flood, a rise of just 2 or 3 feet less would have meant that the canal would have suffered no serious damage. As it was, repairs cost the company $100,000 and grave harm was done to trade.

Right after the flood came political interference as damaging as anything the canal had suffered from nature. Canal "ownership" by the State of Maryland gave the choice of new board members to the political party currently in power. Subordinates all up and down the line were therefore the objects of party patronage. In June, 1852, the state appointed new company administrators who instituted a top-to-bottom spoils system and thereby set a precedent. From then until the early sixties, every time a new board came in there was an orgy of firing and hiring. Concern for the effect on the canal was practically nonexistent.

Bondholders complained that there had been a dozen different administrations in 20 years, resulting in undependable transportation, a failure to dredge when the canal silted up, dilapidated culverts, unpaid interest on bonds, and bonds themselves fallen to a value "below sale or quotation." They put the whole blame squarely on the State of Maryland, as it had "absolutely shaped and controlled the policy of the company." As a group of bondholders summed it up, the great enterprise languished. Nobody has ever questioned their opinion, but only wondered how the canal survived at all.

Mother Nature continued her attacks. Not a year passed without its natural mishap. Severe droughts so lowered the water level that the boats had to stop for weeks at a time. One year low water below Dam No. 6 stopped commerce for two months. A flash flood washed out a culvert and caused a loss of several weeks. One year the opening of the canal was late because of lingering harsh winter weather. A drought in 1856 caused low water and forced the company to build masonry dams to replace the old brush-and-rubble ones.

The old unsubstantial dams had required frequent repair, causing much loss of time. Contracts for the new Dams No. 4 and No. 5 were let in early 1857, and hardly had this been done when a flood of ice pushed its way down the valley. In all, four floods overran the canal in 1857. That year drove the company almost to the edge of financial ruin.* Even when good, the com-

---

*In the same year another depression hit the country, its most terrible blows falling on industrial workers in the cities. American wage earners had come to be in a more perilous position than Old World serfs, who had at least been given some sort of food and shelter. The urban poverty that now burst upon the American scene was on such a scale and so glaringly juxtaposed with riches as to be an altogether new phenomenon in this country.

pany's condition had always been precarious because of heaped up debts and repair costs. Just before the Civil War broke out, it was running on empty and its officials were expecting foreclosure.

The war brought much destruction to the canal and its business. As the waterway was right between Washington and Richmond, it was highly vulnerable to damage from both Confederate and Union forces. In some instances, battles were fought so close to the canal that the company's property was hurriedly made into hospitals and morgues. Besides the harm done by fighting around and across the canal, both sides seized and held parts of it from time to time. Early seizure of the Alexandria Aqueduct by the Union army left the canal without its only practicable outlet to the river at tidewater and played havoc with trade.

In the first year of the war, Confederate troops broke through embankments at crucial spots and attempted to blow up some dams. In *I Rode with Stonewall,* Henry Kyd Douglas, youngest member of Jackson's staff, wrote, "Before New Year's General Jackson made several trips to Dam Number Five on the Potomac for the purpose of destroying it and thereby impairing the efficiency of the Chesapeake and Ohio Canal, over which large supplies of coal and military stores were transported to Washington. . . ."

The Hagerstown *Mail* reported that on December 7 the roar of cannon had been so loud and seemed so close as to alarm the townspeople. It was the sound of Stonewall Jackson's battery attempting to put Dam No. 5 out of commission. According to the *Mail,* "With the artillery he had he was unable to batter down the dam, which was constructed of splendid masonry, but it was greatly weakened." Union soldiers on the Maryland side of the river fired on the Confederates in an effort to protect the dam. What they managed to do was to destroy a barn and a large store of grain, as like as not the property of a Union sympathizer.

Jackson made another try on December 10. With his militia making a feint in the direction of Williamsport, he and his small force left Martinsburg and marched to a spot near Dam No. 5. There the Confederates worked from the 17th to the 21st, digging a channel that diverted the canal's water supply. This dried up mile after mile of the waterway, and for the time being knocked out that area of the canal for both Union troop movements and coal shipments from Williamsport to Washington.

The canal was soon taken under protection of the government, but the Confederates attacked Dam No. 5 again. They took cover behind "Coulston's splendid stone mill," fired on the dam and destroyed the cribbing. At this point the Fifth Connecticut put up a battery, bombarded the Confederates, and drove them from the sheltering mill.

Without these interruptions, the canal's shipping could have continued throughout that mild December. January 1, 1862, was so warm (60 degrees) that fires were unnecessary, but on January 2 "the winter set in very cold." Shooting went on all during the winter, but little damage was done and that to buildings and not people. The presence of the Union army was "offensive" to some locals but good for business, the soldiers buying all manner of products at substantial prices. The army left for Virginia in March, 1862, and a month later paid nearly $60,000 owed for flour and other provisions.

In that same month, March, 1862, "Lieutenant Brooke's iron pot," the startling ironclad *Merrimac,* horrified the Union navy and briefly demoralized Lincoln's cabinet. It had quickly destroyed two frigates in Hampton Roads, itself unnervingly unaffected by their shots; and at six o'clock on the morning after, the cabinet members met to put their minds to what might be done to protect the Union from this "monster."* At the top of his voice the secretary of war, Edwin M. Stanton, informed the others that the war was lost, thanks to the *Merrimac.* "Nothing," he shouted, "can prevent her destroying *seriatim* every naval vessel, laying Washington in ashes. . . . [It is] not

*Communications being slow then, they couldn't know that the Union's own "monster," the *Monitor,* had been completed. More, it had already started out from Long Island for Hampton Roads. There the *Monitor* would confront and defeat the *Merrimac* on the day after the *Merrimac*'s electrifying performance.

unlikely that we will have from one of her guns a cannon ball in this room before we leave it."

Every American schoolchild knows, or every American schoolchild used to know, how mistaken Stanton was; but things being as they were on March 9, 1862, cabinet members were popping proposals right off the tops of their heads. One proposal that was adopted had to do with canal boats. The government commandeered about 100 boats and held them at Georgetown for whatever use might seem appropriate. Some were filled with rocks and taken down to the river so they could be sunk if it became necessary to block the channel. Six or eight of them actually were sunk later; the others were returned to their owners. More boats were seized in the fall and in the following summer, but held for short periods of time.

In 1864 Early, Mosby, and White conducted raids in which they burned boats, stole mules, and damaged locks and aqueducts. In their effort to bring trade to a halt, the Confederates spot-damaged the canal and tried to prevent repairs. This went on from summer to late fall. The same sort of thing continued until close to the end of the war, when boating was no longer disrupted and the canal's trade and financial condition made some improvement.

In addition to the physical harm to the canal, the company suffered other severe losses. Markets and mills along the canal were destroyed, and the coastal trade, which had accounted for a good amount of coal hauled on the waterway, dwindled.

The setback that might have been the worst during the war years was the loss of two-thirds of its flour trade. This was partly due to the war's interference—for four months during 1861 the canal's business all but stood stock-still—and partly to the B&O's continued efforts to get the lion's share.

Flour had been the mainstay of the company before the canal was finished to Cumberland near the coal field, and it had kept the company going during its leanest years. Even after coal became the chief commodity shipped on the canal, flour had accounted for a large part of its business. For this to go down by two-thirds was a body blow to the company's income. The

C&O went through several more thin years, during which it got more loans from coal companies and scrimped and saved, for example by making only partial payment to employees. At the same time workers were on reduced pay, they were hit by a rising cost of living. The company was obliged to pinch every penny. Even necessary repairs were done in a shoddy fashion, and important improvements—for example, the "raising" of the Georgetown bridges—had to be postponed.

Another continuing source of wartime annoyance and discomfort to the canal company was disloyalty, i.e. Southern sympathizing, among company officials and other employees. The wartime president of the company, Alfred Spates, was so open in his sympathies with the Confederacy that he was three times arrested and detained by military authorities. An engineer working on the new masonry Dam No. 5 was briefly in prison on the same charge. George Spates, a superintendent on the Monocacy division, and some of the men who worked with him, were similarly accused.

Fear of loss of employees to the Union draft was rather more than ensuing events warranted. A few lockkeepers were drafted, but they borrowed money and paid substitutes to operate the locks.

Simultaneously with war-caused troubles, the company's old familiar troubles were much in effect. Politics had brought about a massive turnover of employees in 1860 and 1862, and the consensus was that the newly appointed officials didn't strain themselves attending to company business.

Although the continuity of its own work was disrupted, the canal did the Union good service between raids and repair sessions. It transported both troops and materials, especially the coal supply the federal government prized so highly. The canal, being right at the river, was a natural line of defense for the Union and was often used as such.

Despite all this and much more, the latter years of the war were for the canal company the opposite of its early years. Business picked up in 1863 so much that, although it still could not take care of needed repairs, the company raised its employees' pay and made a beginning on discharging its debts. Business continued to improve during the rest of the war, and by 1865 the company had paid off all its debts and around $150,000 of the indebtedness of its predecessors.

When the war was over the canal was in poor physical shape, but repair and improvement began almost at once. One project, which was a physical and financial improvement but an aesthetic disaster, came a couple of years later, the often talked about and long delayed raising of the bridges at Georgetown.

Eager to carry heavier loads (of more than 100 tons) and unable to use wider boats because of the size of the locks, users had increased the height of their boats. Before the end of 1850, the first year the whole canal was in use, the boats had got so high that there was trouble at the North-South pedestrian bridges over the canal in Georgetown. Only fully loaded boats could pass under these bridges. Unloaded and riding high, going back upstream, the boats could not get under the bridges until the water level of the canal was lowered.

This necessitated what is called the raising of the Georgetown bridges; but the Georgetown bridges weren't raised, they were razed. Four of these five well-wrought masonry structures were torn down and replaced with serviceable but not visually satisfying new bridges.* They were finished in 1867. After the bridges were "raised," it became necessary to literally raise some streets in Georgetown. This is why pre-Civil-War houses occupied there today have English basements; the basements were originally the ground level floors of the houses.

During the post war period, trade on the canal made quick and good recoveries from all reverses it had undergone. In 1869 it reached a record level of 723,938 tons. By 1867 the company had paid nearly all debts acquired since the late forties and was ready to take on payment of its long-term obligations. Highest priority was for the 1849 preferred bonds and the interest on them. Payment was begun in 1869. It almost seemed that "balmy

---

*The remaining old bridge, high enough that it escaped demolition, is on Wisconsin Avenue.

and life-giving breezes" were blowing up and down the waterway and that springtime had come to the canal company.

First Years

Best Years:
Five hundred boats bumper to bumper.

THE YEAR 1870 ushered in a period of prosperity. James C. Clarke was made president of the canal company, and during the following five years—covering his administration and that of Arthur P. Gorman—long deferred hopes freshened as a vigorous program of repair and improvement resulted in the best business ever. In 1871, 968,827 tons of cargo were moved.

During this high point in trade, upwards of 500 boats were running. The very idea of this number of boats in a waterway the size of the canal they lived and worked on taxes the powers of belief of some surviving boatmen. Their experience was in days when the canal could boast of no more than 100 craft and that seemed a comfortable number. Five hundred boats! *"Where would they BE?" "Where would they GO?" "How could they make any time?"* These are proper questions. Where they went was in bumper-to-bumper lines at locks and docks, with boatmen weltering in the heavy congestion and turmoil. Time was lost in great chunks.

With the new prosperity, loaded boats formed lines well over a mile and a half long. The certain delays upset everybody. They were highly irritating and they caused money losses for boatmen, shippers, and the company. Traffic jams on the Georgetown level alone were massive thorns in the flesh of all concerned. Often 60 to 80 boats were waiting, lined up Indian file in order to leave room for passage of light boats going upstream. The canal was not nearly wide enough to take care of regular everyday basin and aqueduct traffic plus a row of boats a mile or more long.

All this trade in 1871 and 1872 had the locks in almost continuous operation. It became a problem to get coasting vessels to handle the cargoes at Georgetown. Coal accumulated there in such mountainous quantities that further shipments had to be postponed.

Clarke tried to meet the greater demand for water for navigation brought on by the growth of trade. In one effort to break up some of the maddening congestion at Georgetown, he tightened controls of water leases and attacked the millers' misuses. The millers were unbudgeable in their opposition to controls, and Clarke had only limited success.

Even with all this hurly-burly, the company made remarkable

The Georgetown level, aqueduct-bridge in middle-ground and Washington Monument behind it. Boats often waited here for signals to proceed and unload. But "If you didn't get no orders at the way bill lock to go straight through, you went to Wide Water—at the aqueduct-bridge, where Key Bridge is now—and you stopped there until they give you orders. I've laid there four and five days, waiting on orders."

progress in paying loans and interest during the two boom years. In 1872 came an upheaval: the regular Democratic party managed to get control of the Maryland Board of Public Works, which lost no time in appointing Arthur P. Gorman the new president of the company. This choice did not meet with broad approval, partly because Clarke had given the company its most successful two years and partly because Gorman was a political boss. Historian Matthew Page Andrews writes that Gorman threw his support to Governor William Pinkney Whyte in exchange for ousting Clarke and installing him.

To the astonishment of nobody at all, Gorman ran the company as if it were an accessory to his political patronage. But he also studiously applied himself to the needs of the canal, and under his leadership it reached its peak of prosperity.

In the matter of water leases and sales, the millers and the company continued to be at loggerheads. Gorman's board tried, in the same way Clarke had tried, to tighten control of water consumption by the millers. The best way was to get the water gauges placed on the canal banks, where, according to the original leases, they should have been anyhow. With gauges on the banks, the company could have kept close check on how much water power was being used and put a stop to many abuses. Again, this attempt brought angry howls from the millers. Because of the company's increased need for water for navigation on the Georgetown level, however, it could not avoid exercising the stricter control of water power that so incensed the millers.

A drought in 1872 had shown beyond question that the canal's need for water had to be met before the wishes of the millers could be catered to. A flood in 1873 threw a pitiless light on the precarious quality of the canal's prosperity. Fourteen days of rain followed by a flash flood had the river's tributaries swollen to such dimensions that the canal's culverts could not cope with them. Many were washed out. Destruction was enormous and some repairs were held up while others were made only to be torn to pieces by a series of storms.

During this period enough smaller mishaps accumulated that

it was impressive that the canal's business thrived in spite of them. Heavy rain made the towpath a mass of mud, sometimes impassable; a rough fall and winter brought sand bars, broken lock gates, small leaks in the banks, and caused early closing; strikes delayed one year's opening; sickness of men and death of mules caused loss of time.

In 1873, boatmen organized to fight decreases in freight charges and in 1874 they went on strike, calling for $1.35 a ton from Cumberland to Georgetown. Investigation by the company uncovered enough abuses in the system to indicate that the boatmen's position was a valid one. Compelling need to get on with trade, however, seemed to the company reason enough not to take time to attempt any remedy. Resorting to strikebreakers and police, the company brought the strike to a speedy end.

The new directors had continued Clarke's program of repair and improvement to such good effect that when the levels below Dams No. 4 and 5 (masonry since 1857) disappeared under the waters of a flood in 1874, the banks had been so strengthened that only negligible harm was done.

Business made consistent progress. In both 1873 and 1874, the company's net gain was a cool quarter of a million dollars plus. All but money for operating expenses was plowed back into the company in the form of restoration, improvements, and payment of back interest.

The year 1875 started out to be the best yet. The reputation of the company was enhanced and its fiscal condition stronger than it had been even in Clarke's administration. Gorman steadily continued and intensified the program of improvements. In this all-time peak year, 973,805 tons of cargo were moved. Coal companies added their encouragement by building 91 boats at Cumberland. This brought the number of mule-drawn boats on the canal to 554, with an average capacity of 112 tons.

In that same year steamboats appeared on the canal. Earlier there had been considerable uneasiness that the speed of the steamboats or the action of their propellers would erode the banks. More than five miles an hour was figured to do serious harm, but the company decided that nothing was liable to damage if such a speed limit were observed. Steamboats remained through 1889.[1]

As another stimulus to trade, the company brushed aside the always feebly enforced stricture against Sunday boating, holding that the canal was a public highway and should be open at all times. Other measures included purchase of a steam dredge and the clearing out of the Rock Creek basin, plans to enlarge the locks, and an effort to hurry along construction of outlet locks above the Potomac Aqueduct.

The company's blue-sky period didn't last long. By spring of 1875, the year that began with such bright promise, business was still improving but income was not. To hold its position, the company reduced all charges—tolls, wharfage, freight—but this was only a prelude to a rate war with competing coal carriers. Thanks to these cuts, trade did increase to some extent, but income dropped.

The nationwide panic that began in 1873 darkened the picture, although it was several years before it caught up with the canal. When Jay Cooke & Company, a prominent banking firm, fell, it carried many other banks down with it, and this froze credit in every part of the country. More than 23,000 businesses, nearly all of them small, were ruined.

This depression was part of an era, the second half of the 19th century, which was full of what historians Charles and Mary Beard called social earthquakes. Two-thirds of the period 1870–1910 were depression years, bringing panic and crime, strikes and violence, shocking degrees of poverty and unemployment. The misery was worse and far more widespread than in earlier depressions which had occurred when the vast majority of Americans were farmers. In the agricultural era, there were indeed hard times but they did not spell bitterest deprivation and actual hunger for the great mass of the population. Industrial-period depression wrought havoc with the lives of large numbers of workers congregated in cities, and brought on development of tremendous areas of slums.

The panic of the 1870s was wonderfully helpful to the monopolies, euphemistically called trusts, and the instrument of economic reverses and ruin to small businesses and workers. Business—Northern, Republican, big—ran the country, and there was little questioning of this from any quarter. The heads of megabusinesses held that God and evolution exonerated them for even their most rapacious exploits. The American public, brainwashed by this Victorian principle and with its morale worn to a frazzle by the Civil War, was in no condition to even try to stick up for itself.

On the eve of the depression, John D. Rockefeller, Sr., formed a cartel. His name first became a household word when businesses absorbed by the cartel, i.e., bought out cheap, lost their freedom and identity but survived in a broken sort of way as part of the pool and those outside the cartel were crushed by it. People began to call Rockefeller's organization an anaconda. This showed a breezy disregard for accuracy, as the oversize snakes crush only enough prey to keep themselves alive and doing well. The Rockefeller organization, as a matter of policy, crushed enough prey to amass enormous riches. Rockefeller had never been interested in being financially alive and doing well; acquisition of money had been his driving passion from early childhood. Yet late in life he was still blandly declaring that Standard Oil had actually been "an angel of mercy," offering "less fortunate competitors" a chance to become part of it.

In 1900, John D. Rockefeller, Jr., was only echoing his father when, in effect, he told the YMCA at Brown University that Christianity and big business were not incompatible, no matter what the populists said. His metaphor was that big business was as a giant rose which had reached its size only because many roses ("smaller, less efficient units") had been nipped in the bud for its benefit.

Members of high finance circles talked a lot about survival of the fittest.[2] The prevailing attitude was that predators couldn't be predators without prey, and that those who were prey should be content with their predestined lot in life and realize that they were performing a useful function in the schemes of God and nature. It is arguable how many small entrepreneurs felt useful, or rejoiced that they were carrying out the will of God, as their

107

businesses were swallowed whole to fatten Carnegie Steel, Standard Oil, and the American Sugar Refining Company.

The canal company did not disappear into the maw of a cartel but the countrywide depression caused industry to decrease its demand for coal, and the impact on the canal company was heavy in 1876. There was a drastic falling off of business, and that left was held on to only by dint of lowering the rate of tolls and wharfage again. This time tolls were reduced from 51 cents to 46 cents a ton from Cumberland to Georgetown. Still, business worsened and improvements to the waterway had to be stopped.

The year 1877 came and brought only grief. The depression continued (its dates were 1873–1878), competition among transportation lines was by that time ferocious, there was another boatmen's strike and another great flood. In the spring the company gave up hope of making any profit on coal that year and concentrated its energies on hanging on to the trade it already had. In the rate war with the railroads the company lowered tolls more than once, finally pulling them down to 22 cents a ton by summer.

In June striking boatmen tied up on the first level above Seneca and did not work for two months. During that time so many shippers gave their business to the railroads that the rest of the boating season was practically a total loss to the company.

In the late fall there was another huge flood, the worst in the 150 years during which records had been kept. It jerked the boating season to an untimely close and almost demolished the canal. In addition to heavy damage all along the line, there were large losses of repair materials, stores, and shipments.

Many thought, as many had mistakenly thought before, that the canal was done for; but the company had not only pluck but staying power and it did not spend much time licking its wounds. Financially shaky though it was, it determinedly buckled down to restoration. It set up an austerity program, as part of which the jobs of officials all up and down the line were suspended; but most officials found new slots in the repair program. The company used every red cent it had and borrowed $115,000 from coal companies, banks, and private citizens. A winter of furious effort made it possible to open the boating season only a month behind time. The heroic exertion succeeded, but it cost $238,500 and left the company financially depleted and weighed on by a $196,463 debt. One more such success and it would be sunk without trace.

Recovery could not be easy or quick and trouble piled upon trouble, pressed down and running over. In 1879 there was a miners' strike. Another severe drought in August and September of 1881 brought the river and canal water levels so far down that boats could operate only intermittently. Miners struck again in 1882, and for the duration canal business was practically at a standstill. The miners' agreement to go back to work came while there were still three months in the boating season, but by that time the boatmen had given up hope of settlement and had left the canal. And during the strike, Gorman had resigned as president of the company to accept appointment to the U.S. Senate. The business year 1882 and the canal's best years were over.

[1] The U.S. was the first country to make practical use of steamboats. They performed poorly in rough waters, and the quiet canal was perfect for them.

[2] According to one of the characters in Edna St. Vincent Millay's *Conversation at Midnight:*

The fittest to survive may well derive some satisfaction,
But should refrain from finding cause for pride, in that;
The value of a life is not determined by that life's protraction:
The fittest to survive in a sewer, is a sewer-rat.

Last Years:
"Prostrate and overwhelmed with difficulties."

THE LIFE OF THE CANAL had been one continuous desperate struggle for existence. Even its best years had been polka-dotted with minor, medium, and major misfortunes, and its last years were a dispiriting string of closely spaced ills.

The canal was afflicted with the railroad and stalked by financial adversity from its beginning days to its final hours. Bankruptcy was upon it as far back as 1832. After the Point of Rocks dispute, when the company finally achieved legal freedom to proceed with construction, work hardly begun had to be halted and not taken up again until money was in hand.

The state's famous $2,000,000 loan of 1835 was quickly shown to be pitifully insufficient for completion of the canal. Much of this loan went to pay old debts and to repair finished parts of the waterway. Maryland, the one source of prompt and effective aid, came forward again—this time with the feverishly controversial "Eight-Million-Dollar-Bill" of 1836. The canal company's share, amounting to $3,000,000[1] was given in the form of subscription to capital stock, which placed the state in control of the company by making it the majority shareholder.

It was, however, two years before the company saw any proceeds from the legislation. The state's bonds, issued at six percent, found no takers in the American money market, for, beginning in 1837 and continuing through 1840, the country was in a depression brought on by Wall Street excesses in land and stock speculation. In England, where buyers had been rather optimistically sought, the bonds were not sold until 1838, and then only after they had been converted from six percent dollar bonds to five percent sterling. All things considered, it was small wonder that the canal company was pleading with the General Assembly for further subscription to its stock.[2] The session of 1838 granted a subscription of $1,375,000.

Year by year appeals were made, the state and the canal company lurched along, and it was a tossup which was worse off. Dam No. 6, 50 miles short of Cumberland, was finished in 1839.* The incomplete part of the line between Dam No. 6 and Cumberland was usually called "the fifty miles." Only 18 miles of the section remained to be finished, but partially built structures were all up and down the whole 50 miles. Worse, the unfinished parts included the most massive and most expensive work of all—the tunnel and its enormous deep cut.

By 1841 the company was truly needy again and the State of Maryland was stone broke. Maryland's alarming financial condition was at the very least partly due to its generosity to the canal. Between 1826 and 1840 the state had gone into debt to the tune of $10,000,000 in order to help the railroad and the canal. Altogether, Maryland had borrowed $15,000,000 to help fund a group of transportation projects in several sections of the state. With this borrowed money it distributed grants, some of which were generally regarded as no better than purchase prices for legislative votes wanted for other projects.

By the embarrassed year of 1841 the canal company was mired in debt and took in less money than met its expenses. ("Prostrate and overwhelmed with difficulties" was the description given by its president, James M. Coale, in 1851.) In 1844 the canal company repeated its appeal, made twice before, to the legislature for the state to waive its liens on the canal so as to allow the company to finish the waterway. Officers of the company were about the only supporters of this measure. By this weary time the canal's friends had softly and silently van-

*Dam No. 6 was the end of the canal until 1850 when the whole project was completed.

ished away and its enemies were in full cry. Principal opponents were the city of Baltimore, the highly vocal Baltimore press, and, naturally, the B&O Railroad.

An act waiving the state's liens was passed by the skin of its teeth—on the last day of the legislature's session and by a majority of one vote in each house. This act provided for the state to relinquish claim to liens on the company's property and revenues and gave the company authority to sell preferred bonds up to $1,700,000. As security for these bonds, their buyers held a mortgage on the company's net revenues. Money from this sale made it possible for the company to complete the canal.

The late 1880s were calamitous. In 1886, within the space of little more than a month, three floods bore down on the canal. Then came a disheartening and repetitious series of misfortunes, climaxed by the mammoth flood of June, 1889, which demolished the waterway. Caused by the same unprecedented rains that devastated Johnstown[3] and laid waste seven other towns in the Conemaugh Vallley, it harmed business and life in general all through the Potomac Valley.

It was no secret that the C&O was insolvent and also unsuccessful in its efforts to raise funds for the waterway's restoration. Beleaguered and badgered, the company reacted by denying the reality of its situation. Perhaps because it had become inured to walking close to the edge, it insisted it should still strive to carry on. It resisted receivership right up to the time receivership took place, still clinging to some scrap of hope that somebody, somehow, would respond to its appeal and come to its rescue.

The trustees for the 1844 bondholders (a few banks, the B&O, mostly private citizens) filed for receivership in December, 1889. To preserve their rights, they had raced to beat to the draw the holders of the 1878 repair bonds. The 1878 bondholders, chief among them the B&O Railroad, held a mortgage on the body of the canal; if the canal were sold, there would have been nothing for the 1844 bondholders.

The financial arrangements of the canal company, always complicated, had by the prereceivership and receivership periods

112

Flood of 1889 (companion to the catastrophic Johnstown flood), damaged and scattered boats and threw several hundred men out of work. It left this scene of wreckage at Lock 33.

become incredibly complex, far more so than Chinese boxes or wheels in wheels. By this time they formed a labyrinth through which none but a dedicated financial historian would dare or care to grope. It boiled down to this: the B&O, as holder of a mortgage on the body of the canal, would determine the canal's future. To have the future of the canal determined by the B&O was not unlike having the future of a young tree determined by the honeysuckle vine already coiling around it.

The B&O had always itched to do the canal in, but after the flood it wanted the waterway rebuilt. The Western Maryland Railroad was eager to continue its line from Big Pool up to Cumberland where it could compete with the B&O. That would have

113

had the line crossing and recrossing the canal, and it was common knowledge that the Western Maryland stood ready to buy enough of the canal right-of-way to extend its tracks to the coal fields. The B&O would just as soon have looked at a gorgon as see this happen, and, because of its determination to preserve the right-of-way, it even grudgingly and not really seriously considered buying the canal itself. Its final decision was that its best course was to restore the canal at its own expense.

Neither restoration nor anything else the B&O did about the canal was done formally as by the railroad company. This would have been a legal impossibility. Everything it did, and it did all necessary to protect its interests, was done by action of trustees. It gave the B&O no trouble to work its will through the trustees because, as was its prerogative, it had appointed them.

In January, 1890, the 1878 trustees, acting for the B&O, requested that receivers be appointed, basing their petition on the canal company's having missed payment of three successive coupons of the 1878 bonds.

Then came the difficulty of determining a suitable court to name receivers. The canal company had been chartered by Virginia, Maryland, Pennsylvania, and the United States. It owned real estate in Virginia, Maryland, and the District. There was scarcely any locale that could be thought of as neutral ground.

Receivers were petitioned for in Maryland and the District courts at the same time. In Maryland the railroad by-passed the state courts and took its case to the Circuit Court for Washington County. There was difference of opinion as to whether or not a county court was appropriate or even legally competent to settle the future of the canal which, after all, ran through considerable other territory. The decision was up to the presiding judge of the Washington County Court, Judge A. H. Alvey. Alvey, who later rose high in political and judicial sectors, has been described as proud and ambitious. Be that as it may, he did not hesitate to decide that he was fully competent to judge the case.

The court's decision was for another chance for the canal and for the appointment of receivers to restore and operate it. Robert

114

Bridges, Richard Johnson, and Joseph D. Baker were named. They were to examine the canal and estimate repair costs and prospects for profitable operation. In his decision, Judge Alvey had tried to provide protection to both sets of bondholders by requiring reconstruction and operation of the canal by trustees.

First the receivers were euphoric about the canal's chances of being revivified; then they offered the bleak opinion that the cost of rehabilitation would be prohibitive and that the entire waterway should be sold. In the fall of 1890 they blew hot again and advised restoration and operation. Judge Alvey ordered sale of the canal, to follow through on an earlier pronouncement he had made, but suspended this decision with the proviso that the trustees of 1844 restore the waterway without delay. The District of Columbia court handed down the same decision.

By the following September the railroad, in its indirect way, had the canal repaired and open for business. Trade regained its old level swiftly but failed to grow from there. Gay as the nineties were in song and story, it was in 1893 that the country slid into another deep depression in which four million workers lost their jobs.

Two situations exemplified the times. Coxey's Army[4] of unemployed made its way from Ohio to Washington, boating and

Coxey's army of unemployed in the depression of the late 1800s. In what was then a novel method of attempting to call the federal government's attention to the suffering of a large segment of the population, the "army" came by foot and by canal boat from Ohio through Pennsylvania and Maryland to Washington. They came to urge a nationwide program of roadbuilding by jobless and needy men (another new concept that materialized years later), but members of Congress refused to see them and so did President Cleveland.

plodding through Pennsylvania and Maryland, but was refused the government's ear even momentarily. During a period when the Pullman Palace Car Company had a $25,000,000 surplus and paid $2,500,000 in dividends, it cut wages by 20 to 25 percent and rejected the idea of reduction in exorbitant rentals and utility fees in its company town. When the men finally went on strike, 12 were killed in the consequent rioting.

As for the canal, it never made a profit after 1890. But the court order had required that it show a profit or be sold. To satisfy the letter if not the spirit of this demand, the B&O indulged in a piece of financial sleight-of-hand. It formed a shadow organization and called it the Chesapeake and Ohio Transportation Company. This company entered into a contract with the receivers whereby the receivers promised to keep the canal in working order and the transportation company promised to furnish necessary additional boats. The court ratified the contract over the state's objections. The transportation company was also to guarantee the C&O yearly payments of $100,000 that they called profits. With these "profits" the receivers paid the modest cost of receivership and some of the canal company's repair bills and other debts.

The contract's reason for being was to fend off an order for sale of the canal. The railroad had restored the C&O because this was the least expensive way to keep the canal from going to a B&O competitor. Repairs cost far more than had been figured, and the railroad had seen fit to resort to the shenanigan of forming another company to absorb the operational losses of the canal.

In effect, the railroad lent the receivers money to repair the canal. It then formed a paper corporation through which the railroad furnished the canal company with funds to meet expenses and to pay off the loan from the railroad. Once having paid itself back, the railroad rewrote the contract, with court approval, to provide only that the canal be guaranteed its expenses. This satisfied the court order by showing that the canal company was not operating at a loss, and it ruled out any competition for the railroad.

In 1902 the Canal Towage Company was formed by the Consolidation Coal Company, itself owned by the B&O Railroad. The towage company operated the canal, and it changed the whole personality of the waterway and its boatmen. No longer did captains own their boats and give them the names of their choice and paint them as they liked. Their boats were furnished by the towage company, went by numbers instead of names, and were uniform in appearance. The policy of the new order was regimentation. Uppity or indolent or individualistic boatmen were not indulged, and the rough and rowdy element was banished beyond hope of return. Those expelled were replaced by a less obstreperous group, many of them devoted family men.

Flood damage at Snyder's Landing, roughly a mile from Sharpsburg. Jim Snyder operated a basin, a warehouse where boatmen bought hay and corn for mules, and a wharf. Partially legible date written on back of photograph is April 8; the year is probably 1902. Young boy at lower right is Walter Renner, born in 1889 and in this picture looking about right for 1902. Warehouse on right was built after the one before it was destroyed in the (Johnstown) flood of 1889. This picture came to J.P. Mose through his grandmother, Alice (Mrs. Jake) Renner. Walter Renner was cousin to Mr. Mose's mother, Ella May (Mrs. Jerome) Mose. Renner and Mose are boating-family names known to all canal people of the waterway's last period.

The two-pronged goal of the towage company was economy
and regularity of operation. Its position was that solvency took
precedence over all else, including the welfare of the boatmen.
Freight charges were lowered, pay was cut drastically, and strikes
were not tolerated. It soon became clear that independent boatmen were on the way out. The coal companies built (at Cumberland) most of the boats, and they kept rent and sale prices
as high as possible. This meant that independent boatmen
needed to charge high freight rates. The towage company, in
its determination to cut its costs and to profit by tolls, lowered
its freight rates. The independent boatmen disappeared from
the canal, ground between the stones of boating expenses and
the economizing of the towage company.

118

Left: Flood of 1924. Scene near Shepherdstown, West Virginia. On March 29, the river rose rapidly at Cumberland, where it reached heights comparable to those of the catastrophic Johnstown Flood of 1889 and where it did tremendous damage.

Top: Same spot, same flood—at its peak. Damage along the line of the canal was less than at Cumberland, but it served. For the fifth time, the canal was demolished. More, this flood became the precipitating factor in the situation that brought the curtain down on the canal's hour upon the stage, by giving the railroad a presentable reason for shucking off the burden of its operation.

The boats carried lime and other building materials and a certain amount of flour, but coal made up nearly the whole business on the canal. The Consolidation Coal Company (owned by the B&O Railroad) accounted for more than 99 percent of the canal's business. At Cumberland it took the coal from its own mines to its own dock by way of its own railroad, and sent it down to Washington in its own boats. These boats were operated by the Canal Towage Company (organized by the Consolidation Coal Company) and the receivers.

Having been destroyed as a rival to the railroad, the canal was physically destroyed in March, 1924. A prodigious flood raged over the entire canal and left it in utter ruin.

There was no boating season in 1924 or ever again.

[1] Other recipients were Baltimore and Ohio Railroad Company, $3,000,000; Eastern Shore Railroad Company, $1,000,000; Maryland Canal Company, $500,000; Annapolis Canal Company, $500,000.

[2] Some of the canal company's creditors were owed mountainous sums for work long ago finished and had gone from riches to rags by the company's failure to meet its obligations.

[3] This accompanied the disaster known as the Johnstown flood. After a period of torrential rains, on May 31, 1889, a dam 12 miles from Johnstown, Pennsylvania, broke. This loosed the contents of a reservoir and sent a 20-foot-high mass of water down the valley moving 20 miles an hour. In only one hour it completely destroyed Johnstown (population, 30,000) and seven other towns. A Pennsylvania Railway bridge held firm, and the water heaped up wreckage against it. Many people were saved from drowning by clinging to this wreckage, but were killed when it caught fire. Altogether there was enormous loss of life, 2,200 deaths at a conservative estimate.

[4] The Commonweal of Christ, usually known as Coxey's Army, was made up of about 500 men who were out of work in the depression of the early 1890s. Led by "General" Jacob S. Coxey, owner of a prospering sand quarry and a horse farm in Masillon, Ohio, the army left that town on Easter morning, March 25, 1894, and began its trek to Washington. With Coxey in a carriage were his wife and their infant son, Legal Tender Coxey. The army put on the best face that it could, brave with a brass band and at least one colorful leader—Carl Browne, of California, mounted on a white stallion and wearing a buckskin jacket with silver dollars for buttons—and a mysterious orator never identified but called "The Great Unknown." Nevertheless it was a sight to rouse compassion. Each man carried his blanket and his food supply on his back. They slogged along to Washington to urge Congress to pass a bill, already introduced, which was a fore-shadowing of the Civilian Conservation Corps and its work in the national parks in the Great Depression of the 1930s. The bill proposed that the federal government hire unemployed men in a nation-wide roadbuilding program. The travel-stained and footsore army arrived in the capital on April 26, hoping that their trudging and canal-boating through Pennsylvania and Maryland would focus their government's attention on their dire hardship. Its leaders were roughly repulsed, their effort trivialized, and neither members of Congress nor President Cleveland would even see them.

Since 1924:
Out of the nettle a flower is plucked.

AFTER ITS CLOSING in 1924 the canal remained in the hands of the trustees. Although lying in ruins, it was technically a going concern because it took in enough money in water fees from Georgetown users to pay a skeleton staff. The receivers' court-supported position was that the canal was not abandoned but simply not operating at the time because of insufficient business. Part of this legal fiction was that the waterway could go into operation at any time enough business was offered.

During the thirties, along with countless other businesses, the B&O was hurt by the Great Depression and in debt to the federal government's Reconstruction Finance Corporation. As part of its collateral the B&O produced title to the canal. In 1938, when the railroad found itself unable to pay a due note of $2,000,000, it foreclosed on the canal. As soon as all documents were signed and the canal legally the property of the B&O, it sold the waterway to the government for $2,000,000 and immediately used that $2,000,000 to make its payment to the RFC. It was all a paper transfer, no money changed hands, and it took place almost in the blink of an eye.*

From the time the canal closed right up to the day it passed into the hands of the federal government, the B&O had provided conscientious maintenance. Even when it was not watered, the dams and embankments and locks were kept in order. (At

---

*By law, the RFC had to turn over to the U.S. Department of the Interior (to be used for parks) all assets received from loans.

121

the Georgetown end there was always water in the canal, as this was required by law for the use of the Georgetown millers.) Had it not been for the flood of 1936, the canal the railroad turned over to the government would have been in excellent condition and complete with boats and machinery.

In that flood, many boats were wrenched from their moorings and floated loose downstream, tearing out bridges and doing much additional damage. Locals reacted with vandalism. They breached the canal's banks and pushed boats into the river. They burned boats. They dug holes in culverts in efforts to drain the canal, which had become a breeding ground for mosquitoes. Vandalism continued after the National Park Service had taken charge.

During the few years following the fall of 1938 the Park Service restored the waterway between Washington and Seneca. This section then became a recreational area, part of the National Capital Parks System. The canal was designated a public park in 1939.

In 1954 it narrowly escaped being paved over for a scenic parkway, possibly an extension of the George Washington Memorial Parkway which runs from Mount Vernon to Great Falls. The canal was not totally disregarded. The proposal was that water be kept in certain sections, and that the highway encroach on the old canal bed only when unavoidable. Where it did encroach, meticulous effort was to be made to retain whatever remnant of the canal could be snatched from the paving. The road was to be laid out in such a way as to preserve locks and other structures, most aqueducts and culverts were to be incorporated into the parkway, and a two-lane passage was to be paved through the tunnel. The whole project was to have been a somewhat narrow but adequate highway.

All precautions and considerations notwithstanding, it was a reckless concept because it would have killed a wild area in order to have one more riverside drive in the world.

In support of the proposed highway the *Washington Post* ran an editorial that roused Justice William O. Douglas to protest. He wrote the paper a letter, restrained but made powerful by his stature, and thereby began to make the rescue of the canal a cause.

Douglas invited the editorial writer to backpack with him the full length of the canal, to see and hear what could never be observed from the window of a moving car. He mentioned "...muskrats, badgers, and fox...strange islands and promontories through the fantasy of fog...whistling wings of ducks..."; and he could have mentioned that most of this warm life would disappear, much of it in bloody broken messes under the wheels of cars, if a highway were built. He wrote that if the editor would walk with him, "I feel that...he would return a new man and use the power of your great editorial page to help keep this sanctuary untouched."

The now famous Douglas walk—seven days from Cumberland to Georgetown—was made, with two editorial writers from the *Post* and a group of canal advocates participating. The *Post* writers found their perceptions made finer and their values altered, the change coming not so much from what they saw as in how they saw it. The paper reversed its position, and shortly thereafter the C&O Committee was formed, with Douglas the chairman and Robert Estabrook of the *Post* a member. This evolved into the C&O Canal Association, which worked for years to rally public opinion and to lobby for protective legislation. Out of the nettle a flower was plucked. Finally the parkway proposal was discarded, and in 1971 the canal was declared a national historical park.

It would be a monumental undertaking to restore the entire canal, and it has many forlorn stretches. In them, and even in some of the most visited parts, the canal is remindful of the traces of the dead Persian king's court that "the lion and the lizard keep," and of the final resting place of Bahrám, "that great hunter," over whose head "the wild ass stamps but cannot break his sleep." There are no lions, and perhaps only a stray lizard or two, but a great lot of tramping around by visitors in stout walking shoes cannot break the sleep of the old waterway. The trunk is in many places so nearly filled in that its shape has been obliterated, and in it grow trees 14 and more inches in girth.

123

There are dismal spots where the dry and weedy bottoms of locks and aqueducts are littered with crumpled cigarette packages, potato chip bags, candy bar wrappers, beer and soft drink cans, and other artifacts deposited there by sightseers or local habitués.

In sharp contrast and as a recreational facility, a smartly refurbished portion of the canal flourishes like a green bay tree. The old waterway's first 32 miles (Georgetown to Edward's Ferry), known as the Palisades District, drew close to two and a half million visitors in 1981. Canoeing is popular in the 22-mile stretch between Violette's Lock near Seneca and Georgetown.There are camp sites up and down the line. Locks and aqueducts here and elsewhere are like magnets to nearby residents; and, to those near the metropolitan Washington area, city dwellers and out-of-town and out-of-state visitors come in droves. Every weekend finds the inviting vicinity of Great Falls, for example, crowded with strollers, runners, cyclists, picnickers, museum browsers, river watchers, nature enthusiasts on field trips, and those who sit in sun or shade, depending on the season, and watch the energetic ones disport themselves. The towpath, even in remote and otherwise unrenovated areas, is kept usable, and tourists from all parts of the country have joined area residents to make it one of the favorite hiking, biking, and jogging trails in the eastern United States.

124

Home on the Canal
Part Two
The Hard Good Life

Introduction

LIFE ON THE CANAL has often been described as leisurely. A representative sampling of veteran boatmen and -women says otherwise.

Just as "broke" is all the world different from "poor," "slow" is not necessarily "leisurely." If one goes to bed not unduly tired and sleeps until waking occurs naturally and rising is not difficult, if one carries out one's duties at whatever pace seems pleasant and maybe even carries them out on flexitime, and if there are frequent breaks, then one's work has the ease that goes with leisurely. On the canal boats, it was usual for men, women, and children to begin their work day at 4:30 a.m., and that knocks leisurely in the head right there.

True, the *boats* went "slow and with meanders" and boating people were not hectored by the hustle and clamor of city life, and vicarious nostalgia is seductive. Even now, when it's academic, it is easy to look at watered parts of the canal, envision boats and people gliding at two miles an hour through green country under blue skies, with the world not at all, let alone too much, with them, and slip into a dreamy-drifty state and imagine for a moment that that's what it must have been like. It wasn't.

Superficially observed at the time it was being experienced, life aboard the boats seemed less busy and ordered than it was. The suitable rough clothing and the usual absence of haste gave the whole scene a deceptively Huck Finnish aura. A man sleeping on deck in broad open daylight was not taking his slothful ease, but having time off after doing his stint (which might have been a good many hours of trudging the towpath with the mules), and he well might rise to work again before he was rested.

Mealtimes might be arranged with some flexibility, and perhaps some maintenance tasks could be juggled. The boating proper, however, involved a variety of simple enough but demanding chores. Some of them had to be done as punctually as milking cows, some had to be done in close cooperation with others, and some had to be done right briskly. For example, getting a boat through a lock without harm to boat or masonry or gates required several steps to be taken in rapid succession and the help at just the right moment of someone at the snubbing post. Not the most complicated work in the world, but neither was it work to be done languidly, carelessly, or when the spirit moved, and mañana was definitely not good enough.

The canal never had anything really fit to call a heyday. It was fighting a losing battle every inch of the way, because it never had an opponent its size. Always there were superior forces at work to wipe it out. There was the range of mountains between the Potomac River and the Ohio, and this alone would have been enough. There was the B&O Railroad, which alone would have been enough. There were its financial calamities, which alone would have been enough. There were the Potomac Valley's ever more savage floods, which alone would have been enough. There was the playing out of the Cumberland coal field, which alone would have been enough. And there was more. Still, it staunchly served a purpose for 92 years before its long defeat became final.

It went hobbling through the early decades of the 1900s, with its accumulation of injuries old and new, but it was like Don Marquis's hard-to-keep-down Mehitabel: there was "a dance in the old dame yet." It is these years that are featured in the following reminiscences.

Two interviews in late spring, 1976.

Otho Swain
Potomac

OTHO SWAIN was born on a canal boat on July 24, 1901, at Stop Lock at Great Falls, Maryland, and was to take his place in a family whose working lives revolved around the canal.* His grandfather, John Swain, helped build the C&O. His father, Jess Swain, was both boatman and locktender. His uncles—John, Hen, and Bill Swain—were boatmen. His uncles-by-marriage—Clyde, Bill, and Otho Grove—were boatmen. He himself "stayed on the boat until my father went to tend a lock in 1909. So I was eight years old when my father quit boating, and I boated for other people from the time I was 15 or 16."

As a child he heard his grandfather talk about construction of the canal. "My grandfather and the others were digging the canal. Later a lot of them were driving the Paw Paw tunnel. That means they were cutting through the rock by hand with drills. What my grandfather did, he had some teams that he put in there and helped them to haul the dirt out. They didn't have any machinery to excavate with, just horses and mules and plows and scoops and stuff like that.

"He told me that it was pretty rough going. Saturday was pay day, and he said that on Saturday night they all used to get drunk and get to fighting and sometimes the National Guard would have to come to quiet them down. They were playing cards,

---

*Mr. Swain died in the summer of 1976. This section is largely an excerpt from *Time Was. A Cabin John Memory Book,* published by the Cabin John [Md.] Citizens' Association as part of its bicentennial observation.

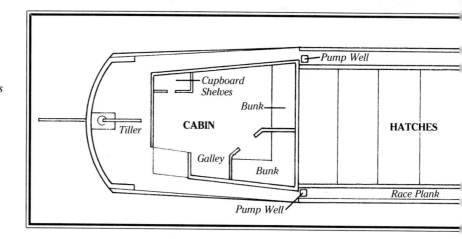

Composite description: "The boats were made usually of Georgia pine. The bottom was oak. A boat was about 90 to 95 feet long and about 14½ feet wide—only a few inches less wide than the locks—and better than six foot high. You walked along the side of the boat (on the race plank). The stable was at the front end of the boat. The bow lamp went right up on the head, at the stable. The stable went down; most of it was underneath the deck. There was a little plank where the mules walked in. Absolutely right in the middle of the boat was the hay house. Then you had 14 hatches; each was about four feet wide. Hatches (covering the cargo), went from one side of the boat to the other and fit tight so the water wouldn't come through. (From the race plank there were) three steps down into the living quarters; on the right was your stove. Behind the stove was your stateroom, underneath the bunk you could set your shoes or boxes with stuff in. And you had another bed on that end (of the boat) toward the coal. And your table on the left hand side between two windows. A cupboard in the corner, between the cupboard and where you went down the steps was a little. . . like a pantry. The race plank was painted gray. The hulls, front and back, would be painted red and white striped. The cabins were all white and green: The hatches were gray like the race plank."

drinking, fighting, everything. It was terrible hard work, and I guess it made them tired and quarrelsome.

"My grandfather used to tell me how the contractors would try to cheat them out of their wages. They wouldn't half feed them. And they'd give them just straw to sleep on.

"The canal company had a lot of trouble with building the canal. My grandfather told me that most of the trouble was in getting lime for cement, and other building materials, but sometimes they wouldn't have enough labor either. And sometimes when they were digging they'd come up on slate—what they called hardpan. That's ground that's just like rock. And they had to dynamite it out. That's hard, and it's expensive to do too. Land cost a lot. They just had lots of trouble."

His grandfather told him about the cholera epidemic of 1832. "It was very catching, and they didn't have any cure for it. He said he'd seen 40 men die in less than two hours. Some who took it got by, but most of them died. Some of them are buried down near the Great Falls on this side of the river, where the tavern is. Up on the hillside right up there, there's only one tombstone left; and all they said about him, they said he was a stonecutter and he was 25 years old when he died; not even his name. When I was a child there was a bunch of stones in there, but there's only one now.

"When the boats were running, when they first started the canal, there were over 500 boats on it and they used to run night and day. They never stopped the boats at all. The mules walked one behind the other. That way they wouldn't take up

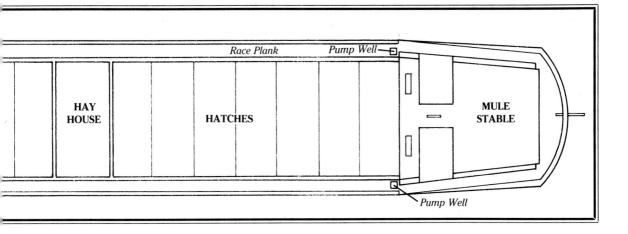

Race Plank   Pump Well

HAY
HOUSE

HATCHES

MULE
STABLE

Pump Well

too much room on the towpath, and some thought they pulled better that way. Most of the men liked their mules; some of them *loved* them. That's what my grandfather told me. He remembered two named Mike and Queen.

"When the canal had first been built and was in operation, my grandfather had 15 boats of his own built and he ran those boats until the towage company, the canal company, sold over to the B&O Railroad. When the railroad took it they kept its name but they put their own boats on it and wouldn't allow anybody else's there; so my grandfather had to get rid of his boats. He sold them to anybody who wanted them for the wood. Just to be destroyed. He even gave some of them away.

"A canal boat was about 90 to 95 feet long and about 14 and a half feet wide—only a few inches less wide than the locks. The rooms were *all* small; but the bunk beds didn't take up much space, and we were comfortable. After you put the cargo on, there were hatches that fit down over the top, went from one side of the boat to the other and fit *tight,* so the water wouldn't go through. Each hatch was about 4-foot wide. You used as many hatches as you needed to cover the cargo.

"Most of the boats had numbers but some had names. My grandfather remembered they had one they called *Good Old Daniel;* they had one, the *Lonely Star;* and one they called the *Morning Star;* and one they called the *Alice May;* one they called the *J.B.;* and one they called the *Farmer's Friend.*

"My grandfather, he had boated coal down Constitution Avenue. There used to be a canal that crossed the Potomac

131

there, and there's a little stone house still standing on the corner of 17th and Constitution Avenue. It was a lock house.* My *grand*mother *lived* in that lock house, and that's where my grandfather met her. After they were married they went to live in Sharpsburg. That was before the Civil War.

"They lived on what a little later was the Antietam Battlefield. They hid some way or other and none of the soldiers hurt them. But I heard my grandmother say that she saw bridges made out of dead bodies of human beings and horses for men to cross on over the crick—there were so many killed there. That was the next worst battle of the war, the worst outside of Gettysburg.**

"Right around here in Potomac, there used to be two old men, Owl Dooley and Pat O'Brian, both of them almost a hundred when they died. They used to tell me about the Union soldiers coming up River Road. They'd come along and steal your horses, cows, anything they could get their hands on. They showed me where the soldiers camped, up here on River Road, one night. Up right at Swain's Lock Road, I think it was. Pat O'Brian was the first blacksmith on the canal right after the canal was built.

"I had uncles on the canal and uncles by marriage, and I used to make trips with them. A trip would take about ten days, round trip. Once you got the hang of steering, it just came to you, but the hardest thing about steering was to steer through a lock. The lock was only about six inches or so wider than the boat. That's not much room on either side, and if you'd gone bumping through all those stone locks you'd have torn your boat up. You had to know how to put a boat in the lock and you had

*On the Washington Extension, built and owned by the canal company. Completed in 1833, it ran from Rock Creek, along 27th Street, to where the old lock house stands now on Constitution and 17th. There it turned east and joined the old Washington City Canal. The extension was not much used, and after 1855 it was allowed to fill up.

**Gettsyburg was a three-day battle with more losses than Sharpsburg, which was fought in one horrible day. Historians agree that Sharpsburg was the bloodiest single battle of the war, with more men killed or wounded than on any other one day of the war.

to know how to stop the boat. If you couldn't stop the boat right, you'd break through the lock gates.

"Stopping's not so hard, once you know how. I've seen a ten-year-old girl put a boat through a lock. Of course, that would be a child raised on the canal. You stop a boat with a rope. They had what they called a snubbing post, and one man would take a rope and put it around the post and he'd let the boat go in the lock real easy and brake it with the rope. It would take about eight to ten minutes to get through a lock. It depends on the lock; some of them were a little deeper than others and it would take longer to change the level of the water. Some of them had what they called drop gates; you had a big wheel and you just turned it and the gate went under the boat. The others had gates on both sides.

Snubbing Post, deeply bit into by heavy ropes—four to five times thicker than tow-lines—coated with abrasive sand and grit. Not one snubbing post remains. This one was at Lock 44.

Bearded boatman rests his hand on snubbing post and observes boat in one of the Six Locks near Great Falls. Because a lock gave only a six-inch clearance on each side, locking through required a neat entrance and the help of a co-worker on the towpath who wrapped a heavy line around the snubbing post at just the right moment. This joint effort steadied the boat in the churning water in the lock and prevented banging up the masonry or the craft by bumping into lock walls, and stopped the boat so that it didn't slam into the far gate of the lock.

"Between locks, the most important thing you had to know was where the best channel was in the canal, the deepest part. It wasn't all the same depth, so you had to memorize the whole canal." And then, as Mark Twain discovered to his dismay after he had just memorized the entire Mississippi River, a boatman had to memorize backwards as well.

"On a long level, they would blow a bugle to let the locktender know they were coming. There was a special bugle call that meant a boat was coming. It said, 'Lock ready, lock ready, lock ready!' and sometimes when you got closer you would holler that too. And the locktender, if it was at night, he would take a lantern and wave it so they'd know he'd heard them. In the daytime, of course, he could see the boat. They'd still blow the bugle, but the locktender would just wave. In places where there were several locks close together—seven are close together around Cabin John—they had bells they would ring from one to the other to let the locktenders know they were coming. And the locktender would ring back to let them know he'd heard.

"The longest level on the canal was 14 miles. What they did on the levels, they always kept the lock set one way, either for a loaded or a light boat. Some locks would stay set for a loaded boat, some for a light boat, and the boatmen knew about each one of them. If a light boat was coming up to a light set lock, it could go right through. If a loaded boat was coming to a light set lock, the boatman would have to make sure the locktender knew they were coming and that they were loaded—so he could change the water level in the lock.

"That memorizing the canal was really the hardest thing about boating. Then you'd have to know the places where some other boat would stop of a night. In case a boat was stopped and you were going on, you'd have to watch out for it. The stopped boats didn't have any lights, and its mules would be tied on the towpath. You could find the stopped boat with your own light, and you'd have to holler back, 'Boat on the towpath!' to your captain or whoever was steering the boat.

"The bow light had a big reflector, and it would show you both sides of the canal and about 50 feet ahead of you. That was far enough ahead, because the boats moved slowly. The average boat would make about three miles an hour. In good weather. That means cool weather, where the mules could work right along. This bow light was just like a strong lantern, and boats never hit each other.

"The tunnel at Paw Paw was *very* narrow; a canal boat could just get through it. In case there might be a boat coming from the other direction, you always put your light on. You always put your bow light on. Night and day you put your light on, because it was so dark in there. If you'd see a light coming, you'd know there was a boat coming. If two got in the tunnel at the same time, it was just too bad. I heard my father tell me that one time that's what *did* happen. And the two of them got shotguns and stayed there and waited, and somebody had to send for the supervisor to come up there and make one pull back. My father remembered that. But generally one boat could see the other one in time; you could see his bow light. If there was one already in the tunnel the other one wouldn't go; he'd pull up to the side of the canal and wait for him to come through.

"There were some powerboats on the canal, some steamboats; they hauled limestone. The place where they burned the lime is right off Pennsylvania Avenue Bridge, right near Rock Creek. I think the old lime kilns are still there, but there were only about four or five of these steamboats. They were *very* noisy. The mules, after they got used to them, they didn't pay them any attention.

"Boating wasn't what you could call hard labor, but it was long hours. In late years boats generally ran from five o'clock in the morning to eleven o'clock at night. That was long hours all right, but it was our living and we had to make it. There wasn't much chance to rest during the day, but we never felt rushed. The mules *could* have gone along by themselves, but they'd be too slow. The man driving them would keep saying, 'Come up! Come up!' That's all they'd have to do to get the mules to go. I never saw anybody hit a mule. They were all good to the mules. All of them would see how fat they could keep their mules and how clean they could keep them. The harness was

Otho Swain

135

always greased and shiny, and they'd get the mules shined up too, with brushes.

"Now, in the winter months they would put the mules out on different farms. The canal couldn't run when ice was on it. They would have a farmer, and maybe he'd take 25 or 30 mules, and the next farmer would take 25 or 30. And they'd keep them through the winter months. Then in the spring the captains would go and get their mules and bring them in. These farms weren't right around this area; most of them were all up country—around Boyd's Station, Slidell, all through Frederick County, and Washington and Allegany [counties]. Some of the farmers would come to the canal and get the mules—walk them over.

"The boats were tied up in wintertime, right in the canal. Some of the people lived on the boats the year round, but a lot of them didn't. My family didn't. We lived in Sharpsburg. Right on the Antietam Battlefield, where my grandparents lived.

"Now, there's two places in the canal where the canal goes out in the river. One place they call Little Slack Water, and one they call Big Slack Water. They're up in the Allegheny Mountains. You just go right out in the river, and there's a towpath along the river. Little Slack is a mile long, and Big Slack is four miles.

"Locking into the river wouldn't change your steering much, but it was different because the river was wide and your boat would run much easier. Your mules could go better. It was nice to be in the river for a while. It changed the scenery.

"Every time a boat would go to Alexandria for a load of coal,* or, say, to Indianhead or Gas House, a tugboat pulled it down the river. They'd leave the mules in a big stable in Georgetown and they'd go get loaded up. Boxcars would be on top of the wharf and the boats would be under it. They'd put 30 tons in the back of the boat first. They'd pull the bottom out of the box-

---

*Besides hauling coal from Cumberland to wholesale buyers at coal yards near Washington, canallers sometimes bought from these same yards for resale in small local transactions. On arrival from Cumberland, the coal had been put into the boxcars Mr. Swain mentions. A boatman would sell a load of it retail to individual families up and down the canal between the coal yard and Washington. See also page 236.

cars and the coal would go down a chute on [to] the boat. When they'd get that first 30 tons on the back, the boat would raise up. Then they'd have to back the boat back, and they'd put another load on the front. That would even it up. Then they'd put on the rest of the load. It would generally take four boxcars to fill a boat.

"Boating was never lonesome to me, because you'd see different things every day. It was really . . . you enjoyed it. It never got tiresome. On the upper end of the canal, up around Hancock, I've seen little black bears. I've seen a catamount at Harpers Ferry. It was a small one; I guess it was a kitten; it was only a little bigger than an ordinary cat. It was beautiful. It used to be Harpers Ferry was full of mountain goats. Harpers Ferry and all the way up to Hancock, all the way up through the Allegheny Mountains, mountain goats and bald eagles. The eagles were beautiful too. Those little black bears wouldn't hurt you; neither would eagles. I've heard there were grizzlies, but I never saw one. Of course you'd see deer—and raccoons, groundhogs, possums, black snakes, water snakes. You'd see birds of all kinds. You'd see ducks, bluejays, robins, killdeers, and cranes. They called water cranes and fishing cranes different, but they looked alike to me. They'd fly way up in the air and all at once they'd dive right down on a fish. They say water snakes are dangerous, but I never had one of them to bother me. They're brown, more tan I guess you would call it, and very pretty. I've seen them as long as four foot, swimming in the canal.

"Of course you'd see all kinds of wildflowers. I remember seeing what they called flax, and there were bluebells, and the arbutus. Arbutus is kind of a pink color. If you had a little bunch, you could smell it all over the house.

"The canal company paid for hauling cargoes. Now, if you were boating grain, one man would buy the grain and he'd bring it down the canal and *he'd* pay the boatmen so-much a ton. The canal company paid for the coal; so-much a ton, but I can't recall just what it was a ton. There never was any trouble about getting cargo. There was always stuff to haul. Always.

"I boated beginning when I was 15 or 16. I would make trips,

Otho Swain

137

about four or five a year. Then I'd come out and go back on the farm and work. My father [Jess Swain] farmed and he tended a lock too. I worked for him. I worked for other people on farms too. We worked from five o'clock in the morning until nine o'clock at night for 50 cents and our board. This would have been in 1916 or '17. We plowed ground, we plowed corn, we planted corn, we planted wheat, we planted potatoes, worked potatoes, planted onions, we harvested.

"My father had been a captain. He got tired of boating, I guess, and there wasn't much way of getting his kids to school; so he quit and went to tending lock. The men that tended the locks before the First World War only got $22 a month—for working seven days and seven nights a week. Twenty-two dollars a month and a house to live in and his garden. He had to make the garden himself and tend it, so what he really got was $22 and a rent free house. In the winter months he got $11 a month. In the winter most of them used to work on the canal, wheeling out mud and stuff like that. They got 11 cents an hour for that. They couldn't do any extra work during the summer because they had to be on duty all the time. My father tended lock for 35 or 40 years.

"First he tended lock at Great Falls, but he didn't stay there long until he moved up to Swain's Lock. That's my father's lock. That's Lock 21. Swain's Lock Road is named for my father, because it led to his lock. I was about eight when he left the boat, but I helped him. I helped him open the gates, turn the paddles up and leave the water in or out. I helped him do anything that's supposed to be done around a lock. We cleaned it up. Any debris that would get into a lock, you'd have to throw it out with a pitchfork. And we always kept the lock whitewashed to make it look good. I helped do that too.

"My father had a pet goose named Jimmy, and that goose lived to be 27 years old. My father would get in the buggy to go to the Potomac store, and Jimmy would get right up beside him and ride out there and back. Mr. McCrawson gave him to my father when he was only two days old, just the tiniest little thing. My father raised him, and he walked around everywhere

138

with my father. If my father would go fishing in the boat, Jimmy would get in the water and swim right out to him and stay out there as long as he stayed. Anybody'd go around my father, Jimmy would bite the devil out of him. If you own them, geese are very good to you; but if a stranger comes around you, they really don't like it. Jimmy was friendly with me, and I petted him, but if a stranger come around—as long as he didn't get too close to my father, it was all right; but if he got too close, Jimmy would bite him. Jimmy was beautiful. Gray and white.

"It was 1919 when I made my last trip up the canal. I quit because I thought I could make a better living, and I started working on golf courses. I liked that a lot. I really did. It was right good money and I met a lot of people.

"I was at Burning Tree club for a long, long time. I met a lot of people there. Eisenhower was the only president I ever met and talked with. I built Eisenhower's putting green down at the White House and after that I kept it up. We didn't get the credit for it, because the club didn't want anybody to know that club employees built it. But Colonel Tom Belshe and I built it. The Park Service got credit for it, because that really came under parks. Eisenhower complimented me many a time; and when I was in the hospital the first time, he wrote me a letter; and I liked him. I was green superintendent at Burning Tree from 1936 until I retired in 1967."

Jess Swain and devoted friend Jimmy. Father of Otho Swain and keeper of Lock 21, the elder Swain raised Jimmy from a tiny two-day-old gosling to a beautiful gray and white adult who lived to be 27.

Thinking back to the canal again, Mr. Swain recalls the hostilities between canal and railroad. "[They]. . .had kept on fighting each other all along—just like from the very beginning. The railroad held up the building of the canal up at Point of Rocks for *years*. There was only room enough for one of them to get through there, because bluffs came right down to the river edge. The canal company claimed the land and the railroad claimed it, and they had to go to court. The court gave the land to the canal company, but the railroad had held the canal up for four years.

"The canal finally closed down in 1924. There *was* flood damage then, but the railroad—it was the railroad that really killed the canal."

Interviews, July 8 and November 18, 1979.

J. P. Mose
Sharpsburg

J.P. MOSE "practically grew up on the canal." As a baby, he used to go on the canal with his mother. When he was 10 he was driving mules. At 12 or 13 he was steering.

At the age of "almost 81,"* he performs an exercise beloved of boatmen: he recites the canal.

"We start out with the nine-mile level at Cumberland. Then we come to the three locks. Then the one-mile level of the Narrows. Then come the ten-mile lock. Then the eight-mile level of Old Town. Then come three locks and two short levels—a lock, a short level, a lock, a short level, and another lock; three locks there together and the two short levels between them. Then come the two-mile level of Old Town. Then come the three-mile level of South Branch. Then come the seven-mile level of the tunnel. Then come the three locks of the tunnel, a short level, then another lock. Then come the one-mile level of the tunnel. (That's where all them goodlooking girls were at.) Then come the four-mile level of the tunnel. Then come the three-mile level of the brick house. Then come the two-mile level of Bill Bell's. Then come the five-mile level of Orleans. And after that come the three-mile level of Sideling Hill. Then come the two-mile level of Pearre. Then come another short level, of Dam No. 6. Then the seven-mile level of Hancock. After that there come another short level between that and the fourteen-mile level. Then come the Four Locks. Then come the two-mile level

*Throughout, whenever given, ages are as of dates of interviews.

140

J.P. Mose

of Four Locks. Then come the two locks, with just a little short level between two locks. Then come Little Slack Water. Then come the seven-mile level of Williamsport. Then Lock 44. Then come the six-mile level of Williamsport. Then come the four-mile level of the Big Slack Water. (There's that 92-mile stake: 92 miles to Washington, 92 miles to Cumberland.) Then come the two locks at Big Slack Water. Then come the guard lock. Then come Dam 4. Then come the six-mile level of Taylor's Landing. Then come the five-mile level of Sharpsburg. Then Lock 39. Then come the one-mile level of Shepherdstown. Then Lock 38. Then the six-mile level of Shepherdstown. Then come the four-mile level of Mountain Lock. Then come the two locks; one of them was a feeder lock. Then what we called the feeder level; that was about a mile long. Then there was another one we called the Goodheart Level; that was at Harpers Ferry. Then the lower level of Harpers Ferry. Then come the two-mile level of Sandy Hook. Three-mile level of Weverton. Then come the four-mile level of Brunswick. (That's where the mule kicked me.) Then come the two-mile level of Catoctin. Then come the seven-mile level of Point of Rocks. Then come the nine-mile level of White's Ferry. (I notice in a lot of these stories that people write, they call the nine-mile level the nine-mile level of the haunted inn. We just always said the nine-mile level of White's Ferry.) Then come the eight-mile level of Riley's Lock, Lock 24. Then come the short level of Seneca. Then come Violette's Lock and the feeder level. Then come the two-mile level of Seneca. Penny-field's Lock. Then come the three-mile level of White Oak Springs. Swain's Lock. (That's where Jess Swain tended lock, the daddy of Otho Swain.) Then come the two-mile level of Six Locks. Then come the Six Locks. Then come the four-mile level of what we called Log Wall. (I hated to be out there, especially at night.) Then come the Seven Locks.* Then come the one-mile level of Cabin John. Then come the two-mile level of Magazine. Then the short level above Georgetown level, which was the four-mile level of Georgetown. Then you come to the four locks that locked you down into Rock Creek. Then come one lock that locked you out into the river. That was the whole thing.

"You had to watch very careful steering a boat, because in a lot of places the canal was very narrow, and a lot of rocks. You'd have to know all the bad places. Right down there at Cabin John, below Seven Locks, there was a big bluff sitting there on a turn. If you happened to meet a light boat there, it was a little bad. Each one of the boats would have to make a swing—very near quarters. And there was numerous places like that.

"The lower lock of the Six Locks was what we called Log Wall.** It's about a mile long. In a lot of places they had to make a good bit of fill to get the towpath in. You come out of the lock,

---

*Beginning with Lock 8 at Cabin John, there are seven locks within the space of approximately one mile. This cluster, ending with 14, called Seven Locks, is the heaviest concentration of locks on the canal.

**Log Wall was a part of the canal made by filling rather than excavating. The river curved in at this spot and, in order to get the canal in, the builders put up a large fill about 60 feet high. First they made cribbing—a framework, a hollow wall, of logs—and then filled it with rubble and earth and laid logs in front of that. The canal here, then, was lined with logs.

and on this side there's a lot of rocks, and on this side there's a lot of rocks—riprap—and the canal is going right between these rocks. Right at the foot of Log Wall the towpath is not very wide, and it's windy—it's *win-dy* up there—and, gee, you'd look way down 50 or 60 feet [to the river and its boulders]. Boy, I hated to be out there, especially at night.

"One of the tricky places to steer was in the Catoctin Aqueduct. We called it the Crooked Aqueduct. The *aqueduct* was straight, but you come in crooked and you went out crooked. And that was the same way with the Six Locks; one lock—that was the fourth lock—was called Crooked Lock.

"The canal average was supposed to be 60 feet, but a lot of places I have doubts whether it was that wide or not. A canal boat was 90 feet long and 14 foot wide and it was better than six foot high, maybe six foot six inches from the bottom up to the race plank. The race plank is what we walked on. Then the cabins was a couple of feet high. The stable was a couple of feet higher from the race plank up. I guess most of the stables was up close to my shoulder. The stable went down. I'll say the stable was about five feet above the deck; the most of it was underneath. There was a little plank where the mules walked in.

"You'd come to a lock, you'd drop the fall board—three to four feet wide. At the lock you'd change teams. So we'd run these out the stable, and then the team that was out, we'd run them in. The fall board, we'd hook it on the inside of the stable and drop it down on the lock wall, and a team would go out and then a team would go in. If you wanted to get a team out on the bank, you dropped the long board and they went out. They had to go and come one at a time. You used the short fall board at a lock. The long fall board you used between locks; on the levels you needed a longer board because you couldn't get [the boat] right up to the towpath.

"The stable was at the front end of the boat. Then come the middle cabin where we kept the hay, and that was absolutely right in the middle of the boat. Of course the hay was on one side, and on the other side most all of them had a bunk for a guy to sleep on. And a place where they set their bow lamp.

J.P. Mose

143

The [kerosene] bow lamp went right up on the head, at the stable; but in the daytime they'd set it in. The back of it was metal, but the two sides and the front was glass. It made a pretty good light; a big reflector on it, and they'd set it mostly to have it shine on the team. You could see the canal ahead of you. They'd set it so [the person steering] could see the team and the canal."

"Then you had 14 hatches on the boat, 7 between the horse stable and the hay house, and 7 between the hay house and the living quarters.

"The living quarters. . . . You walked along [on the race plank] the side of the boat. There was just enough space to walk, that's about all: maybe a foot. Three steps down into the living quarters, into what we called the basement. Then there was another step and you opened the door and there was another step to the floor.

"On the right of the steps was your stove. Behind the stove was a bunk. That was your stateroom. Two could sleep in it very nicely. Two big people. Underneath you could set your shoes or boxes with stuff in. And of course you had another bed on that end of the stateroom toward the coal. And your table on the lefthand side between the two windows. A cupboard in the corner, and between the cupboard and where you went down the steps was a little door where you kept your potatoes, your ham if you had a ham, like a pantry.

"They had to have a small cook stove. It burned wood or coal. We mostly burned coal, but in hot weather we aimed to have wood. [With wood] you could get a quick heat and it would be soon over. Coal was all right when the weather was cold; it just burned along. In the fall of the year or early spring it was very good.

"My brother and I, we were just young men, we kept our boat—the 27—*painted up.* Yes, we kept our boat painted up. We took pride in it. Most of the people did. The hull of the 27 was dark brown. They used some kind of stuff they called carboline to preserve the wood.* It was something like this creosote that

*A wood preservative made of oil from coal tar treated with zinc chloride or chlorine.

144

they use now. The race plank you walked on, that was painted gray. The hulls, front and back hulls, would be painted red and white striped. The cabins were all white and green. The hatches were gray like the race plank.

"The boats were made in Cumberland. They were usually made out of Georgia pine. The bottom was oak. It took a lot of bumping, that bottom. I believe the sides were about two inches and a half thick." Deck and hatches were made of pine, whether or not Georgia pine Mr. Mose isn't sure. They made a point of using Georgia pine for the sides. "Because a lot of those planks were *long*."

This was the canal boat that's among Mr. Mose's very earliest memories. When he was ten years old and driving mules, "I wasn't tall enough to reach up [to a mule's head]. They had a little strap I'd get hold of to stop him and start him." And when he was 12 and beginning to steer, he was learning caution.

"It was lots of places that you had to watch, steering a boat, especially if you met a boat. That was one reason that the loaded boat always kept inside toward the towpath and the boat going upstream kept to the side toward the berm. On the berm side, a lot of times that wasn't too good, maybe a lot of rocks; and of course a light boat could get over pretty close but a loaded boat couldn't.

"Now, Little Slack Water was a right tedious place to steer. You'd come out in Little Slack Water, in the river, and there was a good many crooks in it. You come out into the river and there was a great big bend. And you went down a little piece, and there was another big bend. And right above the guard lock there was a pier—and a loaded boat would have to get around that pier and then you'd have to cut her right sharp around to get into that lock.* Of course now, the light boat went up on the *inside* of that pier, in the channel next to the towpath, but the loaded boat had to go on the outside, in the river. When the river was up, I tell you, you wanted to be on your guard. You wanted to know what you was doing. Believe me. Because

J.P. Mose

*This "pier" was a narrow strip of land.

Children chained to deck for their safety. A sight to shock uninitiated outsiders, this was the way boating families protected their small children. Chains and ropes were long enough to allow considerable movement but not long enough for any chance of falling overboard. Living members of boating families, including some then children, recall that children seemed to suffer no noticeable trauma from this practice.

the current goes right fast. If the driver kept the team up, if he got his mules moving to beat the band, to keep the towline tight and the boat a little faster than the current—then it wasn't too bad. But, boy, if he didn't. . .! The man steering would have a hard time. He wouldn't have much control over the boat.

"Now, if that river was up, it got so-high, they wouldn't let you out. They'd stop locking boats. The locktender would stop you. He had to judge. They had a mark to go by, a mark on the lock; and when that water [reached that mark], no more locking boats. You'd wait until the water dropped. Sometimes you might be there maybe a day before the river dropped.

"The danger would be that you might end up going over the dam. There was a boat went over Dam No. 5 one time, in the early 1900s. I don't know the background of it, but I think the wind. . . I think the boat was going upstream and the wind was blowing and I think it broke the line. He had no control of the boat and she just went over the dam.

"When a boat was loaded and going downstream, you couldn't

146

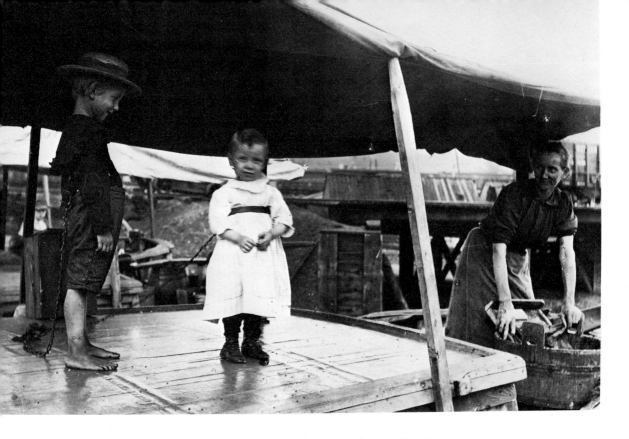

get it too close to the bank [where the canal was getting shallow]. So if the guy was out on the eight-mile level, say, and got tired and dinner time come and he wanted to get on the boat, we'd toss this plank out on the bank—and of course the boat kept moving along. And this guy hit that plank to get on the boat. If he didn't hit the plank, he took a dunking. After he took a dunking a couple of times, he got pretty good at it.

"People was on the canal with families, children. It would get pretty hot for little fellows down in that cabin all the time. We didn't have no air conditioning and we didn't have no fans. I've slept out on the deck a many a time. So they'd have a little harness on them and they'd tie them, and you'd give 'em the limit of the line so they wouldn't roll over this side or that side [of the boat]."

Occasionally people are somewhat taken aback to hear of children harnessed and put on a line, but it was a necessary precaution. "There was a lot of people drownded on that canal. I seen a lot of people drownded. I saved a couple of children from drowning. A boy had gone down on the bottom; I jumped in and grabbed and got hold of him, brought him up. Got him out on the towpath and worked with him. We used to bring them back over a barrel. If he wasn't gone too far, that would work. Most every boat had a barrel on it.

"Most every boat used to have what they called a beer keg on the quarterdeck. That's what we kept water in. Cause you couldn't get water every place. We'd get to a good spring, we'd fill up that barrel. It was pretty big; I think it held 30 gallons, maybe more. We'd lay it down and we'd cut a square hole in the top and we'd put a good heavy canvas, maybe double it a couple of times, and lay it over this hole. And when we wanted some water we'd reach in there and get it. Mostly we used a metal dipper. Of course the water would get very warm, but then it was good to cook with. But now, when we'd get to a place like Georgetown, we'd buy a cake of ice and drop it in that barrel. We'd get a big cake for a nickel."

Accidents were a part of canal life, and boatmen remember those that happened in their own day and think of those they heard about from days past. Little Logs was a place of some special danger, and Captain Tony Singer lost his life there. Mr. Mose recalls, "He leaned over to hang out his bow lamp, and fell in. He was crippled, and he drownded."

Along with other canallers, Mr. Mose remembers the death of the Spong children as the worst accident he knew of. "This was Captain [Samuel] Spong, Boat No. 74. A tugboat, the *Winship,* hooked them on the evening before, and that would have been September 10, 1916, for them to unload the next morning. They locked out in the river at the river lock at Rock Creek, and the *Winship* took them up to the powerhouse—right along the Potomac River. [There was a] concrete wall along there, [which you] pulled the boats up aside of and [where you] tied them, and there's where they unloaded. There was a pipe come out of that wall. I don't rightly know the size of that pipe, but I'll say around four to six inches. It came out straight, and there was an elbow in it, and the pipe went down into the river. They used to blow the boiler off, mostly at six o'clock in the morning."

They did this on the morning of the 11th. "Mr. Spong and his oldest son, Thomas, they were out on the boat getting ready to unload, putting up the hatches. His wife, Nina—they called her Nine—she was up also, but those children weren't."

The children were Johnny, aged 13; Willard, 11; and Sarah, 6. They were asleep in the cabin. The steam was blown with such force that it knocked the elbow off the straight part of the pipe, which then blew a powerful jet of steam straight out from the wall. "All that steam forced right into the boat, straight into the cabin. I don't know whether they had the window open or not, but a force like that would have *broke* it open.

"Naturally . . . a mother is a mother, and she tried to save them. She got scalded pretty bad. I don't know what hospital she was in in Washington or Georgetown, but she was there for several months. The undertaker from Sharpsburg come down and got the three children and took them to Sharpsburg and they were buried in Mountain View Cemetery. Captain Spong never boated any more after that."

Many canallers remember this terrible accident, but sometimes there is confusion about details. "A lot of people want to say that it happened at the paper mill, but that's not true. The paper mill was right on the canal, before you get to the lock at Georgetown. And a lot of them said he had gone shopping . . . lot of them said he had gone down to feed the mules, but I asked Alta [Spong Crampton]. She said he might have *been* down feeding the mules, but Tom and him was both on the boat [when it happened].

"I knowed all three of those children. Thomas, his birthday was in October and mine was in November, and that was all the difference there was in our age. Now, they had an older daughter, Sis. She was home. But Alta had been on the boat. When it got to Sharpsburg [on its way to Georgetown] she got off and stayed with her sister. God's blessing. Or she'd have probably been gone too."

Mr. Mose can remember when Ernie Willard shot Gus Speech.

"He shot him over a woman. It was through jealousy. I think Ernie Willard had gone with this woman Gus Speech had on

J.P. Mose

149

the boat with him. Gus Speech beat his time, I guess. She was on the boat when it happened. That was at Lock 7, Glen Echo. Charlie Shafter tended lock there, and he hollered at Gus Speech that somebody was going to shoot him. Gus run in the cabin, and I guess maybe he was looking out the door to see what was going to happen—and the guy shot him in the hip.

"They took the boat and pulled it over to the side and Gus Speech went to the hospital. And...I don't know...Ernie got a term, I guess; I can't remember back that far. But Ernie Willard shot Gus Speech and Gus Speech never come back on the canal. After that Pat Boyer got that No. 5 boat."

Both sides of Mr. Mose's family boated. "My mother was May Mose. She was a Renner before she was married. My Grandfather Renner was on the canal. And my Uncle Charlie Renner boated on the canal. Uncle Ed Renner boated on the canal. And Uncle Ridgely boated on the canal. And Uncle Clell boated on the canal. And Uncle Ivan boated on the canal, but then he was never the captain of a boat. He was just the same as I was. I was never a captain. But I was just the same as a captain: I could take a boat and do everything, leave home, take her to Cumberland and load her, take her to Washington.

"I was born in Sharpsburg. The biggest part of the boatsmen was from Sharpsburg. And of course when us children were small, my mother spent a lot of time on the boat with my father. As the children got bigger—we had a right good-sized family— why, she didn't go on the canal so much. She stayed in Sharpsburg.

"In the last part of March everybody would begin to get ready to start out. Then round the last week in November or the first of December they'd begin to quit. Maybe some of them might turn up in the second week in December. They all couldn't stop at one time; they wouldn't all get through at the same time. When the fall of the year come, we tied up and we went home to Sharpsburg. Till about the last of March, boats just lay in the canal. They drawed all the water out and the boats laid on the bottom.

"My father got in bad health at one time. He had a kidney

150

condition and he was a right good while getting over it. For a while he was off the boat, sick. And my older brother Lester and I boated the boat ourself. Just us two boys. I guess my brother was around maybe 14, and I was about 12 or 13. My sister went along with us; she did the cooking.

"Finally my other brother, Clifford, he was beginning to get a little age on him and he'd go along too.* Then when World War I come along, my brother Lester went into the army. Then my father, he and I and Clifford, we boated while Lester was in the army. Then when the war was over and my brother got out, he got married and got a boat of his own.

"That didn't mean he owned the boat. The canal company owned the boat. Now, back years ago, past my time, I think there was a lot of individuals that built boats and put them on the canal. A lot had their own teams. But the way I understand it, when the Canal Towage Company took it over, they furnished everything, the mules and everything, feed and all. [But] if you had a team and you wanted to keep your team, you could. Which my Grandfather Renner did. Up until he died, he had his own team. One was named Rose, one was named Mag. One was named Annie, and the other one was named Rose. They called them Big Rose and Little Rose.

"One time of day, my father had his own team. The last five years we boated, maybe longer than that, he had five mules. Buck and Diamond, Mike and Queen. And Jewel. That [last three] was the three-mule team. Jewel was a little black mule. Queen was a gray one. Mike, he was a mouse-colored mule. And Buck and Diamond, they were both bays.

"I was kicked by a mule. He was a young mule; we hadn't had him very long, and I scared him. He laid me out, too. When you're boating on the canal in the summertime, the flies get bad. And of course we had fly nets we'd put on them. A fly net is a thing made with big straps. They'd come down close around the mule's knees, and they would keep a lot of the flies

J.P. Mose

*Clifford Mose, died January 26, 1980.

151

off. Some of them had them over their heads. It didn't seem to bother them. They'd get used to it.

"Well, it was in the summertime, it was pretty warm, it was getting about sundown—right down here at Brunswick—and I was going to take the nets off. It was right close to a lock, and I was going to throw them on the lock. I walked up to Buck to unrig him, and I must have scared him. And, boy, he just— I'm telling you he caught me right in the hip. He knocked me clean across that towpath. It sort of knocked the ball out of the hip socket. I was a couple of months getting over it. He didn't mean to do it. I just scared him.

"A mule is *something*. He's pretty hard to train; but once you get him trained, he's very sensible. I think mules are more sensible than horses. Once you teach them something and they know what they're going to do, they'll do it by themselves. Now, we used to have a little mule, this little Jewel. We'd come to a lock and go to change teams. She was down at the end of the towline, and she'd go on and all you had to do was to holler, 'Come on back, Jewel,' and she'd turn around and come back.

"Once you got them going in and out of the boats, you had no trouble. Because they knew where they got their dinner and their breakfast. Sometimes you had to hold them till you got the others out. If we had all four mules out on the bank, we'd put both feeding troughs out.

"Lots of teams, you could get on the boat and let them go by themselves. Like, if there's only two people on the boat and you come to a nice place, a straightaway or something like that, with no danger, you could get on the boat, eat your meals or tend to the other team, and let them go by themselves."

Mr. Mose found that most mules are quite gentle. "A lot of people thought a lot of their teams. I'll say some people weren't very good to them. You find good and bad people everywhere. As a general rule, most everybody took good care of their teams. You just had to figure it like this: without your team, your boat wouldn't go. Just like a car without gasoline. The majority of people did take care of their teams. *We* did."

Mr. Mose remembers that a mule was good for about 15 years

on the canal. He thinks that a well cared for farm mule had a longer life. "I think they did live longer, because I've known of mules lived to be 30 years old. A life for a mule on the canal didn't last that long, I'll tell you that. In the first place, the reason it didn't last that long. . . when the wintertime came they'd put them out among people to winter and they *starved* them to death. I'm not kidding. When the spring of the year came, you'd go and get your team, and some of them would be so poor they couldn't hardly walk. That's the truth. They had different places to winter these mules, and they'd pay so-much a head. I can't remember what they paid, but it wasn't too much and [the mules] didn't get much to eat."

J.P. Mose

Casting his mind back to how he and his family made a trip, Mr. Mose recalls, "You went up to Cumberland empty. Everything loaded at Cumberland was coal. There were men to load the boats and men to unload them. They'd shovel the coal back up under the cabins and under the stable. You had to do that to get 112 ton of coal on the boat. Or 115 or whatever it might be. It was loaded up pretty thick. The man in the office would give you a manifest. That shows how much coal you're carrying and that's what you get paid for when you get to Washington.

"Then we'd start down the canal. You get to the nine-mile level at Cumberland, that's what you call a waybill lock. The locktender would give you a waybill—the day and the date and the hour you went through marked down. Now at Washington, sometimes. . . we'd pick up something, what we called a backload, and take it a piece up the canal. Maybe along in the fall of the year, with the canal doing some repair, you might haul some sand or gravel. Downstream, hauling coal was the main thing; but upstream lots of times they'd haul fertilizer up to these farmers. Lots of times they'd haul some lumber. Backloads weren't so often. You never would load deep, never drew more than a couple of feet. You didn't want to load 'em down, because it was a pretty hard job to handle that canal boat going against that current; it was pretty hard to steer.

"Most boats went back empty. Wasn't too many people *liked* to go back with a load on, because you never got too much

153

money for it and it was a bigger job to go upstream with a loaded boat than it was to go down.

"But you'd load in Cumberland and start down. Now, my Grandfather [Jake] Renner, he was one of the leading boatsmen on the canal. When he left Cumberland he never tied up till he got to Washington. There wasn't too many boating night and day, but you put in long hours. Most everybody tried to be going by five o'clock in the morning, and they tied up anywhere from nine, ten, eleven o'clock at night. Long hours. It wasn't hard work. The biggest thing was walking, following the team.

"The guys that boated all night long, every six hours they'd change mules and every six hours they'd change drivers and the guys steering. Us boys, we done a whole lot of night running.

"When we left Cumberland, we come along pretty good to Sharpsburg. We'd be coming downstream loaded and we'd always aim to get to Sharpsburg to lay overnight. We'd get to spend the night at home with the rest of the family. My mother, she'd have some pies baked, maybe a couple of cakes, and we'd load a basket and take it along on the boat with us. And we'd get a lot of clean clothes. We never washed clothes; we'd just take them home to our mother. And she'd have us all clean clothes enough to do us until we'd get back.

"It took about three days to go to Washington from Sharpsburg. Us boys were pretty good boatsmen. We were pretty fast. We didn't play along the canal and we put in long hours. Lots of times we'd leave Sharpsburg and the second night we'd tie up at Great Falls. But them was two big day's driving and you better believe it was."

From Cumberland to Washington took "about seven or eight days. Unless you went night and day like my grandfather. Then we'd come to Washington. When you get to Willard's Lock, the locktender signs [the waybill] too. Then he reports it in to the main office that Mr. Mose, Boat No. 27, is on the Georgetown level. When things were going pretty brisk, you didn't have to wait very long [to unload]. Sometimes you'd get your orders right there at Willard's Lock and keep right on through to Rock

Creek. You got to Rock Creek, old man Kingston said, 'J. Maury Dove's unload.' They had a tugboat out there in the river; it would hook to you and take you to J. Maury Dove's or down to Alexandria, to Smoot's. Smoot's took a lot of coal. Or up to Capital Traction Power House. Maybe they'd send you over to John Miller's brickyard to get unloaded. They might send you to the Navy Yard or Indianhead.

"But if times were a little slow, if you didn't get no orders at the waybill lock to go straight through, you went to what we

Typical scene at Willard's Lock (5), known to boatmen as the waybill lock. Waybill showed how many tons were on board and determined the captain's pay. "Without that you couldn't get through." Light boat is being pulled upstream. Mules harnessed together slantwise, which drew the boat straighter than if abreast. In middle-ground, lock keeper's wait house; on right, some vacationing town dweller's tent.

BILL OF LADING.

No. 40   THE CANAL TOWAGE COMPANY   1000-7-05

Shipped, in Good Order and Condition by **The Consolidation Coal Company**, on board

the Canal Boat 57 , whereof J. Bowers

is Master for the present voyage, and now lying at the port of CUMBERLAND, and bound for **WILLIAMSPORT, MD.**

with cargo 114 11 tons R. M. COAL, which is to be delivered without delay in like Good Order and Condition

to **VICTOR CUSHWA & SONS**, they paying freight at the rate of 22¢ per ton. And as an inducement

for the Consolidation Coal Company to ship the above cargo, the Master of the Boat agrees not to allow the whole or any part of the C o, to be taken from the Boat nor to remove the hatches thereof until ordered to do so by the Consignee ; that all detentions in unloading shall be at his risk, and that nothing not herein specified is to be implied between the parties hereto.

In Witness Whereof, The Master or Clerk of said Boat

has affirmed to four Bills of Lading of this tenor and date one of which

being accomplished the other to stand void.

Allowance in addition to above rate
for 4 Boatman's Mules, } $
" 4 Canal Towage Co. Mules, 6.00
" Mules,

Dated at Cumberland, this 2" day of May 190 6

Test :

William Heck

J. Bowers

For the Canal Towage Company.

Waybill.

155

called the wide water. That was at the aqueduct-bridge, where Key Bridge is now. You stopped there until they give you orders. I've laid there four and five days, waiting on orders.

"Of course if you just went to Williamsport and unloaded, you turned around and went back to Cumberland to get another load. A lot of this coal boated from Cumberland to Williamsport. Cushwa's, they were coal dealers. They had a coal yard in Williamsport; they took a lot of the coal. And Steffey and Findlay was a coal company. They're still in business in Hagerstown but not in Williamsport.

"A lot of people liked that short trip to Williamsport, especially the fellows that lived there. There was a good many people in Williamsport that boated on the canal. There was Mr. Shupp. There was Lizer. There was John Tice. The Zimmermans. Williamsport and Sharpsburg took care of the best part of all the boats.

"Now, there was a few that lived in Cumberland, and a few lived here and there different places along the canal. There was a few from Hancock: the Myers family, the Everitts.... They tell me that the *only* man from Hancock still living that boated on the canal is Jake Myers.* And Jake is 90 years old. He used to run his father's boat a whole lot. And my brother Lester, down at Sharpsburg, we figured out that he's *the only fellow that's living* that was captain of a canal boat.

"Three people is what you should have on a boat. Makes a nice crew. You'd have a driver, you'd have a man steering, then you'd have a man that would go out and tend to the team—feed them and curry them—and sweep the boat off. Three is actually what you should have to run a boat right. Most boats had three. Some only had two. Yes, a lot of them. That was working a hardship. The captain would have to get out and drive the same as a mule driver. The captain, he's supposed to steer the boat. But just like my brother Lester and I, why, when we was on a boat alone, he'd drive a while and I'd steer. He'd get tired of driving, and I'd get out and drive and *he'd* steer. The

*Mr. Myers died in June, 1981, in his 92nd year.

main thing is that the captain is in charge. He's responsible.

"We'd make 25, 30 mile a day downstream. You see how many hours you had to put in to make 25 mile? Now, we made 30 mile a day downstream many a time; and upstream 40 mile a day many a time. Upstream the boat traveled faster because upstream was easier, because you didn't have no load on and the boat wasn't drawing much water. The boat would only be drawing about a foot of water; but coming down, it was loaded down about five foot and there wasn't much water between the bow of your boat and the bottom of the canal.

"Now, lots of places there was places that we called wide waters; the water would be wider and deeper, and you could tell when your boat hit that wide water. You could feel it moving easier, a little faster. The water had more room to go around the boat. Same way upstream. Now, upstream you'd be going against the current. The only level you ever had much current on was the feeder level.

"A feeder level, there's where a dam is. Like down at Washington, Dam No. 1. All that set was the four-mile level at Georgetown. Then you come up to Seneca, Dam No. 2. That set the canal from Seneca to Dam No. 1. Then we come on up to Harpers Ferry, Dam No. 3. Dam No. 3 fed it down to Seneca. Then we come up to Dam No. 4; that fed it down to Harpers Ferry. Then Dam No. 5 feeds to Dam No. 4. Up to Dam No. 6, that fed to Dam No. 5. Dam No. 6 to Cumberland was the longest stretch; it was just exactly 50 miles from Dam No. 6 to Cumberland, and Dam No. 8 fed the canal for 50 miles.

"About ten mile below Cumberland, between the canal and the river, they had a pump house. Lots of times in the summertime when there'd be a little drought, not getting much rain, they'd pump water at that pump house into the eight-mile level to keep the rest of it going."

Many boatmen remember the canal water as bright and clear, with certain exceptions. In Mr. Mose's judgment, "It wasn't too clean. Because you'd have your team staying out overnight, and naturally it was just the same as cleaning out a stable. In the water, that's where it went."

J.P. Mose

157

In the canal's busiest days, there were upwards of 500 boats, meaning at least 2,000 mules, on its roughly 185 miles. The mind recoils from the idea of the condition of the water with manure from 10 to 11 mules to each mile of canal. Even in Mr. Mose's day the ratio of mules to miles was high; and even at the final period of operation, with maybe only 50 boats, there would have been a minimum of a mule a mile. And there was also the matter of human waste from each boat. Yet there were children who swam in the canal and nobody seemed any the worse for it.

Mr. Mose considers canal life as roughing it, but by no means altogether comfortless or boring. Of necessity they used a lot of canned goods, but "when you'd get to Washington you'd get yourself a nice big steak. And my brother was a good cook. He could make good Boatman's Bean Soup, and that was one of the best bean soups you've ever eaten. It was very tasty. I ate so much bean soup one day it made me sick; so my Uncle Herb Mose named me Beanie. There's people still today call me Beanie.

"My brother could cook most anything, to tell the truth. I wasn't too much of a cook. He used to make biscuits. And whatever was in season in the way of vegetables, he'd get them. He couldn't stock up, but then there was a lot of places along the canal. And a lot of the locktenders put out gardens, and they'd sell the boatsmen lima beans, corn on the cob. Plenty of corn on the cob. My brother didn't bake pies, but we bought pies. Right down here at Shepherdstown used to be a woman that baked bread and pies and sold them. Home-baked bread. Used to be several places to buy homemade pie—apple pie, cherry pie, mostly pies with crust on top."

Sleeping wasn't as satisfactorily arranged for as eating. "The bunks didn't sleep too good, because all you had was a straw tick in the bunk. That's all. That wasn't too good. I never knew of anybody having a mattress.

"There was a lot of nice things along the canal to see. When you left Cumberland there wasn't much except the mountains. Then when you got on down the canal, the Round Top Cement Mill above Hancock. That was a big building right alongside the

158

Boatman's Bean Soup

1 lb. Great Northern
   beans (or navy beans.
   Most canallers prefer
   navy beans)
2 quarts water
2 medium Irish
   potatoes, diced
1 large onion, chopped

1 pint of canned
   tomatoes or 4 large
   ripe tomatoes, cut up
1 large ham bone or
   ham hock; cut lean
   meat off and put in
   kettle

Soak beans overnight and drain. Add water, potatoes, onion, and ham bone, and cook until potatoes are done but still firm. Add tomatoes and cook 30 minutes more. Season to taste. More water may need to be added as beans cook. Serves six.

After he quit boating, J.P. Mose married 18-year-old Idella Kauffman, who knew nothing of canal life but who soon learned to make the bean soup he was so fond of. Here's Mrs. Mose's recipe.

rock cliffs. A lot of nice scenery around Hancock and Big Pool. And Little Pool. At Little Pool you'd go out in a big body of water. Little Pool was, I think, a mile long. Big Pool was about two mile long. There was mountains. And cliffs. All that kind of thing. Right above Hancock you could look across the river and there was another great big cliff, a beautiful cliff. Some [of the cliffs] were straight [up] as my hand. And a lot of nice farms.

"When you got below Harpers Ferry, when you got below Point of Rocks, the mountains cut off. Then there was some beautiful farm land. Lots of nice farms along that canal, indeed there was. Lot of farms down there didn't raise nothing but cattle.

One of the sights looked forward to by young boatmen was at what they called The Lock of the Pretty Girls. These were the daughters of "Old Man Kasekamp...the fifth lock below the tunnel. One that was named Ann—boy! every boat that came along, she was out there painted like a kewpie doll. I'll guarantee you that every boat that come through that lock—in the daytime;

159

I don't know about after night—Ann was *out there,* sitting on that porch. Flirting with the boys. You better believe she was."

Another family with what old-fashioned novelists used to call a bevy of beauties was that of locktender Darkey, at the foot of the three-mile level of South Branch. Mr. Mose remembers that "Old Man Kasekamp didn't have prettier girls than Hughey Darkey. These were very nice looking redheaded girls—four or five, I think, of the prettiest girls you ever saw."

Less satisfactory was night boating. "After night you couldn't see nothing; you'd just hear tree frogs hollering. If there was three of you, it wasn't too bad. Probably one would be sitting beside you and talking to you. It wasn't too lonesome. But two of you would be pretty lonesome—that boy out with the team and you on the boat. That was lonesome, you better believe it was. Now, in the summer you didn't have to go too long after dark, because it don't get dark until close to nine o'clock. But when the fall of the year come, you done a lot of boating in the dark. Steering would be lonesome [even in daylight], but there was more to look at."

When they were in port, "You were very happy to get off. When we'd get to Washington we'd tie up there at the wide water above the aqueduct bridge. We were just kids, and first thing we'd do is get down on M Street. There used to be a place down there, an ice cream parlor, and you could buy a banana split for a dime. There used to be moving pictures. Ten cents. You could go in and sit all evening, watch the show repeat. We used to like that.

"Sometimes when we went to Georgetown we stayed on the boat until we got unloaded and then started back up. Sometimes you'd leave maybe the next day. And sometimes you'd lay around for a couple of days. Then we'd have a rest. Swim. Go down to M Street and buy banana splits. Swim some more. It wasn't too clean, but it was running water. I was just a small boy, learning to swim.

"I couldn't swim very much, and a cousin of mine—I was swimming between the boats—he [had] shoved me off to swim to the next one, and, by Jimmy's, I couldn't make it. I started down.

I went down a couple of times. A fellow from Hancock, by the name of James Everitt, he crawled out on the side of the boat, reached down and got me by the hair and pulled me up. He was a young man then, in his twenties. James Everitt. He just died a couple of years ago. He must have been right old. I wasn't too long learning to swim, I'll tell you. They'd caution children."

Although Mr. Mose stresses the long hours that boatmen worked, as all canal people do, he looks back to his boating days fondly, as most canal people do. "One time of day I liked to boat on the canal. You was on the move all the time, for one thing. And there was a lot of things happening along that canal.

J.P. Mose

"One time there was a boat went out in the break down there above Seneca Lock, and I tell you we just got back and that was all—before the break went out. I mean a break in the tow-path, with the canal pouring into the river and you could be left high and dry. This time we got by before it happened. The boat right behind us come along and he went out in the break. Right out in the river. Everybody got off [the boat] before she went out, and they never bothered to take his boat out. It was an old boat. If it had been a new boat, probably it would have been a different story. It was loaded with coal. Somebody said that the farmers got most of the coal out of it.

"Lots of times there'd be a break in the canal. That would stop the boats and they'd pile up, and all the boys would get together and go swimming and have a holiday until they could get that break fixed and lock the boats.

"Our boat sunk once. Hit a rock. This boat was the No. 38, before we got No. 27. It was up at the Narrows, right this side of Cumberland. At the one-mile level above the ten-mile lock. [Sometimes there was] stuff in the canal and we wouldn't know it. Well, that's what happened. We come out of that lock and hit that thing and the boat stopped. The locktender, he heisted all four paddles out of them gates behind us and the boat just swung around and hit the rock. My mother was on the boat with us children. We only sunk down about to the top of the race plank.

"We went up to the third lock where they had a telephone

161

The Captains They Knew

When they "saw the handwriting on the wall," as J.P. Mose put it, he and his brother, Lester M. Mose, made up a list of the boats and captains they knew. At different times, the boats were captained by various men.

Spelling of names was generally haphazard among canal people, and it was quite usual to know others well and yet have had no particular reason to know exactly how they spelled their names. Spelling, then, cannot be vouched for in every instance, but identity can.

Boat No.	Captains	Boat No.	Captains
1	Raleigh Bender	17	Wilhelm (Harpoon)
	Tom Kerfoot		Boyer (Later he had
	George (Corky) Price		No. 92)
2	Wes(ley) Lizer	18	John Tice
3	Harry Pryor		John Tice, Jr.
	Tony Singer		George (Tad) Bowers
	(Drowned at Little Logs)	19	Will Colbert
4	Daise Wolfe	20	Dick Haynes
	Clint Zimmerman	21	Charles G. Myers
5	Gus Speech		Old No. 21: Clete Dick
	(Shot and wounded at	22	Tom Hover
	Lock 7)	23	Jake Renner
	Pat Boyer		Charlie Renner
	Oliver Grove		Ronnie Mayhew
6	Gus Hebb	24	Benjamin Hebb
	_____ Keim		(New No. 24)
7	Otha Grove		Clete Dick (Old No. 24)
8	Henry (Hen) Preston	25	Edward Rockwell
	Bill Wooder	26	Ide Crampton
9	George Sandbower	27	Old 27, C.R. Castle
	(and sons Russell,		New 27, Jerome Mose
	John, and Joe)	28	Charles (Scat) Eaton
10	Charley Fox		(Also 80)
	George Swandle		Robert Hebb
11	Taylor Reed	29	Joe Snyder
12	George Knight	30	Harry Zimmerman
	Richard Stevens	31	Will Gloss (Old 31)
13	Charley Fox		Doc Wilson (Old 31)
14	Charley Huff	32	
	(Old No. 14)	33	Ben Snyder
	Albert (Bert) Swain	34	
15	Clyde Stride	35	Sam Atwell
	Oliver Grove	36	Tuden Underdunk
	West Bear		Leiper Price
	Clyde Grove		Jim McKelvey
16	Foster Bowers	37	

Boat No.	Captains	Boat No.	Captains	Boat No.	Captains
38	Bud French	65		94	
	Jerome Mose	66	Jack Stride	95	Foster Taylor
	(Later, New 27)		Lloyd Martin	96	Lafe Dick
39	Pat Boyer (New 39)	67	Will Fisher	97	Edward Mose
	Wilhelm Stull (Old 39)	68			Ronald Schroeder
40	Nelson (Nels) Huff	69	Will Zeigler		(Youngest captain on
41	Bill Taylor		Will Penner		canal)
42	Billie Swain	70	Ridge Renner	98	Sam (Old Man) Kelley
	John (Johnny) Knode		Ed Renner (took over	99	Fred Benner
	Lester (Les) Mose		when R. Renner quit)		Ridge Renner
	Charles (Piney) Delaney	71	Lev Benner		(Then to 70)
43	Tom McKelvey		(Later to 91)	100	Charlie Showe
44	Dan Saylor	72	Jake Bender		Ed Renner
	Will Saylor (son of		(Then to 49)		(Then to 70)
	Dan Saylor)	73	Frank Myers (Went out		
45	Emmert Martin		in Conococheague		
46	Tom Crampton		Aqueduct)	**Other captains:**	
47	Lewis Snyder	74	Will (Boodle) Bowers		Charlie Hewitt
48	Jack Hetzer		(Then to 24)		Commodore Myers
	Newton Boyer		Reuben (Rube, Ruby)		(Brother to Jake Myers)
49	Jake Bender		Castle		Ralph Dick
50	Jake Renner		Sam Spong		Charlie Bowers
	(Also New 23)	75			Robert Underdunk
	Max Knight	76	Will Colbert		Alvey Mills
51	Owen Stickle		(Later, 19)		Fred Stull
	Luther (Lu) Benner		Roy Colbert (Will		Daise Taylor
52	James Hall		Colbert's son)		Sam Poffenberger
	Henry Williams	77	Charles (Piney)		Rube Poffenberger
	Lester (Les) Mose		Delaney (Earlier, 42)		Charles Huyett
53	Ambrose P. McCardell	78	Charlie Shaw		Charles Bowers
	George Myers	79	Bud Crampton		Harry Kuhn
54	Frank Hull	80	Charles (Scat) Eaton		Leif Eichelberger
	Jack Speaker		(Later to 28)		Jim Reed
55	Charlie Bender	81	Mart Kinsel		Jim Everetts
56	Dent Shupp	82	Charles (Beaver) Davis		Turmann Gray
	Orville Delaney	83			Ben Huff
57	Albert (Af) Davis	84	Lafe Dick		Ralph Dick
58	Jack Speaker		Jack Hetzer		Theo Bear
59	Charlie Pearl	85	Gus Speech (Then to 5)		Ab Davis
	(Later tended lock in	86	Robert (Bob) Wright		Bob Swain
	Georgetown)	87			Ed Dunn
60	Sherd Banner	88	Dickie Moser		
	John Crampton	89	Denton (Dent) Shupp		
61	Hen Sensel		(Then to 56)		
62	Bob Zimmerman	90	Sharpie Taylor		
	(Also New 31)	91	Lev Benner (Went		
63	Hen Swain		out at Big Pool)		
	Leonard Swain	92	Will Hen (Harpoon)		
	Links Crampton		Boyer		
64	Ide Crampton	93	John Mellott		

and called in to Cumberland that we'd sunk. They told the lock-tender to pull the plank; so he pulled the plank. They had planks in waste weirs to hold the water, and you'd draw the plank up to let water out. We had to move everything out of the cabin, the hay and everything. They sent carpenters down from Cumberland and they boxed the hole in. Then we went to Williamsport and unloaded."

The boyhood memories are the best. As time went by, Mr. Mose liked boating less. "I spent practically my whole young life on that canal. After I got older, then I began to date the girls; and of course that makes a change in life. I boated until 1920. I got married then. Met my wife and got married. Boating was getting a little on the slim side and my father, he didn't want to boat any longer. My older brother, he didn't want to boat any longer. So my father and I tied up in the fall, and the next spring we just didn't start out."

Jacob F. Myers

(Died June, 1981, aged 91)

Hancock

"SUNDAY NEVER COME on the canal."

Here speaks Mr. Jacob Myers—Jake to his friends—in the 90th year of his life, recalling, with much sadness and little if any pleasure, his 30 years on the canal. "Why, you worked all the time. You'd get up at three or four o'clock in the morning and start the boat. It was a rough life. *Very rough.* People think today—the young generation thinks it was a plaything. It wasn't no play-job. *Very* long hours. I got up four o'clock *many* a morning, [knocked off at] ten or eleven o'clock that night. That was called a day on the canal.

"We stopped a little at night. Some nights you didn't stop at all, you just kept going—to get back to Washington, to get your freight, the money you got paid to make the trip. Back to *Georgetown;* you didn't go to Washington. Rock Creek divided Georgetown from Washington."

Mr. Myers's father was Charles G. Myers, captain of Boat No. 120. No. 120 was painted "battleship gray. That was all over the boat—decks, hatches, and all. The cabin was painted blue inside."

For the Myerses, boating was a family affair, but without women. Jake Myers's sister-in-law Molly (née Shives) boated, but not the women in his immediate family. Jake was the youngest of the Myers boys, though they were fairly close together in years. He had two younger sisters, Catherine and Emma. After the death of their mother, they lived with their Aunt Minnie Sensel and their grandmother in Hancock.

Jacob Myers

165

Early in life, "I went to boating with my pap. I wasn't very big, but I was big enough to holler, 'Come up, Mike.'" Although he doesn't remember his exact age, he's sure he was under nine, "a very young kid."

Young Jake stayed on the family boat as he grew up. "The *long hours*," he repeats. "You stayed up all day and all night. It wasn't nothing to stay up all night. You did just what the captain said. There was four of us—two brothers and Pap and me." The brothers were Columbus and Commodore.

Their time was spent "sleeping, cooking, fixing something to eat. Pap steered a lot. Anybody can cook that wants to; we all took turns."

Even as a small boy Mr. Myers helped with the cooking by making bean soup. "That was the main dish on the canal. The first thing you do, you get the white soup beans and you wash them. Wash 'em off and put 'em in the pot. Had an iron pot. In this pot was a piece of meat. Pork. Hog meat, in plain words. Then, let's see—you put the meat on. You boiled the meat a while and then you put the beans in. You slapped a little salt and pepper in it. The way you tested the beans, you took a bean out and took a fork and mashed it. It had to mash up to be done. Then the soup was ready to serve."

Though they navigated in six feet or less of water and were pulled by mules, the boatmen were in a nautical situation. Sleeping quarters were staterooms, at Georgetown they were in port, and the captain's word was law. If the captain of a particular boat wanted to run day and night, you worked day and night or you signed on with another boat the first chance you got. If he was your father—and the captain often was—you worked day and night and stayed put.

A captain was financially responsible for whatever help he had in the operation of his boat. He himself was paid at the time of each delivery according to the number of tons of cargo he had hauled. If he hired a hand, the pay came out of his pocket. And the three sons of Captain Myers, who paid them? "My pap did if he wanted to. If he didn't, he didn't pay us. That was up to Pap." Mr. Myers was aware that the towage company was paying one man and getting the work of more (three more in this instance), but "you just had to put up with it. I made a good many trips without Pap giving me a quarter. *Twenty-five cents.*"

With mature years, Mr. Myers came to understand that his father, a man with a family to support, had to keep a close watch on his expenditures. When he didn't give the boys their quarters at the completion of a trip, it was because quarters weren't easy come by. "Sometimes they [captains] made more, some months they made less. This depended on the conditions of things you run into on the canal, what stopped you. . . ."

On the Myers boat, work went on seven long days a week. "Sunday never come on the canal," said Mr. Myers again. "You were tired most *all* the time, to tell the truth. I often thought I didn't get sleep enough. I made a trip on the canal in 168 hours in a week. [That means everybody on board was on duty or on call 24 hours each day for seven days and the condition of the mules goes without saying.] I made a trip from Georgetown back to Georgetown in 166 hours and ten minutes.

"Sometimes you did [have some time between trips] and sometimes you didn't." There were occasions, however, when he could be grateful for a period of respite. "Why, you might lay in Georgetown a week." During that week Jake and the others "fished and laid around. You went to this boat and talked to them, and that boat and talked to them." As for the hungered-and-thirsted-for rest, sleeping "was the biggest job you had to do."

Just as "Sunday never come," boating never stopped because of inclement weather. "Weather never stopped you. You just had to put up with it. An awning [sheltering the stern] kept the sun off and the rain. I remember a storm at Antietam Aqueduct—tore the awning down, upset everything. It didn't hurt the boat, but it did the awning. Tore it up." As Mr. Myers remembers, an awning cost about $11, a fair sum in those days.

"There was taverns along the canal" and drinking among the boatmen, "Oh, a lot of it." Nothing in particular to tell about, no untoward incidents to recall, "They just *drank*." But not on Boat No. 120. Besides going to the taverns along the way, "They used to drink in Georgetown too. There was an old Dutch

Jacob Myers

woman sold beer for five cents a quart. But, like people today, they'd drink anything—a lot of them would."

As it does with many old timers, the impasse at the Paw Paw tunnel sticks in Mr. Myers's mind. "Why, a loaded boat pulled in the tunnel at one end and a light boat at the other. They were in there so far—they stopped."

They stopped because passing was impossible and neither one would yield and back up. "*Sure* they were angry. When you set all night and all day with a double-barreled shotgun in your hands, you must not be in a very good mood. A man by the name of Zimmerman, Clint Zimmerman, from Big Pool, was captain, and he wouldn't let 'em untie the line to pull 'em out or in."

Mr. Myers remembers that boats often got partway into the tunnel from each end, "often, but it didn't go that far. You can back up a light boat, but a loaded boat's hard to back up." So it was plain what should have been done. The light boat should have backed up. Most of the time this was done. This time, Mr. Zimmerman, in the loaded boat, justifiably felt that he had precedence. As for the captain of the light boat who wouldn't budge either, "Bullheaded!" says Mr. Myers. "Oh, what *was* his name? He was from Williamsport."

The single solitary aspect of canal life that Mr. Myers speaks of with any degree of pleasure is the mules. He was fond of them and didn't feel the need of any other pet. "I had a *mule* to pet." He thinks back to his father's teams. "Mike and Rose, Tom and Bird. I didn't like Bird very much; she'd kick. I liked Rose; you could ride her.

"I enjoyed being with the mules. I had a lot of fun with the mules. *Yes, sir.* A mule is intelligent. He has more intelligence than a horse. And good. Gentle. If you treat a mule right, he'll treat you right."

Much as he detested and suffered through the cruelly long hours on the 120 and the consequent loss of sleep, Mr. Myers never disliked canal life on grounds of loneliness. "You had all kinds of companionship. Every day you'd meet locktenders and different people along the canal. You see, there was a lot of locks,

74 of them. Sometimes you went 14 miles [between locks]." At two miles an hour, 14 miles can stretch out in time, but on a typical day Mr. Myers would see four locktenders.

In his thoughts he keeps returning to the oppressive nature of the work, mainly because of the hours. "I didn't like it. I didn't like it at all. It was too rough. There was one 14-mile level; that was the longest. And the shortest—a canal boat was 92 feet long, and you had to push it out of the lock at a little short level at Four Locks. You had to shove it out of the way for the loaded boats to get by you.* All such things as that you had to do. You were being drove around all the time, up and down, and one thing and another. It was harder [to keep house] on the boat than it would have been in town. You had so much to put up with. Nobody knows what you went through. Just the ones who went through with it."

Jacob Myers

After 30 years, Mr. Myers quit boating. This was a milestone in his life and he remembers its exact date. "I quit boating August the 28th, 1919. I went to work for the railroad, Baltimore and Ohio Railroad. I labored on that."

And was that better than the canal life? "*Yes.* That damned old canal's been a joke ever since it started."

---

*There was an extremely short level at the lowest of the Four Locks. If a boat were approaching the lock as you were leaving it, you had so little room that you could avoid the oncoming boat only by poling yours out of its way.

Interviews, August 12 and September 1, 1979.

Lester M. Mose, Sr.
Sharpsburg

Lester M. Mose

"I NEVER LIKED THE CANAL. Never liked the canal life," says Lester M. Mose, Sr. "But I took a lot of interest in it. A *lot* of interest."

Son of Captain Jerome Mose, Mr. Mose, like so many others, went on the canal at an early age. "I remember well. I started in 1904. I'd have been nine years old in October, 1904, and I started out in the spring. On my father's boat.

"Ahead of that I was on the canal when I was smaller and I just can't remember too well. But my mother was on quite a bit at that time. Up until 1904 she was on. My mother was Ella May Mose.

"Once in a while she'd get off for half a trip or something and look after home. There was only one in the family older than me, and he never stayed with us. Ernest stayed with his grand-father, Jacob Renner. Then there was the girl, next to me, Charlotte; but she was on with us but very little. Then J.P. came into the picture. J.P. was on when he was very small, with our mother."

Even as a child, Mr. Mose didn't fancy canal life. "No, never did like it. For one thing, when I was a child I was kind of afraid of water. I got out of that later on, but that was one thing. And I never liked those Italians. You'd meet them after night, walking along the towpath. In 1904 they was building the Western Maryland railroad from the head of Big Pool to Cumberland, and they had a lot of foreigners building the railroads. The railroad was right along the canal. They had shanties all along

170

the towpath. I was just kind of afraid of them, that's all. Nervous, I guess.

"There was this too. Above Orleans there was the five-mile level. I was driving.* My dad said, 'You go ahead and drive and we'll tie up down at Orleans bend. This was right above Orleans. It was dark. I had just met a couple of guys walking along. Alvie Mills and Jim Ike Mills, brothers, big tall fellows. They had a scow—wasn't as long as a canal boat but it was as wide—and they was hauling supplies along for this railroad. They had a cabin on the scow, but it wasn't too high, so we carried the tow line over it.

Lester Mose, Sr.

"In the meantime, because it was dark, my mother made up her mind to get off and walk along with me. Jim Ike Mills got her by the hand, and the boat was right beside the scow. There wasn't too much space on the bow of the scow because they had stuff all over it, loaded with wheelbarrows and planks and stuff. When he pulled her, they got out of balance and both of them went in the canal.

"Well, Dad hollered for me to stop the mules, and I stopped. And of course I was a young fellow, nine years old, and I thought the world of my mother, and, boy, I started running back. They got out. Mr. Mills got 'em out pretty well. Mr. Mills could swim. (My mother couldn't swim) and she was a right good-sized woman too. But he got them out, and we tied up there. We didn't go any farther that night. I had run back to her hollering. She said, 'I'm all right. I'm all right. Hush crying.' She was very tenderhearted.

"My daddy, he was a little bit different. He was good to us, but you had to do things the way he wanted you to do them. If he told you to do something, he wanted you to *do* it and do it his way, not your way. We always did. Had to! No question about it. Had to.

"We'd start out in the first of April. I'd go to school in the winter-

---

*Muleskinner is not a word the canal people used. "You got that from other people, people who didn't know [any better]." To the canal people, those on the towpath were drivers.

time. Round the first week in December I'd get to school, and the last week in March I'd have to come out. I enjoyed school in a way, but I was always behind. Wasn't up with the rest of the pupils. They was ahead of me [being there for the whole term]. So I didn't get a good schooling like I should have had. It made a little difficulty. You didn't mind stopping [school] in the spring, but you hated to start in the winter."

On the Mose boat there were the three family members. "We didn't have nobody but me and him and her. My mother steered. She never got out to drive. I walked for miles and miles. We had a three-mule team, and I walked miles and miles. I never did mind the walking. Once in a while I could appeal to Daddy to give me a rest. I'd get a break, whenever he could get out and do it. He would drive on maybe a three- or four-mile level, and my mother would steer.

"After 1905 or '06, he hired a hand. I went on with him, with the hand. In 1906 we had a hand, but only part of the year. And that's when J.P. got into the picture. He might not remember he was on that early. He was about nine. But he wouldn't stay on; sometimes he'd go with us and sometimes he wouldn't. Our mother never got on the boat much after that. She might make a trip to Washington to get some clothes for the winter or for school, but that's about all.

"We had boat No. 38. J.P., he'd get on with us a while, then he'd get off. Dad never forced him, and it was just Dad and I and now and then we'd have a hand. There was a fellow on the canal—we called him Harvey; he talked through his nose—and Dad would get Harvey on a while with us. I think J.P. was on the whole year in 1907, 1908, and 1909.

"My father . . . I believe he did [like canal life]. Frankly, I believe he did. But he had a family to raise. He had to like it or lump it, that's all there was to it. I took a lot of interest in it, but I just didn't like it. It was kind of lonely to me. I was a fellow liked to get around people. You didn't get around too many, only when you'd get to a locktender. Of course in Washington you met a lot of people; in Cumberland you met a lot of them; maybe Williamsport, if you unloaded there, you met a lot of them. But

I just didn't care too much for the life. It wasn't too hot to me, I'll tell you that."

These childhood feelings carried over into youth and manhood. "I had [the same feeling] all my life. I did. The whole time I was on the canal. It was lonely. To me, it was lonely. You'd go for eight or nine miles and see nobody. Only thing you'd ever run into would be a locktender, and you wasn't there but a few minutes. But I always did like the mules. One was named Dick; one was named Aleck; one named Matt; and one named Rose.

"I took a lot of interest in the mules. Mules was always used. Horses wouldn't stand the travel. There were a few horses on the canal, but not too many and they never stayed long. A mule could stand [canal work] better; they had smaller feet; they were tougher. Horses made an awful good team, but they didn't last long. Mules could stand it better.

"Getting a loaded boat started was a hard problem. That's one thing about a team of mules. You start your loaded boat out of the lock, and it's a *dead weight*. If you had a good team, they'd just go up against that towline and stretch that line up so-far, and then they'd just stay there a little bit and lay their weight there until the boat started moving so they could make a step. Then they'd make another step. After they went about 25 feet [that way] they didn't have the boat under good headway, but they had the boat moving.

"If you got a new team and had mules that was never used to the canal, [they] had a little trouble learning to do that. They'd jump around. If you'd talk to them and quiet them down, it didn't take 'em too long. It might take a couple of weeks or a couple of trips, but they'd come to it. Putting them in the stable at a lock you had the same story. After they learned that, the minute you dropped that fall board they were there just like *that*. The others would come out of the stable, and they'd go in. The others wouldn't come out until you laid that hatch back; but then one would come out, and the other would go in, just like rabbits."

Starting a dead-weight loaded boat was a tremendous strain on the mules. Especially if they were afflicted with impatient

Lester Mose, Sr.

173

drivers who would not take the time for the 25-foot process described by Mr. Mose, the mules became spavined. There were a large number of mules on the canal with these painful enlargements of leg bones. "Spasm," says Mr. Mose. "A lot of them. It didn't happen with me. I had one mule . . . but it never bothered her much. She was a big mule; she weighed about 1400 pounds. She had that spasm in one leg, and I used to take Yeager's Liniment and bathe her with that. You can use it for man or beast, but mostly for beasts."

There were several maneuvers that mules often made with a minimum of direction. Mr. Mose cites their dealing with towlines and passing other boats. "There was 35 yards in a line, and it was about as thick as my thumb. They pulled that line and it come up. It was never straight like a cable; it always had a sag in it; sometimes it dipped [into the] water. We never used anything heavier, not to pull the boat. Now, there were heavier lines to snub the boat up. When they got wet, they got much bigger. They were all manila rope. Usually you never used as long a line for a light boat as a loaded boat; you never used as *good* a line either."

In a passing situation the light boat always moved over to its own left. It had to sink its towline in the canal for the loaded boat to pass over; so the boatmen had to make sure that the line had been dipped enough to be wet enough to sink. "I had one team there, two old mules, and they'd go along and that line would *never* dip water. They kept that line above water all the time. I'd see a boat coming and I'd holler whoa to them and they'd stop and I'd let the line get wet. They'd get back about five or six feet from the bow of the boat and stop, and the line would sink. So when [the loaded boat] come up, they would just walk around the loaded boat's team, and they'd take their time, and the loaded boat's team would step over the line."

Occasionally, not often, there would be a mule who needed to change positions at locks in order to do so with any peace of mind. Such a mule simply could not cope with that 16-foot walk across a plank over the water, reaching from boat to towpath or the other way around. "The boat was stopped. [General-

174

ly] they weren't afraid. But some of 'em you couldn't get to use [the fall board]. They *were* afraid. My daddy had a team. . . that gray mule he had—we called her Queen—she'd never use a long fall board. She never would. Before she'd take a long fall board to get to the stable, she'd swim the canal. She never could get used to it. And you couldn't start her out either. If she was in the stable and you [tried to] start her out [on the long board], she'd jump off in the canal. She'd jump into the canal and walk right up the bank."

Lester Mose, Sr.

Much as he liked the mules, Mr. Mose remained ambivalent about them on one point. "I'll tell you one thing: you could never trust a mule. He could kick you with his front feet. So their bridles had blinkers on them, and when you was walking beside of them they couldn't see you. Get in front of them, they could. Some of 'em was all right. But you could never trust a mule. I had a good team. Four mules. One I could never trust; the other three I trusted all right.

"But that one mule, I never did trust her. She kicked that brother of mine, Daniel. Up on the four-mile level of the tunnel. He couldn't drive and she wouldn't listen to him and she was kind of bullheaded. [When she kicked Daniel] she knew the minute I hit that towpath. I didn't even get up to her; she just straightened out and went on. She never kicked me.

"She was all right in the stable. She was fine. You could curry her, walk all around her, do anything; but she would take contrary spells. And she did it with someone like my brother. He was small, he was only eight or nine years old, and she just wouldn't pay no attention to him. She was just that type. But she was a good mule. She was a good leader. Her name was Kit."

Speaking of Buck, the one who kicked J.P. Mose when he accidentally frightened the mule, Mr. Mose says, "He was a nice mule. He did kick J.P. down at Brunswick, but I knew that mule and Buck was a nice mule. But he wasn't no good leader. He was more of what you might call a butt mule than he was a leader. Not all were good leaders. Not all. But it wasn't too much trouble to find a good leader.

"We had bells that went in the hames of the harness. We had

175

screw eyes and we put these bells in them. When the mules were walking, them bells chimed all the time. [Our mules] *loved* them. They'd just walk along there, proud and nice as could be—especially with a light boat. You could tell by their movements. You can tell a mule when he's walking proud. Just like a horse and buggy. You can tell. You'd have four [bells] on each bow. For each mule, and they had three sets. We never used them much after night. Daytimes we kept them on.

"I took a lot of interest in the harness, and seen that it fit good, that the pads on their shoulders were good. The mules, when they started out and had eight miles to go, or three miles to go, four miles, when they tightened up against that towline that collar never left their shoulders. It never left. And they would sweat. If you didn't take good care of them, if you didn't have thick pads on the collars, they'd get sore shoulders. They'd get sores. The only time in the day the collar left them [was], if you stopped for some reason and took it off a little bit.

"The pads protected them a whole lot. But they still sweated and you had to clean them pads and dry them. When you'd take them off you ought to let them lay out somewhere where the sun was shining. It was only in warm weather that the mules sweated so much. In cool weather they didn't sweat at all. But you'd still have to look after them. You had to scrape them and clean them off, whatever stuff had got on [the collars] from the mules' shoulders. You had to take *care* of the mules. And the same way with the harness. You had to grease it and oil it. Every time we come off a trick we curried them down. We fed 'em good. That's how I took interest. I did take care of the animals.

"And the same with the boat. I kept her clean, kept the water out, kept it painted. You always kept the bow of your boat painted up pretty nice so it would look good. And your lamp board, where you put your lamp at night, kept that painted. If you wanted to do decorating, you bought your own [paint]. But if you just wanted to paint the boat, like the cabins or anything, why, they furnished it. That was the Canal Towage Company. They had the boats. The C&O Canal Company, that was the *canal* company. They owned the canal itself—locks, dams, all that.

176

"The towage company boated the coal for so-much. They paid $3.00 a trip a mule—whether I owned them or the towage company owned them didn't make any difference. Three dollars for a mule. When you come [only as far as Williamsport] they only paid you $1.50. They paid you $3.00 a mule for a whole trip; when you come to Williamsport, that was only half a trip. The Canal Towage Company paid us. In other words the whole works come from the Consolidation Coal Company. All the money had to come from there to keep things going. Because [coal was] all you hauled. They mined it up here at Frostburg and Cumberland.

"Those that worked on the canal itself was working for the Chesapeake and Ohio Canal Company. George Nicolson, he was the big shot of *both* of them. The ones that worked on the canal, kept it up, he would come along—he had a pay boat, a yacht— and he'd pay them off, give their money to the locktenders and the superintendents and the section men. The man that generally wrote our checks as soon as we hit Washington was Hassett. He was from up here at Four Locks and his first name was Timothy. He was there a long time. But Nicolson was the big shot of everything. He was the man you referred to about everything, about the canal or the boats or anything. He was a good man, good to get along with.

"We wasn't under contract. [Each trip] you got the waybill and they paid you according to that waybill. Just whatever coal you had on, whatever amount. If you went down the river to Indianhead, you got five cents extra [per ton]. If you boated along right and nothing delayed you too much, you could make two trips a month *easy*. You didn't have to rush. If nothing delayed you. If you're getting 40 cents a ton for coal, why . . . it was between $90 and $100 a month. The average was in there somewhere.

"Now, it all depended upon what else you did. If you brought watermelons back up to sell them, you made a little money. I'd say on the average if you got $100 a month you was getting big. In them times that was pretty good. But you worked 16 hours a day to get it. Plus the time you laid around."

Mr. Mose agrees with Mr. Myers that there was almost never

Lester Mose, Sr.

177

enough sleep for a boatman, and that what made the work hard was the long hours. But, "I was young; I didn't mind it. I could lay down an hour or two and get up. It didn't make any difference.

"The life was interesting in a way. I just never cared for the canal. It was lonesome, and you were in different places a long time. It just wasn't fast enough for me. Even after I married and went for myself, I still never liked the canal. But I took a good interest in it. A boat for myself, four pretty mules—a nice big team—when I quit. The first year I didn't have a good one, but in 1921 when I quit I had a *good boat.*"

He remembers one thing that relieved the loneliness. "The only thing that would happen along the line, there might be somebody that . . . somebody would say, 'We'll run together.' In other words, he wouldn't try to pass me and I wouldn't try to get away from him. It made company for you. He'd catch up to you and he wouldn't be too far behind and you could see him. The distance wouldn't be too far, just enough [behind] to let you get through the lock. Then the front one would loaf along a little bit and let the back one catch up, and he'd walk along with the driver and chin. Or you'd chin to the one on the [other] boat, and so forth. And you'd tie up together at night and start out in the morning together. This did make it a lot better. Yes, it did. It made a lot of company.

"When you come down loaded, you could see in the tunnel. If there was nothing in it, you was clear. But the light boat couldn't see anything until they got right up to the tunnel. Usually I'd run on ahead of my team and see if nothing was coming. If you didn't, you had to take the team right up to the tunnel before you could see. But then you *could* stop; there was a place there to lay over. You could turn your team around in the tunnel by this way: you had to unhook 'em and turn one mule around at a time, turn his head toward the canal. Then after you turned around, you could get one by the other."

A feature of the canal that interested Mr. Mose was the swinging bridge. "There was one at the foot of Big Pool. A farmer at Fort Frederick, he had ground on the towpath side between the canal and the river. He'd come down there and swing that bridge around, and he'd go across with his team. Then he'd take the bridge back, and they had a little overhead bridge, a little walk that he could walk back on to get to his team. The team went across the swinging bridge; it was wide enough for a wagon. Then he put the bridge back; in case a boat would come it wouldn't be in the way.

"Then there was one at Brunswick, and the same thing. Down there they had a bridge that crossed a lock that went over into Virginia. There was farming ground along the towpath there too, and that locktender, he took care of that bridge. I can't think of the man's name to save my neck—I've studied and studied— but I knowed him well. But then he'd put the bridge across, and you could cross with a team and he'd put it back. The bridge was just along the edge of the lock.

"At Goose Creek there was another, and that locktender tended that one.* It was the same story—farming ground.

"These were the only three there was. They tell me that one time there was one at Point of Rocks, but I can't remember about that. I do know there was one [a bridge] in the towpath down there. The old Point of Rocks bridge come across there then, and the farmer would come down the towpath, then went across this wooden bridge over the Point of Rocks. They had a kind of basement there, with water in it. These grain boats would go in there. And there was a bridge in the towpath that you'd swing around and let these grain boats go in so they could load them. They'd haul the grain from Virginia over them. But I never knowed of one to cross the canal there. There was a bridge across the canal, but not a swinging bridge, not a turn bridge. Not to my knowledge."

Once, in 1919, Mr. Mose's boat sunk. "What happened on that, they had a break on the towpath. Right below Dam No. 5. And of course the canal was filled, furnished with water, from Dam No. 5 down to Dam No. 4. The river was four mile long up there at Dam No. 4. So we laid in the river up there until they got

Goose Creek was across the river in Virginia.

Lester Mose, Sr.

this [break] fixed. In July. Hot weather. It was about eight or ten days.

"This boat was old, and she dried out. Naturally we went on to Cumberland. Some of [the boats] didn't lay there long; we happened to be the first one that [got that] far. We went on to Cumberland. We went to load, and when we got about half loaded water was pouring everywhere. So we stopped them from loading it. And she sunk. Right at the wharf. Only the bottom of the boat had been in the water; the other four feet or five feet, that all dried out.

"Next morning the people from the Cumberland boat yard, they come down and pumped her up and went on and finished loading her. We slept out on the deck that night, out on the top. You always had an awning put up, like a tent. We slept out on the deck, my wife and I.

"Some [breaks] were caused—there was a lot of rock formations, and over the years, as water would follow the crevices of these rocks, it would keep eating and eating and eating until it cut the towpath out. Or it could have been from a jar. Then in lots of places it come from groundhogs or muskrats.

"I can remember well enough that in September, 1917, we was going down and we tied up below Goose Creek Lock, above Seneca, between Goose Creek and Seneca. That's below Monocacy. We tied up below the lock and we had the five mules and my dad's boat. The 27; I had it. And J.P. was on with me. And Clifford. So we laid over below the Goose Creek Lock about a quarter of a mile, at the eight-mile level of Seneca.

"Then we started out, and Clifford was driving. It was a good team and they'd drive themselves, pretty near; you didn't have to worry about them. We kept on going and we got breakfast—I ate, and J.P. ate—we carried the team to the stable and harnessed them and fed them; because to go down to Seneca we'd put them up and put the three mules in—rest them, feed them.

"We got down about two mile above Seneca. J.P. jumped out, and he was walking along talking to me. It was daylight. This team we had out had a gray mule in front. Queen. She was an awful good mule, but the team had been hit by lightning one time down at Cabin John. It knocked them down and they broke a brand new line and run off. They run from there to the upper lock of the six at Great Falls. After that, any little thing kind of frightened Queen. Especially a little heat lightning. Boy, she'd look at it!

"So she was down there and J.P. was walking along. Then she tucked her ears. I seen her ears going. I said, 'You better get down to that team. Queen sees something.' So he run down to her, and when he got down there this whole bank had slipped out, over a hundred feet. He hollered to me, and I said, 'Stop your team.' The boat, it just kept going, of course. He got down pretty close to the boat and I thought he'd have slack enough in the line to get 'em across [the break].

"I said, 'Now, you get her by the head, because she's going to take you across.' She was pretty lively. He got her by the head and she did take him across all right. He hung on to her. Crossed this narrow [remaining] piece where the break was. I said, 'Any water coming through?' He said, 'Yes.' I said, 'Go brush them up a little bit.' So he did and they were pulling pretty good. The boat got by [the break].

"I wanted to get off the level. In other words, if the water went down I couldn't get through the lock. It was at the end of the feeder. That division was fed from Harpers Ferry to Seneca. When I got to Seneca and then got off of it, I only had about half a mile to go, a short level, and then it got into another feeder. We went on to Washington and unloaded and they worked on [the break].

"The bank had slipped, a certain portion of it, maybe half of it, and left a little bit of the path standing, enough to get the team across. The river's wide there above Seneca. There's a place a mile wide, they tell me. Well, that's a lot of water down there. The wind a-blowing and the waves washing, they undermined the back of the bank. Of course that weakened it, and the weight of the water in the canal pushed it out.

"The canal was a dangerous job. It was dangerous. There was a lot of washouts. The towpath would wash out, and after night you didn't see it until you were right up on it. There was boats

Lester Mose, Sr.

181

that went out [into the river] in these washouts. Up here at Williamsport there was a boat went out of the aqueduct, went out down in that creek.[1] It was dangerous. Up at Big Pool there was a boat went out up there—a washout.

[With a break] "usually the back of the bank [as at Seneca] would slip out, slip toward the river. As long as the towpath stood there you could get a team across; but when it washed out too you didn't get nowhere. You had to stop." Stopping was easier said than done, however. "That's the trouble. That's why they went out sometimes. They couldn't stop.

"But they had [level walkers] all along the line, in different sections. If a break wasn't too bad, they could draw the water off a little and repair it. If the washout happened after night, nobody knew anything about it. The level walkers didn't walk at night. Just in daytime. Quite dangerous it was.

"There were people that lost their lives [on the canal]. Even around the locks it was dangerous. Them old paddles, they'd break off or something. If you weren't careful going into a lock

Aqueduct wall collapsed, and boat No. 73 "went out" with it, down to Conococheague Creek. This happened on the early morning of April 20, 1920, with no lives lost and no injury to man or beast. The canal was shut off at Dam No. 5 but that left seven miles of water to run, and in addition there was that which backed up into the broken aqueduct from Lock 44; water poured over the break for 24 hours. Tiny figure at right is a Williamsport man on the skiff he rowed out to the boat.

182

and you'd jump on the boat—the boat fit pretty tight, but you could go down beside her front and back. You couldn't fall through by the sides of the boat, but at each end. Wasn't too much of that happened. Very little of it.

"Mules got drowned at different times, when you were changing them [at locks], putting them in the stable. They'd have to step up over a little place. After you got 'em trained they wasn't too bad. Now, if you got a mule that never boated and you had to train him, you had to watch him. He might get balky, and instead of going on the fall board [he might] step in the lock—between the bow of the boat and the lock, and you couldn't get him out. If he went down there, there wasn't no way to get him out. He had just enough space to be in there, and he'd drown.

Lester Mose, Sr.

"[It was] in 1914 my dad got sick. He got kidney trouble and it bothered him quite a bit and he had to get off. That left just me and J.P. That's when I started taking my dad's boat. He was on a couple of times, to make a trip now and then; but from '14 to '17 J.P. and I run it. Then Clifford, he got old enough and he got on with us some. I started out the spring of 1917 and made one trip and I went in the service. Daddy had to get on. Him and Clifford and J.P. run the boat. Clifford could never run a plank. J.P. and I, we was like cats, but Clifford never could run a plank; I'd have to give him my hand or he'd fall in every time.

"I got out of the service in 1919; on March the 21st I got home from overseas. I had planned with the old girl that we'd get married, and we figured on getting married in the fall; but I changed my mind. She did too. So we got married on the 30th day of March. And I couldn't get a job nowhere.

"My wife's parents, they went boating. And her two sisters, Annie and Hazel. We took care of their house in Sharpsburg. I was trying to get a job and I couldn't; so I wrote in to Mr. Nicolson, the general manager—I knew him well and he knew me well—and I asked him for a boat and a team. I told him I couldn't get a job nowhere. He wrote right back and told me there was nothing available at the time, but first one available I would get. That sounded pretty good.

"In the meantime my daddy went to Cumberland and got a load of coal. When he came down he asked me if I'd take the boat to Washington for him. He wanted to set his garden out. I said sure. When I got down to Washington I talked to Mr. Nicolson. He said, 'Well, I don't have a thing, but you're going to get the first.' I brought the boat back home and my dad got on. I worked in my wife's garden, her daddy's garden, put it out. I worked some at my father's garden too. He went to Cumberland to get another load.

"He come down, on his way to Washington, and I got a letter

Loaded boat on its way downstream. (A light boat would be riding high.) In foreground, cabin, at back end of the boat. Awning gave the steersman some protection from rain or sun. (Mules and driver out of sight down the towpath had no protection, but were out there come wind or weather.) In exact center of boat is the hay house, for storage of hay and surplus supplies and a cot for the hired hand. Front of boat is stable. Between stable and hay house, and between hay house and cabin, are the 14 hatches that covered cargo in the hold. Before he was a captain himself, L. M. Mose boated on No. 27 with his father, Jerome Mose.

184

from Mr. Nicolson to go to Cumberland and take the 52 and team. He said, 'Your dad's going to be unloading and you can go up with him.' I did. Dad come up; I got on with him, and we went to Cumberland. We had to buy the [gear] on the boat, such as grab hooks, boat poles—poles if you had to push the boat around somewhere, grab hooks if you had to hook something out of the canal—running plank, surplus stuff that you had to have, the boat pump, the bow lamp, and a stove and table. He wanted $20 for it, all this stuff I needed. I didn't even have $20. My dad, he got it.

Lester Mose, Sr.

"So we loaded the 52 and started on down. Pete—Clifford, we called him Pete—went with me, and J.P. with my dad. We come on home.

"In the meantime my wife was gathering up bedclothes, some dishes from home, some pots and pans. I got a couple of chairs. We got set up pretty well. They had painted the cabin all up. My wife got on and we started out and went to Washington. Next trip, we went to Williamsport. And my dad did too. That's when we got another brother, called Daniel—he's out in Ohio now. He was only a small fellow around 10 or 11 years old. He got on with me, and J.P. and Pete took my daddy's boat and my daddy got off again. J.P. run that boat the best part of that year, 1919.

"We were going to try to go to housekeeping in Sharpsburg; so we had to buy furniture. We had to buy everything. My dad had a house there, and we went in it. We bought quite a bit of stuff. But I didn't have enough [money] to keep us over the winter; we couldn't put up anything on the boat. I got a job then with U.S. Steel. One of their subsidiary plants was up here at Falling Waters. It was a stone quarry. They called it the Nestle Quarry. I'd go on the bus to Hagerstown on Sunday evening and get on the trolley car and go to Williamsport and then walk about six miles to where we were working. Then on Friday evening I'd come home. Get home some time around ten or eleven o'clock.

"I had different jobs to do at the quarry. I could run block drills. I could load stone if I wanted to. I could drive a mule that they

185

pulled the cars out with. We made pretty good. [The quarry] hasn't run for years now.

"Spring came along, of 1920. There was a fellow worked up there by the name of Johnny Knode. He was a captain on the canal and he had a new boat. And he was going to quit. So he said to me, 'Les, why don't you write in for that boat? I'm going to quit and go to the Western Maryland.' He told me around April. I said, 'Are you sure you're quitting?' He said yes, he'd got a job up there. He showed me a letter. Quitting.

"I came home and I sat down and I wrote a letter to Mr. Nicolson that I'd like to have the 42 and keep the team I had. I had an awful good team. They were company mules but they were mine. Frank and Queen. They were real white, and they were big mules. Then I had two that were an iron gray, pretty dark. One was named Kit and the other was named Logan. They were four *good* mules. I wanted my own team.

"In the meantime, my daddy quit. Mr. Nicolson wrote back to me and said, 'Why not take the 27 and that team?' That kind of made me a little mad, and I thought to myself, 'I've boated the 27 enough, and the 27 is getting old.' It was about 12 or 13 years old. They get up like that, they get soggy and they're not too good. Twelve isn't the lifetime of a boat. They wear longer, but you have to rebuild 'em and patch 'em up. So I just sat down and wrote to him that I didn't want the 27 and I didn't want the team; I wanted the 42 and the team I had—or nothing. So he wrote back to me and said, 'Take the 42.' So I boated the 42 for two years and then I left it. I got a better job, with U.S. Steel.

"The two winters I [had already] worked there, it didn't pay a whole lot more than the canal paid. [That was with] limestone. For the steel mills. Limestone is a flux for the steel. So then I went to Pinesburg; they had a plant there. I didn't do no labor there at all. I got into good jobs there. I'd run the hoist. They were dropping railroad cars to load stone. I had a good job.

"I'm getting ahead of myself. In the fall of 1921 we tied up in September. The river had a drought. The canal wasn't getting enough water to run. Things didn't look too good to me in 1921;

so I decided, well, I've got a job here, and they offered me a house up there to move in and to move me up there and I said, 'I'm going to take it.' I wrote in and gave up the boat and team.

"The canal run some and I boated some in the spring of 1922. It run some in '23, but that was the end of the line. It never run after that.

"I don't know what happened in '22 and '23. Soon as the canal started, the B&O started building a railroad to Cumberland, and the railroad beat 'em. But they went on through with it and they had good business on the canal up until [its] late years. It could be that something else interfered with them; but in '22 the canal didn't *do* much, and in '23 they done *very* little. I worked at Pinesburg and I was out there right along the canal and I could walk out there and look at it. Once in a while you'd see a boat go by, but not too many."

Mr. Mose put his mind on his new job and the new life that this job opened up for him. Improvements included better working hours, better pay, and an enjoyable social life. "Lot of social life. I finally got a car, and we'd go to Hagerstown and come back down home here, Williamsport or Clear Spring or any place you'd want to go. And go out on picnics. And met more friends, met a lot of 'em. Made a big difference.

"When I left the canal, I *left* it. I forgot about it. I crossed it a couple of times to go fishing in the river. The boats was all gone. The '24 flood took all the boats away. What wasn't taken away in '24 [the] '36 [flood] cleaned them up. There wasn't nothing there. It was dead. Closed up and growed up with trees. I didn't feel too bad about it."

Lester Mose, Sr.

[1] On April 20, 1920, one entire wall of the Conococheague Creek Aqueduct went out, and with it went boat No. 73. Two days before, Captain Frank Myers, of Big Pool, had left Cumberland with coal for Steffey and Findlay at Williamsport. With him were his crew members, his stepchildren Viola and Joseph Davis. At Big Pool, Viola dropped off to visit the family while the men

went on to Williamsport. On the 19th they tied up at Steffey and Findlay's wharf, about 500 yards from Lock 44, and unloaded. Early the next morning, Captain Myers and Joseph began their return trip to Cumberland. About five o'clock No. 73 entered the eastern end of the aqueduct, Captain Myers steering and Joseph Davis driving all three of their mules, and the boat struck the east end of the berm wall a glancing blow. Captain Myers later told how he saw the aqueduct wall shudder, and shouted to his stepson, who was almost at the opposite end of the aqueduct, to cut the mules loose. The wall collapsed and, as the boat was being swept through the break, Myers jumped onto the berm parapet. Free of the boat, men and mules were unharmed. The boat was dashed down to the creek and, not new to begin with and extensively damaged by the fall, it was left there. In 1936 the flood bore it off down the river. At one point it was washed aground and remained stuck until high waters broke it up and carried the pieces away.

(Information in this note was supplied by Mr. Melvin I. Kaplan, President, Williamsport C&O Canal Club, Inc. It was supplied him in the late 1960s by David Wolfe, former canal boat captain and good friend of Frank Myers; McKinley Shank, eyewitness to the accident; the Hagerstown *Daily Mail* for the evening of April 20, 1920; and Lauren Myers, Sr., son of Captain Frank Myers.)

Interviews, August 12 and September 1, 1979.

Mrs. Lester M. Mose, Sr.
Sharpsburg

"I HAVE WALKED the whole hundred and eighty-four miles," says Mrs. Lester Mose.

When she was 13, she went on the canal with her father, George William Colbert, captain of No. 76. She boated with him until she married Lester M. Mose (See pp. 170–188), later the captain of No. 42.

"My father lived to be an old man. He had us girls on there and we worked and helped him just the same as I did when I was married.

"I started first walking the levels, things like that. Driving mules. I have curried them, I have unharnessed them, I have harnessed them, I have fed 'em, and then at night when we tied up the boat, why, I helped unharness them and put them to the trough— feed them for the night. Mornings, we would get up, we would harness them, feed 'em, get 'em ready to start out for the day. They would go. . . .I would say they'd go about five or six hours. Nine or ten miles was a trick. When we would be out driving, sometimes one or the other would hang back, wouldn't want to work up with the other one. Well, if we was to happen to touch 'em, our father would holler, 'Don't you hit them no more!' We had one named Tom, one named Jack, one named Mike, one named Rock. I liked 'em all. Liked 'em all."

Mary Colbert (Mrs. Lester M.) Mose

On a typical day, "Maybe I would walk one of those whole nine-mile levels, walk beside of the mules. And then I would get on the boat. We would have our dinner. Then maybe I would steer. There was a great big stick. There was what they called

189

Workers swapped chores, and here the woman of the family steers the boat through Lock 15 near Great Falls. Main jobs were steering, driving and caring for mules, cooking—and most captains and crew members could take turns at all three.

cleats against the deck; well, now, that's a square box, so far [five inches] apart. You could sit on that stick and you would put your foot up on those cleats and push the stick whichever way the boat was going to go. If it would start to go one way or the other, toward the berm or toward the towpath, you'd have to keep it straight. If [the boat] was going to the right, you'd have to push it [to the left] to straighten up.

"There was usually a sister. There was two of us girls mostly all the time with our father. These were my sisters Ora and Hazel. The oldest one was Ora. Ora and I was together until she got married; and then Hazel come on." When one sister was out on the towpath, the other was cooking or doing other housekeeping chores. Mrs. Mose remembers very little difference, in quality or variety of work, between housekeeping on a canal boat and at the house in Sharpsburg.

"We would have our cabins to scrub. Every morning. Make our bunks up. Every morning. We would scrub our boats off *every morning*. From one end to the other. All the decks were scrubbed. Everything. The cabin floors, little staterooms. There was a hole bored in the floor, in the boat, and the water that you scrubbed the floor with would drain down there. Drain right down on the coal. It wasn't that much to hurt anything.

"We ate most everything and anything just the same as at

190

home, because we carried *plenty of grub*. We could keep food back under the stern of the boat; and the food, it kept good. It was always cool under there; the boat down in the water kept it cool. Two little round holes in the back of the stern like that [about the size of a dinner plate] that were open. We always put a screen over them. Of course, meat you couldn't keep too long. Except in the fall of the year. We couldn't buy no fresh meat. We'd usually buy hams. Cured. Like that. That would keep.

Mary Colbert Mose

"We had a little half range. It doesn't have a back to it and it's not near as big as a big range. There was a place built for this little stove to be set back in. We cooked everything. Everything. You know, bean soup was a boatsman's great meal. Bean soup and rivvels* made with eggs. Fried chicken. Fish. Coffee. Anything at all. If we wanted to bake, we had our little baker—a regular oven.

"The stove burned coal. Because, see, we could use coal off the boat. If you wanted to cook something quick, you used corn cobs. We had a lot. We fed the mules corn, and we'd save the corn cobs. If you had something that didn't take a whole lot of cooking and it was hot, we'd just use the corn cobs; because that would soon die out; the coal would last.

"We heated water on the stove, and of course we had our dishpan and our soap dish. We set the dishpan on the table and washed up our dishes. We used Octagon soap. And we'd redd up our table. Leavings from the table went out in the canal."

Along with women and children all over the country at that time, young Mary Colbert and her sisters were saving Octagon soap coupons cut from the wrappers. "We would get a little book from the Octagon company—there were pictures in this little book—and they would [call for] so-many coupons for every premium. Then all we had to do . . . whatever we wanted, pick out and mail them in. They would send the premiums back by parcel post. To Sharpsburg. We got knives and forks. Spoons. Things like that. Dish towels. Dish cloths. We got rings. The ring was a plain ring; it had your initial on it. It was supposed to be

*See pages 215–216.

gold, but you know it wasn't real gold. They lasted very good."

For laundry, "We heated our water in the wash boiler, on the stove. It's a good size, oh, I would say 20 gallons. We would carry the water out and put it in the tub, right outside of the cabin on the hatches, and we would wash our clothes there. We'd have to put our clothes line up; and when we got done, clothes dried, we'd have to take it down. We'd keep it in what we called the grub house. That was the middle cabin. There was a bunk in there, and if you wanted to keep feed in there you could. One half of it was for a hand to sleep, and the other half for hay. And any surplus of things that you used—stakes that you used to tie your mules to, hay, anything.

"We grew up knowing how to keep the cabins and how to do everything on the boat. Our mother taught us from small up to learn how to do; and our father took just as much interest in showing us how to do, and we had to do everything right. We always kept our bunks made, kept the bedspreads on them. They were oldtime spreads. They were plain, but then they would have designs around in them, like maybe there might be tulips all through it. All of them was white.

"In our cabin we had little curtains up at the windows. We had screens on the windows. Some of the curtains were white, some of them had kind of a figure in, and like that. We kept our cabin painted nice. We'd paint [the walls] different colors. Blue and green. Our little cabin door had a little screen door. When we came down off the quarterdeck, we stepped down into what we called the recess. We stepped down into there to come down into the cabin. We kept the recess just as clean as we did the cabin. We had pictures on the wall. They were maybe like a pretty dog or a cat, something like that out of a magazine.

"And then our little cupboards. We had one cupboard that was built out. We kept white scarves on that. We had the oldtime oil lamps, and at night when we lit them they sat mostly on the cupboards. I kept oil in them. Washed the globes up. Every day. We had to watch our wicks. When they'd get down we'd have to put new ones in. If they got straight across, then they'd start to smoking; so we'd keep them trimmed sort of a little round

192

on each side. If you don't trim a wick, it will smoke your globe. The smoke will come up all over your globe.

"Washing, there wasn't much difficulty to it. We got along very good with everything. I can't see that it was done any different [from home in Sharpsburg]. Not for them times.

"We didn't get too much schooling, you know. The first of April, why, the boats would start out. Then the children mostly that was on. . .My mother wasn't on too much. We had a family at home and she was usually home with them. And she had heart trouble too. But once in a while she'd go on the boat. From 13 on, every April when the boats started, I went with my father."

Mary Colbert Mose

All during the spring and summer, boatmen and their families were mindful of the cold months to come. They gleaned enough to keep them toasty through the winter. It was a foregone conclusion that no boatman ever bought coal.

Mrs. Mose remembers that the men hired to unload the coal from the boats were none too thorough. "They always left so much coal in the hull. Then that coal was ours. Ours to get down in there and scrape it up. There's a place along the side of the boat about two inches long, and the coal would lay along there and they wouldn't fool too much with it. [This place] would hold a good bit of coal, and under the cabins there was some [more] we had to clean up. Sometimes you'd have a ton. Sometimes three-quarters. If you unloaded at Indianhead, you didn't get any. They swept it plenty; they cleaned it out. That was the government getting the coal. Other places, they'd leave a little." Her brother-in-law, J.P. Mose, recalls that "If you had a half pint of whiskey to slide to them, they'd leave you a good ton."

At Sharpsburg, Mrs. Mose continues, "We'd pull in beside of the bank at Snyder's Landing and we'd unload it. There'd always be a couple [to unload], one down in the hull. [We] had to pull it out and dump it on the bank. Everybody had their own pile of coal. Nobody didn't bother it."

Although nobody would dream of helping himself to anybody else's coal, sometimes a pile would get too high during the summer. Then, recalls Mr. (L.M.) Mose, Jim Snyder would haul it in to town. "Jim Snyder run a coal yard out there; he had two horses and a wagon. It didn't cost too much, maybe a dollar a load or something. In the fall of the year, you'd use your own mules and get a wagon. There were wagons around there and you just borrowed them."

As a young girl on the boat, Mrs. Mose didn't have much time of her own. "Not a whole lot. The most time we had was when we went in port in Washington or Cumberland. I'll tell you, we didn't do a whole lot of anything outside of keeping our cabins up and things clean.

"But then, in port, during the afternoon, our friends off of other boats—there was one special one that we thought so much of and she thought the same of us, Viola Snyder from Cumberland. We would go under the culvert and go over to a store and we'd buy sacks of candy. All kinds, mixed. Some of it was hard candy; some of it was wrapped in paper; some of it was candy bars. We would take that and we would go right over the bank, from where our mules was at the trough, and we would sit there under all the shade trees where we could look right down on the river and see all the boats and canoes and things going up and down. We would spend our afternoon out there.

"There was a Mrs. Safford. She had a little church there on the towpath. Just ahead of the wide water, near the culvert, there was a little village in there. And she would get some of these children on Sunday. I don't know what it was [before it was a church]." A small frame house, "It was very common, just benches. Mrs. Safford would have these Sunday School papers she would read to us and things like that; and she had little books she would give us.

"Sometimes we might, maybe, lay in port for a week. We would go up on M Street. We liked to walk up and down and look in the store windows. We'd do our buying there. Was there a store up there by the name of Rosenberg? We bought all our clothes mostly there—skirts, waists, everything like that.

"One place we used to visit very much was the Candy Kitchen. Oh, I thought they had the best candy up there that ever was. They had all kinds and, oh, there's none today could touch it. They made candy and sold ice cream. There's where my first banana split came from. It was delicious. It couldn't have been any better. No matter what they tried to do, it couldn't have been any better." She still loves banana splits.

"Then another thing. My father bought boxes, whole boxes, of candy there. There was a taffy—one was chocolate, one was vanilla, one strawberry. That was the flavors of it. He would buy a box each. It wasn't pulled taffy; it wasn't that type. We used to get it in blocks. They wasn't even. More like chunks. Then there was another kind. He would buy coughdrops—the little long ones, only they was bigger [than now]. They'd be licorice, strawberry, lemon, and orange. He'd buy maybe a couple of boxes of them. He'd buy [these things] in the fall to bring them home for our Christmas too.

Mary Colbert Mose

"And peanuts by the can. He'd buy them there too. They were in the hull. Every time we went in port, he'd have to get that gallon of peanuts. We really lived good on the canal, and when we come home we didn't have anything to buy but coal oil."

Mr. Colbert would bring supplies home. "...bring it home, and buckwheat we would buy at Hancock. He'd buy so-many pounds. I just can't think any more how many pounds, but he'd buy a big amount of it because there was a good family of us—nine altogether—and we all ate hearty. We always had hogs at home. And then in the winter when we come home we would butcher. We made our own food—pudding and pinehorst and all like that.* And he would buy eye potatoes and sugar and various things in Washington and bring them home."

While Captain Colbert was shopping for supplies, young Mary and Ora or Hazel "would go up to Glen Echo. That was one of our places. The streetcars was on then. We'd go out there and spend the day." They did "a good bit of eating. All kinds of sandwiches and ice cream and candy. They had all kinds of rides, roller coasters and everything. But that was one thing we never bothered. I never felt as though I wanted to. I was afraid of it. Now, the flying horses we liked very much. Merry-go-round,

*Pinehorst is also called scrapple.

195

some call them today. The horses moved up and down. They were white with black spots on them, and different colors. Some was black. [There were] sleighs too. We went on both. We used to go more than once [during a week in port]. We'd probably put a couple of days in up there."

The Colbert sisters got on well together, and life on the canal boat, which they regarded as home, was as harmonious as at their home in Sharpsburg. "These three—Ora, Mary, Hazel— we were mostly the ones with our father. They liked it too. They were very well satisfied. We just all agreed together. Wasn't ever one to go one way and one another way; we all pulled the same way. There was nothing too much for one to do. You know how some grumble today.... We didn't do any of that. We just went on and did our work and that was it. And we liked our work and we were kept busy all the time. We knew just what we were going to do [every day], and we always felt good."

Mrs. Mose stayed on the boat with her father until she married at 19. She didn't exactly meet Lester Mose; they lived on the same street in Sharpsburg and had known each other as children. "When he started going with me, that was just before Christmas in 1917. My sister Hazel, wherever you saw the one [of us] you saw the other one. Nobody seemed to know which one he was going with, because we was all together. He always walked in between us; so nobody never knew who was the right girl. We never said nothing. We just never talked about it. Then we were married in 1919.

"We wasn't married long until he got a boat, and I did the same on our boat as I did on my father's. [Except that] after I got married, I never did no driving. We kept the cabins clean, and kept the little curtains up at the windows, kept the little screens on the doors and windows, and scrubbed and cleaned.

"We had two children. The boy was born down here at the Falls. Great Falls, down there at the Six Locks. Lester Marion, Jr. He come a little before time. I was supposed to get off [the boat] when we come back up home. But I didn't make it. So that's why he was born on the boat. [Our daughter], she was born here in Sharpsburg. At our home. I named her Hazel for my sister.

"At that time there was a canned milk for babies. Eagle Brand. It had to be diluted—so-much of it and so-much of water. That's what they used to give the babies." The matter of baby bottles, Mrs. Mose simply took in her stride. "Not a bit [of difficulty]. We carried all of our drinking water and cooking water in kegs. We'd take the water buckets to the springs and the wells. Mostly at all the locks there was wells and springs. So therefore it wasn't no problem for the water." And the matter of baby laundry "wasn't too bad. But, you see, we were used to it. And nothing like that didn't seem too bad to us.

"There was no babysitters . . . like today. Children was brought up with their parents. And they didn't have the mischief to get into like they do today. They didn't get out that much. They was more for home. They didn't think of going every night like they do today. A canal boat was a good place to raise children.

"Lots of people think it was a hard life. People that didn't boat. The boatsmen never, I don't think, thought it was a hard life. We all thought it was a good life. Which it *was* a good life."

Mary Colbert Mose

197

First of two interviews, October 6, 1979.

Harvey Brant
Williamsport

"THE 1924 WATER was about three foot deep in the house, and I had a piano in my parlor."

Harvey Brant had been locktender at Lock No. 44 in Williamsport for the eight years preceding the flood that precipitated the closing of the canal. He was anxious about his piano, but "the superintendent of the canal kept saying, 'Oh, don't move it out. The water's falling up above and it'll soon be falling here.' And it raised for two days after that, about an inch or two to the hour; and I kept putting the piano up on trestles, higher all the time. Finally it got as high as I could put it on trestles, and I knowed I had to get it out of there some way. I got a man's boat, a little scow that he fished out of, pretty good-sized boat, and I brought it in. I couldn't get it clear into the house; so I tied it up against a yard bench and got some planks and laid them [from] the steps to the scow. Four of us got in there in water up above our knees and carried [the piano] out and put it on these planks and got it on this scow and hauled it away. It was safe and dry. I never took it back after that. I [had] bought it for my girls to take music lessons on, and I gave it to my daughter. Trying to move it around in those high waters, I just was disgusted with it."

Until that flood, "everything went along pretty good." One thing that went along at Mr. Brant's lock was the sightseeing on Sundays. "They came out on the streetcar—there wasn't many automobiles then—they come out on the streetcar and they'd stay there all day but what they'd see a boat going through. Sometimes there was so many on the lock walls I didn't hardly have enough room to shove my gates open. I sold soft drinks on Sundays, and ice cream."

These sales were part of the multiple activities that brought in Mr. Brant's whole income. "I had worked up a pretty good business of my own, besides the canal, and the canal wages didn't mean anything to me much then. I had a canoe club. Hired out canoes. I'd have them hired out two or three weeks ahead of time. I made five times as much [as canal wages] and more.

"Then in the fall of the year, I put a fish pot in the feeder— where you feed the water to keep the next level up alongside of the lock—a spillway they called it. It had a board floor in it and the water went through there swift. I built a fish pot and I put [it] down on the bottom of that spillway and I caught about $400 worth of eels every fall.

"The eels come down at night mostly. Sometimes you'd catch some in the daytime. One night I caught 720. I sold them to the fish man the next morning for $85, and that was money in those days. I was pulling eels out all night. It rained as hard as it could rain, and the water was just running out. I almost

Harvey Brant

drownded that night. It had poured down rain and the leaves were.... That's when they come down, with the trash, coming downstream. I'd pick eels out for five or ten minutes and then I'd go rake leaves for that much. If the pot got clogged up it might break out or the eels could swim out.

"There ain't no eels up there any more. They really breed in salt water, and they come up the canal. There ain't no way to get them up here now; we don't have eels no more. [But then] the canal was just full of them all the time. They'd come up through the locks. My father-in-law said when he was boating that when he'd pull into a lock the eels would roll out of the crevices in the rocks beside. He said they'd be over the race planks and you had to shove them off with a shovel or you'd fall and break your neck. They were coming upstream in the spring of the year, coming out of the salt water.

"They come up the Potomac River, I guess, to Washington and got into the locks there and just kept coming through. I guess they come up from the bay. People claim they breed in salt water. Some want to say they breed in Siberia.[1] *I* don't know. [But they were] a help too.

"Then I got my coal off the boats. A boat would come in the lock, I'd throw back one of the hatches and get three or four big lumps of coal off of it. Wintertime come, I had all the coal I wanted to burn. Everything like that figured in.

"I used a lot of their corn too, out of the corn crib, to fatten my hogs. I raised hogs every year. When my family was home I always had three big hogs to kill, and we had our own meat. I didn't have to buy much feed. There was so much shelled corn that I'd just gather up that shelled corn and feed it to my hogs. They didn't keep no tab at all. Some of the boatsmen I know were taking some home to feed their hogs because they never fed that much corn to the mules.

"The ones that owned their own teams, they got more for the tonnage than what the other boatmen did. They got a lot more for the tons they hauled, because the company [paid for the use of the mules but] still fed them. The ones that had their own teams, they were beautiful teams because they took good care of them and they fed them good.

200

"I'll tell you the mules were smart. [Boatmen] would pull in to that lock down there, and they'd snub the boat and stop it at a snubbing post. Throw a rope around it and stop. Soon as they snubbed that boat, the mules would turn around and come back. They knowed it was their time to get in the stable and the other team to get out.

"I used to sell bread to the boatsmen. Caskey would bring it out every morning fresh from Hagerstown; and every boatsman, when he'd get inside that lock, he'd hold up five fingers or four fingers—he wanted that many loaves. Caskey's Bakery. They're out of business now. Loaves *that* big around, he sold them for ten cents. I bought them for seven and sold them for ten cents. [The boatmen] were tickled to death when I sold them bread. Best bread I ever ate. Just like a loaf of homemade bread baked in a brick oven. It wasn't sliced, of course.

"Then I sold other stuff to them too, stuff out of the garden. I had a nice garden every year.

"And I used to sell some hound puppies. I raised dogs. I got as high as $50 for some of my hunting dogs.

"I always went to work over here in the tannery in the wintertime. W.D. Byron's tannery. The Byrons was here for years. I'd always get a leave of absence in the spring to tend lock; and soon as they drawed the water out of the canal I'd pick up my old clothes and go over there and they'd put me to work. I was a leather finisher. I used to finish patent leather. Before I retired, I was running an automatic spraying machine."

Although Mr. Brant earned money in several ways, his duties at the lock always took priority. Earnings from his varied endeavors "figured out better than wages I could have made working [at one place], because they didn't pay nothing then. The men worked on the canal—fixed the towpath, fixed the leaks, and kept the brush [cleaned out] and the grass mowed— got $1.25 a day. And they had to pay the foreman for their board; and when they got everything paid, they only got 87 cents a day. That's awful.

"I don't know if that was a bad time or not; your money was worth something then. Back when I was a young fellow, the highest price pair of shoes you could buy was Walkover shoes—

Harvey Brant

201

and they cost $4.00. Probably cost $120 today. That's how much difference it is.

"When I went there [to the lock] in 1916, we got $22.50 a month; seven days a week, night and day. About ten or eleven o'clock you'd go to bed, and about the time you got the bed warm, why, you'd hear an old bugle blow. 'Can't Get 'em Up in the Morning.' And I'd have to get up and get the lock ready and lock him through." Mr. Brant generally slept in the lock house rather than in the shanty, and the bugles would wake his family too. "They didn't mind.

"I had a log shed across the lock. There was a big corn crib there, where I put feed on [the boats] for the mules. They'd get, I guess I'd say ten or fifteen thousand barrel of corn in there and I'd have to dribble it out to the mules, help put it on the boats. In front of the crib was one room, with a chimney, and I had a stove in there and sometimes I'd sit over there. I could see up and down the canal, both ways. But at night I stayed in the house.

"Sometimes [I wouldn't get waked up] for a week. I tell you what it was. It was people that was trying to get home here to Williamsport and stay overnight with their families. They'd be maybe 20 or 25 miles down below, they'd boat to get home here so they could stay with their family. Sometimes it would be twelve, one, or two o'clock when they'd get here. That's the most I had to get up for. And the same way coming downstream.

"The boatsmen had a hard life. But the locktenders did too, because they couldn't go nowhere. They had to be on the job all the time. But if I wanted to sleep in the daytime, I could lay down and sleep. My wife would hear them if they come. She could tend lock as well as I could. She'd relieve me and I could go some place, a ball game or something like that. It was tied down though. We didn't get to go much together, only in the wintertime.

"I had an old Model T Ford. Sometimes I'd get Johnny Spigler, the boss carpenter, to tend lock for me and we'd take a Sunday off and go away. My wife and me and the kids. We'd go over to Pennsylvania to see my relations. Wasn't no traffic to worry about. It was very seldom you ever met a car. I was my own mechanic. I kept tools in the car, and if anything got wrong I fixed it myself. I done almost all the work on my car in them days. I didn't learn; I just picked it up. I used to grind the valves on my car. Anything that needed fixing, I fixed it myself. Didn't have to pay for it.

"The canal was *beautiful*. They kept the grass mowed just as pretty, and the trees trimmed even. If you'd get on a long straight lie say, a mile or two, the trees would be trimmed and it looked just like a straight line on the trees. It was kept up beautiful. Each foreman tried to make his division look better than the other one did. The water was just about six or seven inches from the top of the bank. You had to regulate it to keep it that way. Each locktender regulated the next level below him. Along swamps and stuff like that you'd see some flowers. Not too many, but some places you'd see some flowers.

Harvey Brant

"We had one of the nicest lock houses on the canal. I had a kitchen stove, a big stove; then in the dining room I had a big stove. They both burned coal. People who lived around Hagerstown tried to get this coal, because it was the best soft coal in the country. Mined up above Cumberland. George's Crick coal it was called, I think. It was soft coal but it was clean-burning coal and it burned good. It was the best coal you could *get*. Of course them mines have run out now. . . . Those big stoves, I could fill up with coal and they'd last two or three days. But of course the upstairs was cold.

"We didn't have no bathroom in the house. We had an outhouse. We didn't have water in the house until, oh, long after the canal stopped. We had to go to the spring and get it. About a hundred yards below the lock there on the berm side. It was pretty tough in the wintertime, going down there getting water. I generally got the water; I'd bring two bucketsful, one in each hand.

"We got the water to wash with and everything right out of the lock. There was always water in that lock, about two feet. There's three different springs in that lock; you could feel the cold water coming up. That's the reason there was always water there. They wanted to get rid of it, the canal people did, but they couldn't. They wanted to get rid of that water altogether. I don't know why. It was nice clear water. We had a bucket with a rope on it, and I had a couple of planks across the lock, and we go out on those planks and dip up a bucketful and bring it right in.

"We had to bathe with a basin or a tub. We had tubs like wash tubs. Our tubs would hold, oh, 30 gallon. They were galvanized—galvanized iron, I guess. We heated on the kitchen stove. My wife would heat her wash water. She had a big wash boiler. My tubs, washing machine, everything, is still down in the cellar. I haven't used them since my wife died. We set [the boilers] right on the front part of the cook stove. Didn't take too long to heat them.

"[The house] had a shingle roof when I first went there. But it got to leaking and they put a metal roof in over the top of the shingles. Galvanized tin roof; I think they painted it green. The same weatherboarding is still there. All the time I lived in that house it was never [re]painted and the paint was still pretty good. That shows you how good the paint was in them days.

"Locktenders a way out from town, they never seen anybody except when a boat went through. There's a six-mile level down here, and then there's a four-mile level. The fellow who lived down there at the six-mile level, he never got away from there because he didn't have no way of getting away. I don't know *how* he got anything to eat, him and his wife. He used to catch eels out of the canal before I put my fish pot in down here at this lock. He used to catch them by the barrel down there. When I put my fish pot in, he didn't get any more eels. I cut him off. His name was Reuben Hornsby. It was out in the country, away from everything, this lock was. I'd say it was six mile anyhow to the nearest store. It was back a long ways from civilization, you might say. People must have brought him stuff there. They were old people, too.

"[It was] not too bad here, because there was always some-body coming to see a boat come through. Always. Always a bunch of people. And we knowed all the boatmen. They were

204

mostly all nice people. Very few of them drank anything. They were Number One citizens.

"There was *one* fellow, he used to get drunk a lot. Boy, every time he'd come to Williamsport he'd get drunk. He was a booze heister.

Harvey Brant

"The boats were loaded up here for Cushwa's; they were loaded at Steffey and Findlay. And then Cushwa's had another place to unload down here at Powell's Bend, down at the Cumberland Valley Railroad. That's about two and a half mile below Williamsport. Anyhow, this fellow pulled in up here at Cushwa's, and he didn't know where he was going to unload at until he got his manifest and they told him he had to go to Powell's Bend. Well, him and his crew went up town and got drunk. They come to the lock that night and I got the lock ready for them; and the boy that was driving the mules, he heisted two paddles of water to draw him in the lock—because he knowed he couldn't *hit* the lock. He was too drunk to hit it. Well, that drawed him in the lock—he come in there a-flying, with two paddles of water drawn out. He went to snub the boat and he fell on his face and I seen he wasn't going to get [the boat] stopped. So I run and got a couple of wraps on the snubbing post and the fire was flying out of it; the rope was burning. I almost got the boat stopped, but it hit the lower gates and it almost knocked them out. Pushed one gate past the other one. Well, I got him out of there, but I don't know how he got to Powell's Bend."

Usually the mechanics of getting a boat through a lock were easier on the locktender. "There's a wicket . . . when it's turned around, it turns the paddles in the bottom of the gates [at one end of the lock]. There's two square paddles on each [of the two sides of the gate], down at the bottom. That leaves some water in there and the lock fills up. When the lock fills up, you get against the beam and push the gates open on each side. The beam is about 20 feet long and 12 by 12 inches. You push them gates back open, the boat could pull in the lock.

"The lock would be full. Then you closed these gates and you closed the paddles in the bottom of them so no more water could get in. You went down to the lower end of the lock—you had to go down to the other end to cross—and you got wickets to open the paddles in the *lower* gate. You turn them paddles and you leave the water out of the lock down to the lower level. Then you open them gates down there and the mules will pull the boat right out [into the main part of the canal].

"When you opened one of the gates, you had to go down to the lower end of the lock and cross them boards, a platform, and come up on the other side to open that gate. You used that platform all the time. If you wanted to go up town for anything, you had to cross the lock. In the wintertime the platform would get icy sometimes. I fell in one time it was icy. I was clearing the line for a boy who was driving, and the line got caught on something and jerked me in. Boy, I mean that was chilly. It was frost on the ground.

"There would be high water or something and trash would come in the canal; it would come down in there and get fastened on the paddles. They'd get so tight you couldn't get them turned. Then you'd have to take a big long grab hook, about a 20-foot pole, and reach down in there and kind of keep working that stuff until you could get it out of there.

"I've never knowed no danger around a lock. Unless you fell in. The only time I seen anybody fall in. . . . I had a swinging bridge—I had built it myself—that I could swing across the middle of the lock, to keep from walking clear around. It was about two feet wide. There was this drunken woman come up there one night. She was with a man and he didn't want her to try to get across there, but 'Oh, I can do anything,' she said. She said, 'Oh, I can walk that damn plank.' I said, 'You better stay over there.' Oh, she was cocky, and she said, 'I'm coming across.' And boy, she started across and down in the canal she went. The lock was full. I just grabbed her by her hair and pulled her up. She was the only person I seen fall in.

"Generally I'd keep the lock full because a loaded boat couldn't hold back in the lock as easy as a light boat could—couldn't hold back because the current would keep driving it. A light boat coming upstream didn't have nothing on, and he could [slow down] very easy. So I generally kept it full. Over the weekends I could put the canoes right in the lock and they could go right out. They were mostly Old Town canoes. I don't know where they were built, but that was the name of the canoes, Old Town.

"They had level walkers on the canal. He had a 21-mile trip to make every day with a shovel on his back and his dinner bucket. And don't you think that ain't a job. Sam Fowler got sick one time and asked me to take his route, and I wasn't used to walking and it nearly killed me.

"If he found a leak along the towpath where you could fix it with a shovel, he fixed it. It if was a bad leak there'd be a big whirl in the water where it was going through. [Then] he'd have to notify the company boat, and the workmen would have to go out and fix it.

"One night they reported a break down on the lower end of the six-mile level, the level below Lock 44. I wasn't working on the canal then, but I was down there that night and I went with them. It was right after I got married. There was a whirl there on the canal bigger around than my living room here, just like a funnel. Water was going out and through the top of that culvert. We cut tree tops and got them all up in a bunch and we'd climb up with ropes and throw them down there in the river. And boy, we worked there all night. Finally we tied a bale of hay on tree tops and this finally choked it off and the water wasn't going through. Then we piled it full of dirt that we got off the scow. It held.

"The next boat that come along, he'd hit it, mash it down. A loaded boat. It held. If it wouldn't have been for that, if we hadn't fixed it, the whole thing would have went out in the river. The whole bank.

"One night when I was tending lock, there was a boat over here waiting for the lock and I got it ready and hollered for him to come ahead. He said, 'I can't come. I'm fastened. Get me a back swell.' He meant to heist the paddle and shut it off and throw a swell up to get him off the bank. I gave him a couple of swells, but he couldn't move. I took my light and walked down along the lock wall, and the canal [had fallen] off by two feet. I knew right well there was a break somewhere.

Harvey Brant

207

"I telephoned Mr. James.* We called him Dick. He was the general superintendent and he was the dumbest man I ever saw. He got that job through pull some way or other. I said, 'There's a break somewhere. We'd better draw the water out. If we draw the water out, it might not get too bad.' He said, 'Oh, hell, damn. We'll have to go and see where it is. Can't draw the water out without going to see.' He was just that dumb.

"So I get in my Model T Ford and I get him and take him up the canal, across the aqueduct; and, narrow as the aqueduct was, you only had *that* much room for each tire on each side.** When we got to the aqueduct, he said, 'I'll go on ahead of you and look for the leak.' And he did. He took his flashlight and went across. He thought maybe the break was in the aqueduct right above us. And while I was driving my Model T Ford along the aqueduct wall with eleven inches on each side of the automobile, he shined his flashlight in my eyes! [The towpath had] an iron railing on the lower side, next to the creek, but it didn't have any next to the canal.

"We went on up the canal, and the further up we got the more down the water was getting. You *know* he was dumb, when the canal was getting emptier all the time and he kept going on looking for the break. I wanted him to draw the water here [at Lock 44] and go on up through the country to Dam 5 and shut the water off up there. It would have saved half that break. But you couldn't tell *him* nothing.

"We got clear up to Miller's Bend—that was about two miles below Dam No. 5—and he said, 'Oh, you can speed up a little bit along here. I think this is a pretty good bank along here.' Just about the time he said that, my lights shone on the bank where the break had gone out. When I got the car stopped, the ground was cracked. I backed up real quick and got off of it and you could hear stones hitting against the West Virginia shore, there was so much water pouring. That bank washed out about

*Not his real name.

**The part of the aqueduct that was a continuation of the regular towpath was at most seven feet (or 84 inches) wide. From the outside of one tire to the outside of the opposite tire of a 1924 Model T Ford is 62 inches.

208

250 feet long. Up here on this level, up here at Miller's Bend. [The canal] drained itself. By the time I got home there wasn't any water here.

"If he'd listened to me and drawed the water and went up to the dam and shut the water off, it wouldn't have been one-fourth that bad. But he had to know it all. He was the dumbest man I've ever seen. I can't help it. He was *dumb*.

"We had just got that break fixed and put the water back in when the side of the aqueduct went out. That was a double dose right there.

"Frank Myers had unloaded at Cushwa's, and it was just lucky.... When they unloaded they always put all four mules out on the towpath to feed them instead of leaving them in the stable all the time they unloaded. So, as luck happened, Myers had all four mules still out on the towpath. And his daughter, a big 250-pound woman, she was out on the towpath. I'll never know whether he might have hit the side of the aqueduct or not, but something funny went on just as his boat was going through. The side of the aqueduct went out and his boat went out through Conococheague Creek more than 20 feet below. He hollered at the girl to unhook the towline on the mules, not to pull them in. She unhooked them. Frank, he jumped off on the towpath. So nobody got hurt.

"It shut the canal out for several weeks. They had to bring a contractor up here from Baltimore. They put a board siding in the aqueduct, planks 5 to 6 inches thick and 14 inches wide. They put logs down in there, from one side to the other, and concreted them in and let these logs stick out on one side. These logs run out far enough that they could put a prop up, and they used the aqueduct that way until the canal stopped. But, my, it wasn't but a couple of years after that it was all rotted away. It was poor lumber. It wasn't hardly worth putting in—and *I mean they worked!* to put it in. And it cost a mint of money.

"Mr. Nicolson* was a big shot. We had a break down here

Italic in right margin: *Harvey Brant*

*George Nicolson was general manager, Chesapeake and Ohio Canal. He held this office from 1890 until 1938.

209

on the four-mile level one time, right along the cliffs, and it was an awful place to get any dirt to fix it. The old woman had the farm up at the top of the cliff there was named Miss Bishop. She didn't want to let him have that dirt to fix the break. She even come out there with a shotgun and said, 'Ain't *nobody* going to take any of *my* dirt.' Mr. Nicolson was a pretty nice man, but he was smart. He had it condemned some way, the place where he was going to get the dirt. Her property back there wasn't no 'count at all anyhow; she was just that contrary she didn't want to let him have it. He offered to pay her good money for it, ten times more than what it was worth; but she was that kind of woman, she didn't want to take it. Anyhow, he got it condemned some way and he got the dirt.

"We had to haul that dirt on scoops by mules down over them cliffs and fix that break, and I mean we was three or four weeks fixing [it].

"I helped on a lot of things. I'd go and help because I'd get paid extra for that. I'd get my $1.25 a day. One time there was a boat sunk in the aqueduct, the aqueduct here over Conococheague Creek. We worked in the rain all night up there. Somebody throwed a big rock in the water, in the aqueduct, and it sunk to the bottom. The rock wasn't much bigger than your head; [but] this boat was loaded and there wasn't much space between the bottom of the boat and the aqueduct, and this rock sunk the boat. We had to shovel all that coal out on to the bank, the towpath, and dig down there. . . . We had to shovel coal all night to hunt for where the leak was. We worked that night till we was just about ready to fall over. We finally found the place, and we patched it enough that we could get the boat out of there and unload it at Cushwa's and take it to the boat yard to get it fixed.

"Mr. Nicolson came along that night. He must have come up from Washington to see whether we was going to get it fixed. He had a big bottle of liquor. He knowed we was all pretty near froze, working there in the cold rain, and he passed that around. Oh, boy, it was something!"

Mr. Brant tended lock eight years, but all told he lived in the lock house 45 years. "I stayed there [after the canal closed] and I only had to pay a dollar a month rent—just to show who it belonged to. A dollar a *year*, I believe it was.

"My garden was behind the house. But when Potomac Edison bought these bottoms over here and started to build the power plant—that was just about the time the canal stopped—they got a bulldozer in there and just covered up my garden, and knocked down my fruit trees and my grape vines and everything.* I had a hog pen back there. They knocked it down. And they never said a word to me.

"They took everything back of the house. And they took what didn't belong to them. It was canal property. The canal company owned 100 feet at the edge of the canal back behind there; but they were big shots and they could get away with it. They took it right up to the back of the house; they [left] little more than room to walk around it. They took all that and covered it with cinders. That hurt, when they took all my ground away from me. And trees and vines. They never said a word. Just put a bulldozer in there and crushed everything."

*With the consent of the court, the receivers disposed of canal properties as occasion arose. They gave the Potomac Power and Light Company permission to put up a power plant near Williamsport.

Harvey Brant

[1] "The American eel is quite common in local waters and has a very interesting life history. Usually considered a typical freshwater species, the adults must migrate about 1,000 miles to their spawning grounds in the vicinity of Bermuda where both the American and European species spawn in early spring. The tiny larvae which hatch in February are about a quarter of an inch in length and grow to about two inches in September, by which time they have reached fresh water and have completed their development from an elver to an eel. Instinctively, the myriads of elvers of the American species are able to separate from their European cousins and make their way westward to our Atlantic seaboard." From *Potomac Trail Book* by Robert Shosteck, Potomac Books, Inc., Washington, D.C. 1968.

Interviews, September 16
and October 27, 1979.

Theodore Lizer
Williamsport

Theodore Lizer

WHEN THEODORE LIZER was 12 years old he was steering his father's boat in Little Slack Water. "And that's pretty bad steering up there," he says, meaning that it's pretty fancy steering. Any C&O boatman will bear him out.

He first went on the canal at "about eight or nine, something like that," with his father, Wesley Lizer, and two brothers. At that time, the beginning of 14 years of boating for him, he was with his father and "Brother Charlie and Buddy. Charlie was the oldest. Then Orville. Then I'm next. Then George. And my brother Frank. Then we had two sisters. They never were on the boat. Mom didn't want them on the boat. Mom never went.

"We started with a Cushwa boat. That was a private boat. Belonged to Cushwa. That was an old leaky boat, No. 36. Then we had a chance to get off that and get on with the canal company and get more money; because we was only getting 35 cents a ton to Williamsport. After we got on with the canal company boat, No. 8, then we got 35 cents to Williamsport, [plus] 80 cents to Georgetown. This was around back in . . .'12 or '13, I guess it was."

Mr. Lizer still has the oak table at which he and his brothers ate so many of the meals their father prepared. When Wesley Lizer bought the equipment needed for the change of boats, he got a large assortment of items for eight dollars and the drop leaf table was among them. "That table didn't slide around," Mr. Lizer remembers. "When the boat hit, that table didn't slide

212

around. It's heavy, and then we had clamps on the side of the cabin that held it."

Like many others, the Lizer boys all steered young. "My father [taught us]. We had to do it because we could steer, but we couldn't harness the mules up. After we got bigger, then we harnessed our own mules. You had to follow the team.

"After we got up big enough, up around 12 or 14 years old, then we got two boats. Had two boats running. My brother Charlie had one and my father had one. We had four mules on each one of them. We changed mules at locks; we never dropped the fall board. Lots of the boatsmen changed every six hours, another team every six hours. We just went so-many miles to a lock and changed. You followed your team in. You had to go unharness them. [Our boats] kept running night and day. We never stopped. Never stopped unless there was a break or something like that. Both boats."

As Mr. Lizer remembers, the mules were treated well. During the boating season, that is. "They was taken care of. Fed good. The canal company furnished the feed. When we'd take them [to the farm where they spent the winter] they were nice and fat. We'd go up and get them in the spring and we had to *walk* them back home. We couldn't ride them back. We just had to drag along with them. Their backbones would be bad and we couldn't ride them because they'd get sore.

"They were at Four Locks. They didn't know what an ear of corn was till we got them down here and fed them. They didn't eat nothing [at Four Locks] but straw and water. It would take us a couple of weeks to get them [properly] back on their feet again. They were *poor*. We had to feed them two or three days [at least] before we could leave. If we were going to leave on Easter, why, we'd go up the first of the week [before] and get them.

"The canal company put them on these farms and paid the farmers to feed them. We kept telling them. Pop told them, 'Our mules is coming in poor. They put them in the barn and they ate straw and drank water and that's all they got.' Pop would raise the devil when we'd go down [to Georgetown] for the first trip. He'd tell Mr. Nicolson down there how they starved them all winter. Nicolson would say, 'They're supposed to feed them corn and hay and work them in the wintertime. If they can work them they're supposed to work them—and *feed* them, keep them fat. We'll have to check on that and change the farms if they don't feed them.' Oh, but the canal company didn't do nothing. They wasn't worried about them. They didn't care.

"We didn't run that old boat [36] but about two years. It was an old government boat. They made them down near George-town, South Carolina, out of pine wood. They leaked all the time and you couldn't keep them pumped out. Pop didn't want any more. These boats were made during World War I. They was half sunk when they brought them in here. They were just no good. They were new but made out of green lumber and they [only] half caulked them up. They didn't know how to make them. Up there at Cumberland, when they made a boat they caulked it; and they knew how far to put two boards together so that water would swell the boards tight. Down there in South Carolina some of those seams got open. You'd have to stick rags and everything in there. We run it a couple of years but it was too much work for us."

When Mr. Lizer thinks back to his early days on the canal, he thinks first of driving mules and of getting through locks at night. Driving, he loved. "You didn't have no boss; you was out there driving and you didn't have to worry about nothing. We-e-ll, screech owls out there at night. . . you'd be setting up on a mule about half asleep and one of them up in a tree would give a whooooooo. You were scared of *them*."

He never found driving lonely. "You'd see everything, see the sights going along. People walking and people out in boats. Lot of people camping. You'd see people camping *all along* the canal. They'd come up and talk to us, walk along with us, and the women walked along and wanted to know how long it would take [to get the] coal from Cumberland to Georgetown. They'd walk maybe half a mile with us and say, 'Well, this is as far as we go. We'll go back to camp. We'll see you when you come down next time.' They'd be there for a couple of weeks, on their vacation.

214

"[You'd see] people traveling out of Georgetown in canoes in the summertime. They could get a waybill in Georgetown. City people. They traveled the canal. They'd get a two-weeks' vacation and they'd come down in boats and camp along the canal and the river.

"A lot of sights. We'd see a lot of deer on the towpath. They'd swim across. And turkeys. And big pheasants walking down the towpath up above Hancock. They weren't wild turkeys and pheasants; they were raised up there at the Rod and Gun Club."*

Animals that occurred naturally in the area included "a lot of foxes. They come down to drink water. Swim across the canal. Gray foxes, silver foxes, red foxes. They'd never bother you. That's about all the wild animals you'd see. I enjoyed them. Never saw no wildcats. We heard a couple of 'em up there in the mountains. Those cattioes, kittyoes, you could hear them up there hollering at night.

"Driving, you could see everything along the canal. Farms on each side. There was big farms, raised white corn. [We could hear] singing at nighttime, over at a farmhouse. Oldtime songs. They sounded good."

The Lizers didn't do any singing themselves. "We never had time. We fished after night. We tied up and fished. We was always fishing. Down on the nine-mile level, above White's Ferry, we used to dip carp about as big as your hand. We had a dip-net, we'd bring up eight or nine carp. We used to catch bass [out of the canal] up at Hancock, big bass. We had a turtle net. We made turtle soup. Or fried them . . . get the little ones. That's what we lived on. We lived off of bass and snapping turtles.

"Father done the cooking. He'd make a big kettle full and that's what we'd eat until it was all gone. We ate a lot of bean soup. [With the bean soup] we used them old Kingham hams. Get them up there at Four Locks. You could buy them for about a dollar apiece, a whole ham. We cooked on a coal stove. You had to keep a coal fire all the time; it was hot in the summer; that's why we always cooked on cool days.

"Lots of times we put in [the bean soup] what you call rivvels.

Theodore Lizer

*To be shot by hunters later as "game birds."

215

Take some flour in a dish, break an egg in it, stir it all up, let it get heavy, keep working it till it gets heavy. Just flour and egg; just like you were going to make pot pie dough. That's all you use—egg; no water. Then it'll all get up in a bump, and you pinch off little pieces about as big as the end of your finger and keep dropping them in the bean soup. It's yellow; the eggs made the flour yellow. And that's what they called rivvels."

After mule driving, Mr. Lizer's thoughts are of "trying to get *him* out of bed." Coming to locks all through the night . . . "getting those locktenders out . . . you'd have to holler and holler. Of course we had a hard time; we was only kids and a lot of them wouldn't get up for us. We'd have to stop and run ahead. We had to change the locks ourselves."

This didn't happen often. "Ninety percent of all the locktenders kept the locks set for loaded boats after night." But when he did come to a lock set for a light boat, Mr. Lizer recalls, "Many a time we'd have to bring her in along the bank. We never had to snub, just bring her in close to the bank and let her drag. We knowed just about how long a distance it would take to get that lock changed, get the water in the lock, and get the gates open for a loaded boat.

"A loaded boat was worse to get to a lock. A light boat, when you stopped the mules it would stop; but a loaded boat was going downstream and it wouldn't stop. The water was running behind the boat all the time and it would keep the boat moving. The water was running maybe a couple of miles an hour. A light boat was coming *in* to the water. The water was going downstream all the time and a light boat was going upstream all the time.

"If the lock wasn't set for a loaded boat you'd have to run down and check the lower gate and [try to] get the locktender out, then run down the other side and get the other gate. The lock had to be full for a loaded boat. If it was set for a light boat you'd have to fill the lock back up. You'd get the loaded boat in there, open the paddles, the loaded boat dropped down in the lock, go down on the other level and you pulled it out.*

---

*"When you open the paddles and draw water off, you're drawing the boat faster. The water is pulling the boat faster."

Water was going on each level *all the time*. Lots of times you might have to put the boat on the bank—a loaded boat, if you couldn't stop it. It wouldn't be hard to get back off. Once you hit the berm side you bounced off."

Hassles at the locks paled in the presence of his generalized feeling that the canal life was a good one. "That's one thing about it: best life we had. We'd stop at Georgetown, the boats was all together, and the kids got together off the different boats. [And we got our] big pay. Fifteen cents! That's what we got for a 184-mile trip. A big pay. Get a bottle of Coca-Cola pop for three cents and a bag of peanuts for two cents and go to see the show— a nickel for the *show*. . . Tom Mix. And we had a nickel left. Then we'd get a nickel's worth of peanuts—a *big* bag for a nickel—and come back and eat them on the boat. We'd sit on the boat and finish them up. We thought we had more money then than the president of the United States! We felt rich.

"And we made money down there in Georgetown, helping people at those big club houses. We'd help them put canoes in, help them clean canoes up, wash canoes. They had those racing boats down there, with paddles; about ten of them would get in one of those boats. [That money too] we had for ourselves. We'd go back up the street, to the stores, to see what we could find. Bought that old licorice. Old black licorice. In straps. You'd get two of them nearly a yard long. Then we'd smoke. Nobody didn't know it. We bought Duke's tobacco, a nickel bag. We couldn't buy cigarettes; we rolled our own. We used to buy Duke's and hide it on the boat. And we'd buy a big nickel box of barnburners, those big matches. We used to hide them too. We'd put matches in our hip pocket and take a sack of tobacco on the towpath. When we did that we kept away from my daddy.

"We'd get up on a mule's back and dive in the canal. Only wore a pair of shorts—cut the legs off pants. We swam all the time. That was clear water. That was *clear* water. At Hancock up there you could see down to the bottom of the canal. Up by eight-mile level, Cumberland." Some are puzzled by this, because a lot of stables were there to be cleaned out and the manure went "right in the canal. That wasn't much. It washed away. You had overflows, water running out over the towpath;

Theodore Lizer

217

then you had waste weirs." Human excrement too went into the canal "and down to the lock. All went through that lock and down on the next level; and time you got down on the next level, it was just all gone away. Up there at Cumberland, and the level of Old Town, you could see fish down there. Come on down to tunnel level, South Branch, that three-mile [long] wide water; at Hancock, 14-mile level, you could see bass swim-

Breathing spell. Boat tied up, mules unharnessed on towpath, boys set to swim in canal where garbage and contents of stable floors were regularly dumped. Unaccountable though it may seem, children swam and fish lived in the canal and seemed none the worse for it.

ming alongside the boat. From Dam No. 6 *down,* you could catch bass and see clear water."

It was not clear everywhere. Footer's dye plant, at the feeder lock at Cumberland, "dyed clothes and goods and everything. The dye was blue." And the plant's waste went into the canal. "That dye come, looked like big marbles. We used to go up there and get the marbles. Wasn't no fish lived there. And the canal was growed up with grass. It come out of that dye and the sewer and stuff. It grew on the bottom. You could see it. They had to cut it; you couldn't get through it with a boat. The canal company had a big grass cutter on a scow. It was like a hay mower. They'd use that grass cutter to cut up through the center [of the canal]; then they'd come back and cut the sides." To find fish living in the canal again, "you had to go down to eight-mile level."

Theodore Lizer

If the boys "swam all the time," they pretty much walked all the time too. "Barefoot. Course we could tell you every stone in the towpath, because all you had to do was look down at your toes and you had them wrapped up." Mr. Lizer remembers that many people went barefoot on the towpath "in the summertime," and, even though he sometimes felt that he'd stumped his toes on every stone on the path, he never felt that this was in any serious degree rough on the feet. "No! It was dirt, and the mules kept it dug up all the time. And grass growed there. There was a mule path and a walking path; you made your own path, walking.

"It was a good scene, with all the trees—and the canal company kept them trimmed so the boats wouldn't get into them. The towpath was cut, the weeds kept down. It was pretty. They kept it clean. They'd cut the weeds with scythes. Cut them down along the water so the towlines wouldn't get fastened. Lots of times they had these old push mowers. Down around Six Locks they used to have them, and they'd cut the grass on the towpath."

There was one view he particularly admired and remembers vividly. "It was a beautiful spot—head of the eight-mile level, foot of the nine-mile level. When you looked out there you could see that lock down there just as plain. On a clear night . . . [or] the moon would be out, you could see the locktender coming, carrying this little lantern. Just a little lantern. Looked like he had a match; I used to say to him, 'This is one beauty spot. When you come out of that trunk up there and come around that bend and hit this, and look down for a mile.' He'd say, 'Everybody says that when the moon is full. When that moon ain't full, it's one of the darkest spots.'"

In Mr. Lizer's youngest days, when his father gave up the old leaky Cushwa boat and ran the canal company's boat No. 8, "Then we went to Indianhead. That was 30 mile down the river. Then you got more money. You got $35 for a load. A lot of boatmen wouldn't go down there with families; that was dangerous. You'd travel all after night. You'd take four boats down there. It was a tugboat pulled us down. We used to call it *Winship*. I think it belonged to the canal company too."

It was a twitchy business being towed to Indianhead by the *Edith Goddard Winship*. "You went out in the river all the time and it was all after night. We were *in the river*. You'd meet these big boats and waves would come up over us. The government had a lot of boats out there, big boats, and they threw waves up! Brother!

"Then you had big pleasure boats—they would haul about a thousand people—going out of Washington down to that big [amusement] park below Alexandria. It was lit up . . . [and there was] dancing and everything over there all night long at Marshall Hall. The tug would go past the Marshall Hall boat.

"We were down there one night and we had a brand-new boat and that boat started leaking. The tug was pulling four boats; we tied the boats together. We [the tug] was in the middle; two boats on each side of us. We were setting on the tugboat talking to the fireman, and this boat kept going down. Somebody looked over and said, 'Hey, that boat's disappeared!' And that boat wasn't a foot from going down.

"The fireman hollered to Daddy and said, 'Better get somebody

*Loose fiber; raveled hemp rope.

220

on there. That's boat's sinking.' We jumped up and took the measuring sticks, stuck them down in the hold, and there was two or three feet of water in the boat. We had pumps, wooden things with handles; they had leather suckers. They made them up here at Cumberland. When you pulled up, that would bring the water up; when you shoved down, water was trapped in the bottom of the pump. I've pumped many a gallon of water.

"We went down there below Alexandria to Occoquan. There's where we pulled in at. There was a wharf and we had to pull in there and get to shallow water. The one that was sinking was next to the tugboat. We had to get to shallow water in case she'd go down and we'd let her go. You never know what [a sinking boat] is liable to do. She had 110 tons of coal on her and a light boat on each side of her. She could have pulled them down.

"After pumping, we got down in the front of the boat, down in the mule stable and down in the front. We found out the oakum was coming out.* It had washed out of the seams and the water was coming in. We got down there and drove oakum back in. Each boat always carried chisels and a lot of oakum in case we hit a leak. After we got the caulk mended and we got the water out of her, then we went down in the front and checked her. Captain Tom said everything was OK so we got her back out. After he seen she wasn't leaking, Captain Tom backed her out. We started down the river again. We watched her all night down to Indianhead, and unloaded and brought her back. When we come back, they took it back to the boat yard in Cumberland. Then they caulked the outside. We had caulked the inside. They put tar on it; that tar is to hold the oakum in. And that was a new boat. That was the first trip for that boat."

The Lizers' boats always had four of the family on each: "one steering, one driving, two resting." They "divided up the family. We'd drive so-many miles, then we'd bring the mules in and lay down on the deck and sleep and rest. When your team went in, then you went to bed. And you rested five or six hours because the other team was making its five-hour run. And that

Theodore Lizer

221

kept changing. You might have to get up at twelve o'clock and get back on the towpath. Then you slept some in daytime too. Whenever we changed tricks. You'd lay up on the deck and sleep, or go in the grub house. About an hour or an hour and a half, something like that." It averaged out to "about 7" hours of sleep in 24. "We [changed] by the levels. We got plenty of rest.

"We always kept going. We'd try to get home for a big time, Decoration Day and stuff like that. We wouldn't get there. Something would slow Pop up and we wouldn't get there.

"At the beginning of a season, we always left on Easter Sunday. That was the day we'd leave home. *Every* year in April. One Easter Sunday, I think George, my brother, was driving. We went up on this level, the sun was shining, pretty Easter morning, on up to Four Locks, changed, put my three-mule team out. Then we hit the 14-mile level. I drove the 14-mile level; that was my trick. She got cold and started to snow. We had to put the awning up. The boat had an awning over it. We had to take it down for bridges, on light boats for bridges; loaded boats, you never had to bother. A light boat was too high to come under the bridge. Well, we put the awning up. At Big Pool she was snowing. I was walking in the snow and the mules had snow up in their hooves. They were walking on balls of snow. They could hardly walk. We stopped there below the aqueduct. At the head of Big Pool. Zimmermans all up there. They had one Zimmerman never boated on Sunday. Well, we cleaned the mules' hooves out; got sticks and dug the snow out. We crossed the aqueduct. Pop said, 'There's no way we can change mules. Let's go up here to Hancock and we'll tie up there and put the mules over on that overjet.'

"When loaded boats started out, they had overjets to drive underneath. Big buildings come out to the canal edge, and they had overjets—all open underneath.* The boat went up side of it and the overjet was just over the bank. There was one up at Hancock bridge, and he said, 'Bring the mules around, cross

---

*Warehouses here had broad sheltering overhangs.

the bridge and bring them up there and we'll tie up and put the mules under there tonight.' It was still snowing.

"So we drove on up there. The mules stopped and I pulled the line in. It was *cold,* and the mules were walking on [newly formed] snowballs under their feet—Belle, Tom, Jewel. They were black mules, big fat mules. I said, 'Tom, come on. We're going over here tonight. You can't walk and I can't either.' So we cleaned them all good and put the harness on the boat, covered it up, put troughs out and got them fed and watered. They was tired. They just laid down in the hay we threw out for them. When you take the harness off a mule, he likes that, and the first thing he does is roll. One side to the other. And he'll kick. He likes [being free of the harness]. . . . We never got away from there till the next day at eleven o'clock. The sun got up and melted the snow and the mules could walk."

Mr. Lizer remembers considerable drinking from place to place on the canal, but rather moderate drinking on the part of the boatmen. "Up there at Darkey's Lock, up at the head of the tunnel level—that big tire plant was across the river there. Saturday was pay day. Those Italians, they used to come across the river, have a sack, get a gallon of whiskey. Buy whiskey by the gallon jug. Over at the saloon there at the lock. I don't know what the name of it was. They didn't have much of a name on them; they just had saloons. They had boats, but lots of times the river was only about *that* deep in summertime and they'd just wade across it. Any Saturday, pay day, you could find them, you could fall over them, laying down there on the towpath drunk, passed out. It happened every pay day."

Memories vary on this point but, as Mr. Lizer recalls, the men on the boats didn't do much boozing. "When they got to Cumberland, why. . . they'd have to wait overnight to get [the boats] loaded. . . . Three saloons right there in Shantytown, and they'd go over and drink beer. Nickel a bottle for beer. Lots of times Pop would take a 10-quart bucket and get a growler.* And we

*Ten quarts of beer.

Theodore Lizer

223

used to sit out there on the hatch and drink that beer at night. Kids. Course you could drink a lot of beer then and it didn't hurt you. Beer back in them days didn't hurt you. Oh, no, it didn't hurt you. This beer nowadays, you drink two or three bottles and you're drunk. It's got stuff in it.

"They had breweries up there in Cumberland in them days. They had Export and Old German beer. It was made up there, but they called it Old German.

"[Boatmen] didn't have much time to drink. They bought whiskey sometimes. I think Pop bought a fifth of whiskey down in Georgetown. He'd take a drink now and then, and a lot of times he'd bring it home. But very little drinking they done *on the boats*. If they wanted any beer, they'd drink it when they were in port in Georgetown. There was a saloon every other door on M Street. We never stopped; we wasn't allowed in them. Too young."

Thinking back to himself at that age, Mr. Lizer remembers that in the winters he and the others would "go to school when we could. We didn't get much school. We liked it when we were there, but we didn't get much until after Christmas, and then we had to leave in April. We got what we could. It was the only thing we could do to pass the time away, go to school. I liked arithmetic. We did multiplying and stuff like that. We had to figure all that out. Course Mom was always helping us.

"I liked being with the other kids, that's about all. We didn't really like [school], because we didn't get much education; the other kids was ahead of us. We had A and B classes, and we was mostly in the B class because we hadn't got enough education to be up in the A class. And when we did get enough to get up in the A class, we had to go on the boat. So we didn't get much education in the A class. So we quit."

If he could have stayed in school throughout the school year, it might have been different, he feels. As it was, however, "that's all we could do, just get on [the canal] and drive mules again." And as it was, he preferred this to school "because that was the best life. You wasn't in any one spot all the time. Outdoors, and driving the mules, and seeing people, and talking to the locktenders." He carries this feeling with him now. "One thing about it: you hear that on the radio, 'Where are your children at tonight?' [On the canal] "when dark came, if you had *14* little kids, you knowed exactly where [each] was, because you had 14 sets of harness and they were laying there asleep on the blanket on the deck. When [the mothers] would go to bed, they'd take them in the cabins. Everybody on the canal was friendly and neighborly, too. Never had no fights.

Theodore Lizer

"They have these big times now at Lock 44 in Williamsport. They have it every year. I went year before last. People from Washington were down there, asking a lot of questions, trying to learn. I said, 'It would be worth a million dollars to you people to stand right here—we were standing on the berm side—and watch a loaded boat coming down with three mules pulling it and this lock getting ready for it.'"

First of two interviews, August 4, 1979.

Raymond M. Riley
Seneca

Raymond Riley

WHEN RAYMOND RILEY, 82, enters his house from front or back, he steps along a walkway made of red sandstone sawed by his father, John C. Riley, at the Seneca sandstone quarry. He lives next door to the house he grew up in, about a mile from Riley's Lock, 24, where his father worked from 1892 to 1924. He maintains a keen interest in the river and the remains of the canal. Except in foul winter weather—and sometimes then—he often rambles in the vicinity of the stone lock house where he was born. It's on the canal at Seneca Creek.

"Red stone," says Mr. Riley reflectively. At the sawmill "they sawed them [individual stones]. They had big gangs in there and they'd lay it [a large rough piece] on a little car and bring it in there and put it under the thing and let the saw down on it, and it just worked backwards and forwards, just like people saw wood. They'd saw that stone off. Then they'd take it back out in the quarry, outside the mill, and turn it over and put it on the car and bring it back in and saw *that* side off. If they wanted all sides sawed, they'd just keep on until they sawed it square.

"Then they'd lay it on a big round wheel and that wheel would turn. You pour water and sand on it, and that would smooth it down, make it real smooth. A planing wheel, they called it. All the red stone in Georgetown came out of this quarry up here. The Smithsonian building—all that was sawed out at this sawmill."

Not only did Mr. Riley's father work at the quarry-sawmill,

226

but "*his* father worked there." That was William Riley, who came from Ireland at the age of 16. "My father's name was John Riley. He lived over on Reddens Hill; way back over yonder on the hill, on River Road."

At that time, "Will Benson tended the lock. He left, and my father took over, and he was there when the canal shut down. Mr. Violette [who had also worked at the quarry] went down to Violette's Lock, Lock 23, and he was there when the canal shut down. Ap Violette was his name.

"I was born at the lock house. Most of us was born there." The house is still intact, and carries the date of its completion, 1829, chiselled into a stone near the roof at one corner. It is made of the rosy sandstone referred to locally as Seneca stone; the inside walls are plaster. "Red stone," Mr. Riley repeats. "We used to whitewash it. We liked to make it white."

Most hold that lock houses were painted white for the sake of visibility to boatmen, but Mr. Riley believes that it was for the sake of appearance. "[Visibility] had nothing to do with it. The little old shanty, we used to whitewash that too. The canal

Workers at Seneca Stone Cutting Mill, circa 1890. Those who can be identified now are: 1, William Riley; 2, Harry Reeves, timekeeper; 3, Ran Sager; 4, George Goode; 5, Tom Berry; 6, John Riley; 7, Alfred (Ap) Violette; 8, Pete Mitchell; 9, Pete Tony.

227

company would whitewash all the houses' wooden banisters; and they'd give us lime and we'd whitewash the whole house because we liked it that way. Made it look a whole lot better. Brightened it up every year or so. *All* the canal locktenders, they whitewashed the houses. The old Pennyfield house was whitewashed; Swain's is whitewashed; the hotel down there to the Great Falls, it was painted or whitewashed.* Far as the boats were concerned, they didn't pay no attention to that. They wasn't interested in that. It just made the places look good."

The lock too is made of Seneca stone from the once nearby quarry and sawmill, and some stones bear carved signature symbols. Full authenticity is dubious, but Mr. Riley believes in them all. "Every man cut a stone [that's] down in that lock, he had a mark and he chiselled it [in the stone]. One man, he's got his initials and the date he cut the stone and everything. Each man, he's got a brand, and the brand is on [his stones]."

As described by Mr. Riley, the lock house had "two rooms down there in the cellar. Two rooms up next floor. And two up on the next floor. Every one of them had a fireplace in it, but the government went to work and changed it. They've only got one down in the cellar and two upstairs now. In the two rooms in the cellar, that's where we [kids] cooked and ate and people would come and sit."

On the first floor above the basement, "One side was the kitchen; one side was the dining room. And stair steps right in the middle went up. There were two rooms upstairs. My mother, she slept in that room upstairs, and all us boys slept in this room. My father, he slept out in his little cabin."

Each lock house had its "little cabin," sometimes called the wait house, sometimes called the dog house. Here the locktender sheltered in rough weather, and here he often spent entire nights in the hope that his work wouldn't disturb the sleep of his family. Locktenders were on duty day and night, seven days a week (during the boating season). "Mr. Nicolson, he was president, and when they got the last boat up to where it was supposed

*A tavern during canal days, now a Park Service museum.

to be, he'd send word: 'Draw the water.' On a certain day. They had places to draw the water off. The whole canal."

Mr. Riley has an old photograph showing the shanty very near the house, the only thing between being a bench made from a split log. Another of his pictures shows a picket fence on the canal side of the house. "He had to stay in the shanty [at night]," explains Mr. Riley. "When a boat come. . . he could look down the canal and he could look up. If he seen a light coming or heard a bugle blowing, well, he'd have to get up and let that boat in. He had to watch out day and night.

Raymond Riley

"My father, they said they never had to call him. Always seemed like he could judge a boat was coming, and he'd wake up and lock it through. He always had the lock set for a loaded boat. The light boats, they'd run up in the evening. The boats from Cumberland, you wouldn't know when one was coming. You *did* know when the boats from Georgetown would come up. They'd always go through before dark. They'd [leave] Georgetown in the morning. The tugs would bring some up from Indianhead. Say they'd leave town that morning; by nighttime they were all gone. Unless some stray boat was unloaded some place and maybe he'd be a little late."

To help round out his income, the elder Riley raised and sold produce, and he rented rowboats. "A locktender only got $35 a month." This was perhaps not such very bad pay for that time, but the Rileys had a large family.

"My father had a big garden. Used to raise all kinds of stuff and sell it to the boatsmen and sell to people who'd come. He had a little bench [the one at the lock] to put this stuff on. People would buy his tomatoes, potatoes, onions, pumpkins, corn, watermelon, everything you grow in a garden.

"He built his own boats. People went up in the canal and fished. Up there was a lot of bass and all kinds of fish, just the same as there was in the river. Sometimes they'd go out in the river and fish, or go down to the dam and fish. My father would rent a rowboat all day for 50 cents. That was when I was a kid, and 50 cents was a good bit. I've thinned corn for 25 cents a day. From sunup to sundown. For farmers."

Not for additional income but to feed the family, "he raised hogs. And we had a cow. We always kept the meat. We'd have five or six big hogs, weighed about 300 pounds, every year. We used the milk too. We used to make butter. And bread. Mother had to cook all the bread. She'd have big pans, put yeast in them, set them up on the mantelpiece behind the stove and let it raise. Supper time would come, or dinner time would come, she'd just reach up there and get some and take a breadpan and fill it up. And we had hot rolls all the time. Sometimes we'd take potatoes and make our own yeast.[1]

"We had a spring. We had to go way over across the lock and up the road a ways to get water, a little farther than from here to the house next door.* We had water buckets. It was good water. Good. Nice and cold. Everybody around here had to get water out of that spring.

"When my mother washed clothes, she'd just go right out to the canal and get water. The canal was just as clear as crystal. Just like spring water, in them days. You could throw a dime down in that lock and we [could see to] dive down there and get it. Every Sunday we'd go down there and swim. They learned the kids how to swim. They'd throw you overboard and let you come up. There wasn't any danger; too many of us around. If one come up and didn't try to swim, we raced out there and got him. We was right there all around him."

Swimming for children was even more important to the Rileys than to other canal families, for the saddest of reasons. "Katie drownded down there, right out there where they put boats in [the lock]. What happened...she was three...she was making mud cakes and had to get some water to mix them up. We had a fish box [in the creek] and the water was deep behind it. When she crawled out on the box to get the water, the box sunk and she went over. It was over her head and she couldn't get out. They missed her and they got to running around looking for her and they couldn't find her; so Poppa went down and he seen the box gone. He went back to the house and got the

*About 100 yards.

230

rake and reached down by the box and caught her by her little shoe. There she was." Mr. Riley was five years old at that time, and he has only a hazy memory of little Katie; but he remembers the family sorrow, and the change it made in their living arrangements was a permanent part of his life.

"We moved away. We had this house up here [next door] on River Road rented out. So we put the people out and moved up here. My father was still tending the lock. He stayed down there and kept batch. But some of the kids would take something to him every day, something to eat. Some of us was down there with him every day."

Raymond Riley

When Mrs. Riley was at the dark red frame house, "we carried his meals. Mother would pack a basket and we'd go down across the field and take it to him. He could cook, and he had a cookstove. If he wanted eggs or other stuff, he could cook. But Momma would fix him a lot of different stuff that he couldn't cook—bread and all like that. I stayed down there a lot with him. When he was over in the garden—if my mother was there or some of the kids, we'd see a boat coming and we'd just call him and he'd come on up and lock him through."

As Mr. Riley remembers it, the frequency of arrival of boats at the lock was variable. Occasionally boats would bunch up. "Now, if they'd have a break on the canal, all them boats [that had been held up] would be coming right after each other until he locked them all and finally got them through."

Remembering that this father kept the lock set for a loaded boat, Mr. Riley says, "Every evening, after all the boats go by, the last light boat comes through, my father would just leave it set for a loaded boat. All a loaded boat had to do was come in.* He'd come in the aqueduct [over Seneca Creek] and then he'd come on down to the lock.

"My father could look way up there for half a mile and see a boat coming. If he seen a boat coming, he'd just change the lock, shut the gates, fill the lock up, open the gates. . . . He had a bridge, a little old footbridge, and he'd walk across and go

*Seneca Aqueduct and Riley's Lock were built as one structure.

231

up there and open *that* gate, then come back and go up there and open *this* gate. Now, lots of times they had a foot board on the top you could walk across. But after you opened one gate you couldn't get across; you couldn't step from one part to the other. You had to take and go all around and come across the bridge."

Mr. Riley's father had to stick close to home, as did every lock-tender, but he didn't have to be right at the lock every minute. "I was big enough. When he'd be over in the garden, I'd lock the boats through. Lots of locktenders had kids big enough to lock the boats when they was out doing something. Ain't no hard work. The biggest thing is if you could hoist the paddles. If you're just big enough to hoist the paddles . . . you had to pull them paddles around. The lower paddle was big, and that was right hard. You had a big arm,* and the paddles was way down, and that arm turned the paddle. That other paddle wasn't much trouble."

Mr. Riley doesn't remember that 24-hour-duty was overly burdensome to his father. "Some would tie up about eight or nine o'clock, then get up the next morning. He didn't have to worry about them till next morning. Lots of them tied up just below the lock. When boats did come [at night], of course he had to get up and lock them through.

"He got along good with them. They used to have an old horn they'd blow. He could hear that blowing, but very seldom they had to blow for him. They said the lock was always ready, all they had to do was go in. He was a good locktender.

"And Mr. Violette [his situation] was just the reverse. That dam was right down there and that water would run, and the roar of the water, he couldn't hear it [the shouting or bugling].** His shanty was sitting right up there on that hill from the lock, and he couldn't hear for that dam a-roaring.

"Many a time I'd come up there. . . . We'd get our load out in the day, go down to the office and get the waybill and come

*The "arm" was a windlass.
**Dam No. 2.

232

back, and get up there some time during the night. And I'd go ahead of the mules and go see if the lock was ready. I'd change the lock and go over there and holler to him. When I'd go to shut up the gates, I'd holler, 'Hey! Mr. Violette!' and he'd come out and help me."

As with boating, lockkeeping tended to run in families. "Old man Pennyfield himself, George P., he was there, and he died,

Lock tender Violette and pet, Rags. Ap (Alfred) Violette worked at the Seneca Stone Cutting Mill in earlier days and then at Lock 23, still called Violette's Lock. This was so close to Dam No. 1, which fed the canal from Seneca to Georgetown, that its noise made it difficult for him to hear bugles and shouts through horns from approaching boats. "His shanty was sitting right up there on that hill from the lock," recalls Raymond (Ray) Riley, born at Riley's Lock (24), "and he couldn't hear for that dam a-roaring."

and the boy took it over. Charlie Pennyfield. The Swains tended lock. Mrs. Sipes, her husband died and she would tend lock. She had a boy. [They] left; went down to Great Falls. Aleck, he tended the first lock at the Falls and she tended the next lock to that. [When] she moved to Great Falls, Jess Swain come. Then he died, then Bob Swain come; then *he* died, and Mrs. Swain and her boys are down there now. Jess Swain and Bob, they was two brothers. The boy down at Swain's Lock now, he's Bob's son."

Mr. Riley never felt that being a locktender's family made for any degree of loneliness. "There was always a big crowd around there, all the time. Mrs. Good lived right across the road from us. And another family lived right down below that a little ways. Oh, we had plenty of company. In them days, people knowed my father, all around Gaithersburg, Rockville—people come up here fishing and had cottages. I knowed *all* the judges down at Rockville—Bob and Ed Peter, two brothers; Judge Woodward; Nippy Prescott, he was a judge."

As a young boy, Mr. Riley had the usual rural recreations. Along with other boys, he swam, fished, had picnics, ice skated, played ball. "Down in the basement we had a big fireplace and [on the hearth] a big thing to turn around, an arm. The kids every Saturday would come down and we'd take a boat and go out in the river and get wood and bring it in and cut it up and put it [in the fireplace]. We'd have little picnics down there.

"If you wanted to put a pot on this arm, you could swing it into the fireplace. We used to take an old tea can—tea used to come in cans—cut the top out of it, put a piece of wire on it, and boil an egg in it. Just us kids. We'd have a big time down there. We'd cook fish—catch fish and cook 'em; and stuff you buy out of the store that would have to be cooked, like hot dogs. There used to be a big store by the lock, on the other side.*

"We did play a little ball once in a while, back there in Harry West's field. It was right down below the lock where the warehouses used to be. But kids was most interested in fishing, because you could catch plenty of them. Now, up there where the quarry was at, there was water there; and in the winter we'd all go up there and skate."

Because the boatmen and their families were just in the locks and right out again, Mr. Riley doesn't recall having any really close association with them. "I knew some of them," he recalls. "There were two colored men on the canal, Andrew Jenkins and another fellow. Jenkins and Williams, they were the onliest two colored people who were captains. They got 60 cents a ton for running the boats and delivering the coal. Lots of people

*Fred Allnutt's store.

ask me, 'Was there any colored people?' They were the onliest two. They had family [on the boats]. The man would steer, and his wife would steer, and their sons were big enough to drive the mules."

Mr. Riley never was a boatman in the full-fledged sense of living on a canal boat eight months of the year, but he did a certain amount of independent hauling within a small area. He began when he was 15.

Raymond Riley

"This boat was down at Georgetown, left down there that fall after the canal company drawed the water and they couldn't get it back." Ernie Darby and Will Tschiffely had grain warehouses a little bit down the river from Riley's Lock, and they needed this boat because "they had wheat to go away." Young Ray Riley went to Georgetown and made his maiden voyage bringing the boat back.

Between them, Mr. Darby and Mr. Tschiffely had a boatload of wheat to go to Wilkes and Rogers Mills in Georgetown. "But they couldn't get nobody. I had the boat loaded—4,000 bushels of wheat—for somebody else to carry back to Georgetown, but they couldn't get nobody. They come up and asked Poppa. They said, 'He could bring the boat up here; we don't see why he can't carry it back.' Poppa said, 'Well, now, I'm leaving it to you all. If anything happens, it's just your luck; you can't blame the boy for it.'

"I went on. We got down here to Angler's Inn, and a girl had drownded there at the Falls and they had brought her over and put her in the canal. We weren't supposed to go past a body; so we waited until next morning. Mr. Darby went down to Tom Reeves's wharf [in Washington] and found out we weren't there and thought something had happened. So he come looking for us. We told him what was the trouble.... Then we went on down and tied up and unloaded the boat. That was the first [delivery] trip I made.

"I knowed what to do. I'd been around the warehouses and I'd seen them load. And I could steer the boat. Wasn't no trouble to steer. I had two fellows on that could steer. I was only loaded down to about four feet; and where other boats went, I went along where they went. I felt all right. I knew pretty well what to do. I wasn't afraid. The old boat didn't leak much. Anything I've got to do, I don't get excited over it; I just go on and do it. But I was tickled to death to be a captain of a boat. They give me $35 a month, and after I made that trip I run it for two or three years. [That was] the old *Seneca;* belonged to Darby. She was built down to Muddy Branch, next to Pennyfield's Lock. Later Mr. Darby busted up and the Bryan Fertilizer Company, they bought it; and I was running it for a while, and then it got so bad we run it up this side of the bank and just let it sit. Somebody came along in the wintertime and burnt it up, set fire to it one day and burnt it up.

"Now, one time I went down to Alexandria and got a load of coal.* They had the boat on the dry dock. She sat so long on the dry dock she dried out. And when we got the coal put on and come up there...O-o-h!...Long as I pumped on it, I could keep that water down. Got up to Swain's Lock. Swain's got a flume there, where the water goes round; and when the water goes around and a boat strikes it, if you don't lay over so far, that water hits you and brings you over and you miss the lock.

"We had a time getting it in the lock. We just kind of sideswiped it. Will Nugent, he was a colored fellow, he was driving the mules and Will Vide was steering. I told him, 'Lay over close to the towpath; you're going to run on that bar.' Oh, he was going to bring it over. Instead of him swinging the boat over, he didn't do it. There was a big sand bar there and the boat run up on it and had a big hole in the back. And she just filled up, and I saw rats coming up.

"I said, 'She's sinking.' Because the rats stay down in the bottom of the boat. The water got deep down there and they had to come up—and we run them down the race plank. Then they jumped overboard and swum to the shore.[2]

"I knowed she was going down. Swain come up there with a boat and took us over to the towpath; and Nugent sat up on

*Mr. Riley bought this load of coal for families living between Alexandria and Seneca.

236

the cabin all night. She didn't go clear down, just down to the race plank. So we got on the mules and come on home.

"Went down there the next morning, and the canal company they come up and drawed the water down below this hole [in the boat] and they just pumped out and pumped out. We started up and come on and delivered the coal. That was the only time I ever sunk a boat. It was the onliest load of coal I ever hauled.

"I hauled straw, hay, corn, all stuff like that. Cross ties, cord wood, telephone poles, anything anybody wanted hauled. [I remember] going down to Washington at night to get a boat unloaded next day. Got the locktenders up going all along! [We'd shout] 'Hey, lock!' or 'Whoo-eee!' Some had a horn to blow, but we didn't.

"I liked being on the canal. I'd been around water all my life, and that was the reason I liked it. I stayed about two or three years with Darby. At the end of that time, Mr. Nicolson had No. 1 boat laying down at Georgetown and I went down and seen him and he said he'd sell it to me. In the spring I got two colored boys and we went down and got it. The canal company would sell you an old boat when they got done with it. I paid $100 for mine. The bow was bad, but that winter me and my father we worked and put half a new bow on it. Fixed it up.

"Used to be an old steamboat on the canal. One old steamboat named *Addie Wilson*. She used to boat lime from Antietam Mine above Harpers Ferry down to Rock Creek, big chimneys. Used to make some kind of stuff out of it, and the core of it they boated back up here to sell to farmers for five cents a bushel. To put on the land; it would make grass grow. They called it gas lime.

"The steamboat didn't bother the mules. Onliest thing, when it passed a [canal] boat he had to go on the outside, on account of the towline. The blade down in the water would have cut the towline. He always went on the outside.

"We had lots of floods, and the boats would have to shut down. Every time they had a flood it took a right smart while to fix the canal up. The way it is now, there are lots of places [needing repairs] but the government don't fix them up, just lets them

Raymond Riley

go. But just as soon as the water went down, Mr. Nicolson, he'd take them mules off them boats and they'd go there with scoops and haul dirt and fill that place right up. Fill it right up. We had lots of floods, but we didn't have no *big* floods here [until 1924]. From here to Georgetown we didn't have much floods. Now, way up the canal, places would give out and it would take a week or so to fix up. Then the boats would start again.

"I hauled wood for a while. Up there at Second Island[3]—the power company's got a golf ground up there now—a fellow named Rhodes owned a farm. He cut wood off and sold it and I carried it up to Harpers Ferry. I had to pole the canal boat up the river [to get the wood] and back. That was the onliest way we could get it. I'd take a pole and stick it down, pole the length of the boat, then stick it down [again]. Didn't have no towpath along the river. We had to go out Violette's Lock and out in the river. I used to go up there and get 31½ cords of wood. That's as much as I could put on and get out in the river with. The water wasn't deep enough [for more].

"I went to Harpers Ferry [with] a load and they were on strike. I laid up there a week. Just one man was unloading. There was an old man in a houseboat. He had gone up there that fall and they'd drawed the water and he couldn't get back. I told him to wait and we'd tow him down. We unloaded the boat and piled [the wood] on the bank and then we come on. [I told him I'd] tow him to the lock that night and I'd go on through and wait outside till he come through; then I'd hook to him and tow him again. Brought him on down here. His name was Arch. He lived on this little houseboat.

"Far as I went was Harpers Ferry. There's a little lime kiln up about Harpers Ferry. Used to go up there and boat lime down for some farmers. And haul wood up there to that pulp mill right across the bridge from Harpers Ferry where they used to make paper. They had an electric plant there too. Then the flood of '42 come along and carried that all away.

"I run it [No. 1] about two years. Trucks and things got started and put the boat business out. It got so it didn't pay me to boat wood way up to Harpers Ferry. So I sold [the boat] to the man I was hauling the wood for.

238

"Most of the boats on the canal were owned by the canal company." There were, however, a good many other boats plying the canal, owned by their operators. Mr. Riley was one of these operators. "Mr. Hatton Waters, he had a boat. He had an old scow at first, then he had the *Alice May* built. Old man Linthicum had a boat. Old man Billy Thrasher, he run a grain boat. Will Hempston, he run a boat one time. Years ago when I was just a little teeny kid, he had an old boat. He was the agent for Baker Lime Company in Virginia. Different ones had boats, boats that belonged to them.

Raymond Riley

"The last boat built in Cumberland was built for Mr. Hatton Waters down here at the river. He owned a store in Travilah and ran a boat too. The canal company built it and loaded it with coal and delivered down to Georgetown, and turned it over to him. It was the *Alice May,* named for his wife." Mr. Waters used the *Alice May* as a grain boat for maybe as long as three years, as best Mr. Riley remembers.

"When the canal closed, all the company's boats had gone up and docked and they drawed the water. They always drawed the water off above Seneca first." The *Alice May* was at Georgetown delivering grain or on the way back. "Mr. Nicolson held back as long as he could, and then he drawed this eight-mile level off at Harpers Ferry. That wound it up.[4] The *Alice May* had just enough water to get her through Violette's Lock. Pulled right outside the lock, just over the miter sill, and that's where she stayed. Stayed there about two years and then they tore her up."

IF HIS LITTLE SISTER'S drowning had anything to do with it, Mr. Riley doesn't say; but over the years he made so many rescues—25 he figures conservatively—that his activities almost assumed the proportions of a calling. More than once since he gave up boating the local fire department's truck has come by his house, blowing its horn as it approached, for him to join firemen on a rescue mission. He has picked people off logs in the river, out of trees in the river, and out of the river itself. "Some of them didn't even say, 'Thank you' or 'Kiss my foot' nor nothing else." That doesn't unduly ruffle Mr. Riley. "I got pleasure out of going and getting them."

One of his happiest rescues was clearly a lifesaving act. He wasn't boating at the time. He had just got out of the army. "I went downtown for something, and I had to wait half an hour for the streetcar; so I walked up to Tom Reeves's wharf. Got up there and I hear these kids a-hollering and I went to the bank and this little girl was in the canal. I jumped over and went down the steps and got on the edge of the towpath. She was out there, had this big heavy coat on and it was a long time sinking. She was laying on top of the water and the coat was spreading out. She was screaming. I got on the edge of the towpath—there was a wall—I don't know how I didn't go over; but I got my foot out somehow and she come to me. I reached down and caught her by the head and pulled her over to the bank. The other little girls, they helped me get her walking and we carried her up the steps and I turned her over to Mrs. Reeves and I got on the streetcar and come on home."

[1] Mr. Riley couldn't remember how they did this. According to Marlene Anne Bumgarner in the *Washington Post* in November, 1979, however, "Potatoes are a popular place to grow yeasts.

"My favorite way is to chop up three or four medium-sized potatoes (scrub the skins really well, you don't need to peel them) and cook until they fall apart. Drain and mash them up, adding enough potato water back to make three cups of mashed potatoes. Add ¼ cup of honey, stir it in well and cool until just warm to the touch. If they are too hot to touch they will kill the yeast seeds. Add 1 cup of starter saved out and stored (covered) in the refrigerator from the last time you made yeast, or 1 tablespoon of dried yeast dissolved in a cup of lukewarm water. Mix well and leave at room temperature, covered with a wet cloth, for at least eight hours. Take out your one cup of starter and use the rest of the yeast mixture to make a batch of four loaves of bread."

[2] [We had rats] "because we'd go down to Georgetown and they were just thick down there. At Tom Reeves's wharf was an old rotten wall and they lived in it. You could see them any time. They'd walk around in the daytime, and swim across the canal. They'd get on the grain boats. The coal boats now, they were different."

[3] First Island is one mile north of Riley's Lock, i.e., toward Cumberland. Second Island is one and a half miles north of Riley's Lock; it is one mile long. Third

Island, three miles long, is seven miles north of Riley's Lock. Fourth Island is at Edward's Ferry.

4 Longhand notation in a book owned by Raleigh Bender's daughter, now living in Sharpsburg and operating Bender's Tavern: "Raleigh Bender made the last trip down the canal on #1 in December 1923." Captain Bender's was the last round trip of a coal boat.

Raymond Riley

Interview, November 13, 1979.

Mrs. Helen Riley Bodmer
Seneca

Mrs. Helen Riley Bodmer

ALTHOUGH SHE WAS THE DAUGHTER of veteran locktender John C. Riley, Mrs. Helen Bodmer never lived in a lock house. The family moved after the death of little Katie, who had drowned in Seneca Creek at the age of three. Mrs. Riley was expecting a baby in the fall of that same year, "and she decided that she couldn't keep another child around the water. So she moved to the house up on the hill."

Never Mrs. Bodmer's home on a live-in basis, the lock house was part of the home scene and important in her young life because her father was there most of the year and his job was a night-and-day matter.

The old lock house "was simply a four-room house," she recalls. "The two basement rooms were never used; they were just dirt floor. The first floor was two nice-sized rooms—a kitchen and dining room combined and a living room—and the second floor was two nice-sized bedrooms. The flooring was very wide boards. My mother used to mop the floors, and she kept them real, real white.

"The cherry furnishings that my mother brought up to the house on the hill, that was her good wedding furniture. She didn't bring the wood stove, because my father had to cook [some of his meals] for himself. We went down to visit him two and three and four days a week. We never stayed at night, just stayed the day. My mother had a colored woman who watched after me, and she was free then to go to the lock and cook."

At the lock house "there were double beds in each room be-

242

cause my father rented the rooms out to campers. People would make arrangements to come up to fish for the day. My father would outfit a boat and have it ready for them. He would put minnows in the boat for them to fish with. Some would stay a day and some would stay as much as a week. If somebody wanted to stay overnight and didn't have a place, he let them stay in the lock house. [Some] would have their tents and their cabins up along the river, and of course you couldn't get to them without a boat. He had one couple that came for a month every summer.

Helen Riley Bodmer

"The [canal] boats didn't interest me. They were just something that came right on into the lock and were let down and went out; and as far as even noticing that they were coming in and going out, that wasn't of any interest to me. I used to feel awfully sorry for the little children that were strapped onto the cabin. Little children sitting up there with a harness on."

When Helen Riley went on her frequent visits to her father, she was more at the lock than in the lock house. "My father had a long bench out by the shanty in front of the locust tree where people would come and sit and watch the boats go by. It was a big wide board and it was usually filled with people. I sat on it lots of times and watched the boats go through. And listened to the people talk.

"Most of the time I'd just sit around with my father and talk, in between boating. My father's boats that he made and rented out to fishermen, they were in the creek. [I'd] get in a boat and row up the river. That was my playground. You just went out under the aqueduct if you were going out into the river. The aqueduct was right over the creek.

"If I had a book, I would sit in the bottom of the boat and read. Much of it was my schoolbooks. I'd do my studying that way. There were no motorboats, so you could just simply put the oars in the rowboat and let it drift down the river. When I'd get opposite the lock house, all I had to do was to get up and row myself right in. The only time you couldn't do that was when a wind storm would come up. Then you really got behind the oars!

243

"The boys would watch the lock while my father used to row up to the [general merchandise] store. And I'd go with him. Allnutt's store was right up on the crick, about halfway between our house on the hill and the lock house. It's still there. Mr. Poole runs it now." Her brother, Ray, remembers that "you could buy anything down there at Allnutt's, even calico."

"My father would row right up the crick and buy whatever was needed. He didn't have to go out in the river. The mill was right there, just across from the store on the crick bank. Tschiffely's. We bought our flour and corn meal from them."

Riley family group. Left to right, Frank Case (brother-in-law of lock tender John Riley, center); standing behind him, Mervin Riley, son of John and Roberta Ricketts Riley; Helen Riley, daughter; Mrs. Riley; Mrs. Lizzie (Elizabeth) Riley Case, sister of Mrs. Riley and wife of Frank Case.

"My mother did all the cooking for our family. We baked bread all the time. I can't *remember* when I was small ever having a bought piece of bread. On Saturdays she always baked pies and cakes—all kinds of pies, apple, pumpkin, according to the season. In fact she stayed in the kitchen all day on Saturdays. She was a great lemon pie maker. That was my favorite. Coconut and chocolate and lemon-topped cakes, any cake that you think about. Layer cakes; I don't remember loaf cakes of any kind. Of course pancakes was usually our morning breakfast, [with] butter and cane syrup. I remember a great deal of King syrup.

"The family had coffee at every meal. I don't remember that she ever bought any packaged coffee. Coffee beans were kept in a large can, and every day the coffee was ground fresh. Coffee was boiled then, but later on she used a percolator. I have her large drip coffee pot that she used in later years.

"My mother and I, whenever she had a spare moment, we'd sit on the front porch and watch the traffic go by." Her brother remembers that River Road was "no pike, just an old dirt road" and that only a few cars went by. "We had a swing on the porch and we'd sit and swing. And talk. In the evenings especially.

"We had a meat house out at the corner of the yard. Meat was put in there and my father used to salt it and smoke it. I remember his building a fire in the middle of this house, and the smoke would just come pouring out. [The fire] was built right down in the middle of the floor, in a hole—the meat house had a dirt floor—[and he] kept the doors closed and the windows closed. My mother used to buy roasts and put them in a brine. I guess you would call it corned beef. Beef was the only thing we didn't have, and the store sold that. We always had chickens, and my mother used to have a couple of hogs, and my father had a hog pen down at the river and he'd fatten hogs down there also.

"We had a big garden, a real large garden at our house up on the hill, and my father had a large garden down at his place. Every vegetable you can imagine. We had potatoes at both houses, radishes, lettuce, carrots, beets, broccoli. We even had cauliflower, and in the fall we had turnips.

Helen Riley Bodmer

245

"In the fall when we gathered those things, we dug a big hole out in the middle of the garden and put straw in it and then put turnips and cabbage and all the things in that. Just lay them on the straw, different things in different places, laid around in the straw. It was one big layer; you couldn't pile things on top of each other. There was a hill of dirt that came up over it, and there was a doorway made into [that], a door that had a covering down over it."

Mrs. Bodmer remembers her father as "a very tiny man" whose presence in the house up on the hill warmed and brightened every winter while the canal was closed. "My father came home in November and stayed until March. That was a real joy, to have him home all winter. My father just stayed at home and worked around the house. He had to go down to the lock every day to see that everything was all right and that the lock house was kept locked up. He walked down in the morning and came back. I don't know what other [chores] he had down there; you got up early and went to school, and you didn't know what your father did all day.

"We had a Victrola. I've still got the records, very thick, heavy records, one side blank. A new record would come out, and [my father would] get it and play it. He used to love to play—what is it?—'old gray bonnet with the blue ribbon on it.' We didn't go in and play the Victrola in the evenings. My father was the one who played it. He would come home in the fall, then the music would be played. He was a joy to be around, my father was. We hated for March to come, when he had to go back down to the canal."

246

Interview, October 13, 1979.

Mrs. Sam Liston
Williamsport

"I HATE THIS OLD DITCH!" Thus spoke Evelyn Pryor, 11 or 12 years old, during her first day on a canal boat. She was keeping house, together with her slightly older sister, Hazel, on Captain Harry Pryor's No. 69 and she didn't like it one bit.

Evelyn Pryor (Mrs. Sam) Liston

The Pryors had "seven girls and one boy. We were all put on very early. Just as soon as school was out, there was always two of us girls on together. My brother used to have his own boat when he got older, about 18 or 19. His name was Frank. He lived in Harrisburg.

"Momma used to stick us on there. [First] I'd go on with one of my older sisters. Then when I got old enough, the younger sister, Genevieve. I was the next to the youngest.

"The reason we was taken on, my daddy didn't like to cook or wash dishes or anything; and it was mostly to do the cooking and the dishes and keep the cabin clean. As we got older we could steer the boat in certain places when it wasn't loaded, while he would take care of the mules. He'd always manage to get to a level that didn't have so many bends in it. He would manage that way. My daddy never liked to use us. He always had a hand, a man."

Young Evelyn Pryor didn't really hate the "old ditch." She was wounded by homesickness and she was hitting out. "I was so *mad*. I got that way every time we come home and left [again]. The first day I wouldn't eat anything. My father was an easygoing man, and he was always good to us. He'd do everything to make it nice for us. At a lot of the locks they had stores, and he'd always buy us candy. And he said, 'Now, you know you don't get all this stuff. . . . Your mother don't buy you all this.'

"Of course she *didn't*. She had a big family. But he'd take every penny he'd have and buy us kids candy and stuff." It didn't work too well during the brief but intense homesick period. "I used to say, 'Pop, if you just let me off, I'll walk back to Williamsport.' He'd say, 'Aw, now, you know I couldn't let you do that.' And he'd say, 'I wouldn't take you if I didn't have to.' The first day I was always [miserable], but then the next day I'd be all right. The [only] reason I didn't like it was that I got homesick. And my daddy used to say, 'OH! This is the best life!' He said it was a good life, a healthy life. And he boated, it was either 30 or 35 years. I was small then; I didn't get homesick the last year the canal run."

After she made her beginning, Mrs. Liston went with her father every boating season "until I got old enough—I think I quit in my third year of high school. And then I went to work.

"My daddy couldn't swim a stroke. But when we'd get down there at Georgetown—that's deep water down there—my father used to tell [our hand], 'Now, I want you to teach every one of these girls how to swim.' Tommy Jenkins was the hand's name, and he could swim good. So Tommy would put a towline around our waist and put us out on the deep side. He'd say, 'Don't be afraid of the water, because I've got you hooked good. And you swim.' He'd tell us how to do the strokes, and we'd swim. He'd say, 'Now, when you get tired, just say so and I'll lift you up.' And that's the way we learned to swim.

"My daddy fell overboard one time. That was in the fall of the year when I wasn't with him. He just stumbled, I guess, on the race plank. I can't remember how he got out. I guess the man on there helped him or he just got out himself. But he boated all them years on that canal and he couldn't swim a stroke, and he only fell overboard one time. I thought that was remarkable."

Apparently there was a good deal of falling overboard. "Because sometimes you had to be running out, to do things real quick, and the race plank wasn't very wide. You could fall over your own feet.

"He just loved that old canal. He really loved it. He always said, 'It's a good healthy life and I don't see why you don't like it.' My sisters never said they *dis*liked it. They never said nothing. They knowed there wasn't much use."

Mrs. Liston remembers her father's buying provisions that would keep without ice, which no canal boat had. "We used to buy those big long sticks of like-leather bologna. And these hams would come cured and wrapped up in heavy paper, and we'd hang them up and they'd keep." They did have one cupboard-like place where other things would keep for a short time. "Under the stern there was a small door, and it would stay cool underneath the stern of the boat.

Evelyn Pryor Liston

"Now, there was not any store from the time you left Williamsport until you got up to the Four Locks. One of the big canal families—I can't think of the name—tended the lock and kept the store. They had everything. But what we were interested in getting was candy. It was old hard candy, which we liked. Penny candy. Like those big old sticks of licorice. And then they had what they called Jaw Breakers; you got two of them for a penny. Oh, we were smart that way; [we'd buy] whatever you got the most of for a penny. I remember the long sticks of licorice because we used to love that. We used to get feed for the mules there too.

"There was one place that my daddy wouldn't let us stay on the boat. We had to walk. It was only . . . I don't know, half a mile or three quarters of a mile. Because way back, before I could remember . . . there was an overhead bridge where the mules had to walk across to the right-hand side at the upper end of the guard lock. Dam 5. A boat went over that dam. I think the wife drownded.*

"It was the same at Charles Mill and Big Slack Water. Them's the only two places that the boats ever went out into the river. They were both dangerous places and he would never let us

*Not the wife. A daughter drowned and Captain Keim was fatally injured.

steer the boat, even light, in either one of them places. He wouldn't let us stay *on* the boat. [When] he went back into the canal there was another lock and we'd get back on the boat there.

"I was always scared to death of the tunnel near Cumberland, across from Paw Paw. It was cut through the mountain, and water would be dripping down and it was just creepy. It was over a mile long and it was spooky in there. Of course I wasn't very old."

Young Evelyn's life on the boat was not without regulation childhood pleasures. She had a special friend, Clara Hebb; the family dog, Bounce, was on the boat; and they had friendly "neighbors" on other boats.

"Clara's father had a boat, and we always played together. Ben, I believe her father's name was; there's lots of Hebbs in Sharpsburg. There were three girls of them and we always, when we stopped together [at night], we'd always get together and play and make swings. Clara had the prettiest curliest hair. Dark brown. Her father had three girls, but he never had a hand.

"The lady that had owned Bounce, she passed away. Her husband gave him to my daddy, and said he knowed he'd have a good home. He was a collie, I think. He wasn't too big. He had long hair, brown with a little white. Not dark brown. Reddish brown."

Evelyn Pryor, 11 or 12 years old, with the family dog, Bounce. Sometimes, but only on a short level, Bounce would keep Evelyn company on the towpath.

Sometimes Bounce would keep Evelyn or Hazel or Genevieve company on the towpath. "Not too far. Like if it was a two-mile level or something like that, we'd take him." Mrs. Liston felt that being on the boat wasn't dangerous for the dog. "He got off at locks [not by the long fall board]. If we thought it was any place dangerous, we'd take him down to the cabin. He lived to be right old. When we were tiny, my father worked over here at W.D. Byron's during the winter months when the boat wasn't running. When that whistle would blow—they worked till four o'clock—Bounce would come up and walk every evening home with my father. That's how close he was.

"After my daddy died we never could get Bounce any farther than the kitchen; he'd never go in any part of the house but

250

the kitchen. And very seldom could we get him in the *kitchen*. When it got cold we'd put him in the wash house. My mother had a nice quilt for him and she said it was warm enough in there. We missed him so, but Bounce *never* came inside the house again after my daddy died."

There were sometimes traveling companions. "We knew Mr. Shupp very well, as we always run together close. His boat was the 89. Mrs. Shupp used to bake bread and she gave us a loaf or so every time she baked.

"Everybody heated with coal back in them days. You'd have a heating stove in one room and a range, a cooking stove, in your kitchen. What we cooked with [on the boat] was an oil stove, a Perfection. They were the best made. That's what we cooked on in hot weather. Everybody had them around town too."

Other facilities weren't as convenient as the Perfection oil stove. Boating people not only slept on straw but used chamber pots. But Mrs. Liston remembers conditions as none too hard to put up with. "Now, there's people that won't believe it, how people lived on the canal, what you had to deal with. The bunk— you know what it was filled with? Straw. A straw tick. *Every* year my mother would wash them and they'd be filled with fresh straw. A straw tick was right high, maybe a foot and a half, but then when you'd sleep on them a while. . . But! I slept just as good on that as I do now on a Posturepedic. I probably wouldn't now, but then it wasn't bad.

"My sister still has the little drop leaf table that my father used on the boat—in the kitchen, between two outer windows. Then there was a cupboard across this corner, and a chair. We had linoleum on the floor, and the kitchen was painted nice inside."

Garbage went into the canal, as did the contents of the chamber pots. "That's about the only thing you *could* do with it. Even the manure from the stable was throwed into the canal. That's the reason you couldn't use that [water] to cook with.

"For washing up the floor we had a small bucket with a rope on it, and we'd just dip water. And then we'd just throw it down in the canal. At locks they had springs; and for drinking or

Clara Hebb and Bounce. Clara and Evelyn Pryor were best friends, and their fathers' boats often "ran together."

washing dishes and cooking, we never used nothing but the spring water. We'd always have two buckets. We just washed the floor with a cloth. I got down on the floor to wash it and I still do; I don't like that mopping business; I've got to get down on my knees. I wash my floor like we washed it back there. We used to use this Octagon soap most all the time. We would bring the coupons home to my mother. She'd get all kinds of different things, pans and things like that. We didn't do laundry on the boat. We had clothes enough that when we'd come home my mother would always have clean clothes for us.

"My dad used to take newspaper and shine the glass on the bow light. The bow lamp made a good light, because it had a great big reflector in back of it; but my daddy wasn't much for going after night. Once in a while he did, but not very often. There were lots of them that would try to make it [in a hurry], and kill the mules; but my daddy took care of his mules.

"My daddy had goodlooking mules. My gosh, that one big fine mule, that Belle, she was just three or four years old. My daddy treated his mules just like he treated human beings. Not because he was my father—anybody could tell you that knowed him on the canal—he had the healthiest looking mules of any boatsman on the canal. This lead mule, Kate, she was a hard worker; she'd pull. But this big enormous Belle, she was just a young mule but she'd get lazy. They had a big roller with a hook on it to the towline, and they called that a butt roller. My daddy used to say when we were driving, 'Belle's a-riding that butt roller. Give her a little touch there.' He just merely wanted us to touch them. 'Give her a little touch. Wake her up.' So that's what we'd do, but oh! we wasn't allowed to *hit* the mules. *Uh-uh.*

"We'd just say 'Giddy-up.' I can't speak for all of them, but for ours, our lead mules, you didn't have to say anything. But some of those drivers would take that whip, and, oh —. Pop said they worked them to death too. He said, 'It's not right.' And they were nothing but skin and bone. They were thin because they were worked too hard, worked to death. Too many hours. Lot of them used to go half the night. My daddy always had big mules and he would change them often. *He* wouldn't drive them 25 or 30 miles without changing them. He put them in the stable and give them a rest."

Mrs. Liston doesn't remember knowing of boatmen owning their mules. "There was a man by the name of Higgins. Now, he owned my daddy's mules. He had a big farm you could see from the canal, not many miles this side of Cumberland. In the fall of the year, when it got too cold for the boats to run, my daddy and the man that worked for him always rode the mules up [to the Higgins farm] and they'd ride the train back—when the Western Maryland train ran from Cumberland to Williamsport."

Evelyn Pryor Liston

She remembers that "Mr. Higgins was good to animals too" and that "their" mules looked *fine,* always in good shape [in the spring after a winter with Higgins]. The canal company was paying him, I guess, so-much for them, but they belonged to him."

The mules and their drivers were out regardless of the weather, and Mrs. Liston remembers caring for mules brought in soaking wet with rain. "We had to wait until they dried off. Their hair was short and it wasn't no time drying. You had a brush with a handle; you put your hand through the handle and brushed them. Now, in real hot weather, we had to wait too. My daddy would say, 'Now, don't you girls go in there while them mules are hot.' Because it wouldn't have been good. It's just like anyone else—putting cold water on them when they was hot wouldn't be good for them. He'd say, 'Wait until they cool off.' We used to have big sponges, and oh, we'd make over them! We'd get a bucket of water and wet the sponges and rub them down. Oh, they loved that.

"We got up early in the morning, o-o-o-h, my gracious, yes, about 4:30. We didn't eat for a while. Sometimes it would be hardly daylight. We got up and got the mules hitched and we started. When the boat was loaded, that was *slow going.* You see, you had 118 tons of coal in that hold, and two mules pulling it. Sometimes they would put the four mules out [to get the boat started]—just every so often.

"For breakfast, we'd [have] meat, and of course we had eggs.

Slippery Pot Pie

Boil beef or chicken until done, then take out of broth and let broth cool.

Dough for pot pie
1½ or 2 cups of flour
A little salt (I guess at it)
Crisco the size of a walnut

Work Crisco through flour with fork, like making pie crust. Gradually add broth, mixing with a fork until the dough starts to form a ball. If the broth doesn't make it wet enough, add a little cold water; but do not make dough too wet.

Divide dough into three sections. Roll out very thin on floured board, and cut into squares. Place the squares of dough on plates; they won't stick together. Have broth boiling hard before adding squares of dough. Repeat (layering) until all dough is added. When adding a layer of squares, use a large fork to make sure the first layer is wet.

If you want to add some potatoes, have them ready before making dough. Cut in very large pieces. If you don't they will cook up before the dough is done. It takes about twenty minutes. Add all of the potatoes at one time, making sure the broth is boiling again before adding dough. Serve in soup dishes, because there's a lot of liquid.

Mrs. Evelyn Liston's recipe for Slippery Pot Pie.

Eggs would keep good underneath the stern. And cereal. I think it was oatmeal we used to have. For lunch we'd have what we had for breakfast, big sticks of bologna and stuff like that. I always liked the slippery pot pie that my mother used to make. I said, 'Tommy, I think I'm going to try to make slippery pot pie.' A lot of people make it with chicken. Or ham. You can make it with ham. You had to use whatever you had. Well, I mixed this flour and stuff and I had the broth ready and I knowed you had to have it boiling to put the dough in. Oh, my land, I *did* all that. But what I hadn't done, I hadn't put shortening. When you're making the dough up, you take a little lard—now I use a little bit of Crisco—but before you mixed it up with the water you've got to take a fork and put all that through the flour. It's almost like making pie crust. But I hadn't put any shortening. When I put the dough in the pot it all went into a big ball. I just dumped it right over in the canal.

"Slippery pot pie is still a main dish around Williamsport. It's a favorite dish in all the restaurants; they have special days for

254

it. I made some the other week; I like the dough.

"When we'd leave [home] and go up to Hancock—the canal runs right along Hancock—my daddy used to go the meat market. He'd walk up there and he'd get a piece of beef to fry. Steak. He always liked cooked meals. Then he'd always get us some bananas, because we were crazy about bananas. Oh, he was a good old daddy, so easygoing. He was the best old soul that ever was.

"Now, my mother was German descent and she was just *fiery*. I mean she was very strict with all of us girls. When she told us to do anything, we *did* it. Right there and then. It was no 'I will later on.' It was do it right now. I used to get so mad, but after I got older I appreciated that."

In Mrs. Liston's early youth, almost childhood, gripped by first-day homesickness on every trip on the boat, it rather rankled that her mother, Mary Ensminger Pryor, was at home. "She never went on the boat much. I don't know, but I don't think she liked the boat too well. I used to say, '*You* never go on the boat!' And she'd say, 'Well, now, that's all right. I've got stuff to do here at home.' She always had a big garden, and she was always canning."

Mrs. Liston recalls that she had been very curious about the paymaster, partly because of the rather grand boat that carried him up and down the canal. Undoubtedly she heard his name mentioned frequently too. "'I want to see this Mr. Nicolson,' I said. Curiosity, you know. My daddy said, 'All right. You get yourself ready. You can go.'" So she had the chance to go with her father to pick up his pay and she could get a look at the almost legendary Mr. Nicolson. "I imagine maybe he was 35 or 40, something like that. He was nice looking—big tall thin man. Very nice man. But as far as seeing inside the paymaster's boat, no canal man I don't think ever got to see in it. All you could see was when he passed you.

"The only way I could describe the payboat is—it was something like a yacht, but it wasn't that big. He had a chef. He had to have a chef; he had no other way; he went from one end

Evelyn Pryor Liston

255

of the canal to the other. A lot of them places, I don't know how the people ever got their mail. Mr. Nicolson would come and pay the locktenders and the scow bosses.

"The scow had a little cabin on it, and then the rest of it was just a flat barge. They fixed the towpath or anything like that. Harry Kreps [who lives across the street in Williamsport now] was a foreman on a scow. They would take in so-many miles of the canal, each scow. Each had so-many miles of territory to take care of, to repair.

"The boatmen, of course, when they got their pay, they had to go up to Mr. Nicolson's office.* After our dads come back with the pay, they'd always give us kids so-much money; so we'd just go up on M Street to the Candy Kitchen. We was all crazy about these banana splits. And then, when we had any money left, we'd go in the dime stores and spend the rest. Oh, we spent it *all*. I got this little dining set. It was a little round table, dinky little thing, with two little chairs. It was made of wood. It was real small and the legs looked like toothpicks, but I thought it was so cute. My daddy said, 'That thing! You just had to spend your money!'

"Then one time we went up to the shoe store. It was when my older sister was on. We saw this pair of shoes in the window. We didn't have any idea of what they would cost, but we was thinking about buying them for my younger sister. They were high, over the ankle, and they buttoned up the side. They were patent leather down below, and leather. We was going to give up the banana splits to get these shoes for Genevieve.

"We didn't have money enough. I believe they were $4.00 or something like that, and we said, 'Oh, my land!' Hazel said, 'My gracious, isn't that too much for those shoes?' My father gave us the devil. He said, 'Now, you *know* you kids didn't have money enough to buy a pair of shoes. What did you go in there for?' We said, 'We didn't think they'd cost that much money, and we just thought they'd be pretty for Genevieve.' We *might* of [had enough money] if we'd put it all together. But we never did get them.

*The Canal Towage Company building still stands on Wisconsin Avenue, adjacent to the canal.

"That used to be what we looked forward to—going up there on M Street, looking in all them windows. Most of them was old secondhanded stores, but there were some clothing stores. There were furniture stores, but so many of the secondhanded stores carried furniture. There were shoe stores. Oh, we really were tempted to buy those shoes. They *were* pretty. They took our eye. We thought sure we'd get them for Genevieve.

"We went to movies in Georgetown. We had to go to the matinees. My daddy always said, 'Don't wait till it gets dark.' Coming down from that bridge—I think it was the Key Bridge*— there were steps that came down underneath there. Even at that time, which there wasn't so much stuff going on like it is now, he never wanted us away at dark. He was always particular that way.

Evelyn Pryor Liston

"We never had musical instruments. We might sing school songs. One of them was 'Juanita,' and we used to sing 'Maryland, My Maryland.' We had song books in school. I remember that I even had that 'Juanita' when I got older and took piano lessons."

Mrs. Liston's last season on the canal was in the nature of a return. It came after she had given up boating for high school and then a job. "The 69 was the boat he had for years when we were kids. It went bad—hole in the bottom—and my father sure hated to give it up because he had it so long. But he had no other choice. The canal company gave him the No. 3." Young Evelyn went that last time, on the No. 3, because her father needed help. "His hand took spells. When my daddy would be coming down from Cumberland and stay overnight at home in Williamsport, lots of times my daddy would go down to start in the morning and [the hand would] be gone. He'd just take off. He wouldn't tell my daddy anything. Dad took us that last time because he couldn't get nobody. That's how I happened to be on the boat in 1923, the last year the canal run."

*This would have been the Potomac Aqueduct, generally spoken of as "the aqueduct-bridge." The Key Bridge, completed in 1933, replaced it.

Interview, September 16, 1979.

Benjamin Garrish
Williamsport

"I DIDN'T LIKE SCHOOL," recalls Benjamin Garrish. "Daddy said, 'You'll have to go on the canal, then. The whole year.'"

Before that, Mr. Garrish had been on the canal only when school was out. Then "about 1917 or '18 I quit [school]. I only went to the eighth grade. I boated about nine seasons."

Beginning when he was about 15, Mr. Garrish was a hand. "I worked for John Bowers, George Bowers, Foster Bowers, Den Shupp, and I went on one trip with the Lizers. A trip was about 17 days. I rode mules, put harness on them, and steered. I was paid by the trip. The captain paid me. Two dollars and a half. Of course, you got your feed, three meals a day. You made about two trips a month. We didn't run night and day, just from say, about 4 or 4:30 in the morning till 10, 10:30 at night [when] we'd get to a tying up place."

Those nine seasons on the canal left Mr. Garrish with both good and bad memories. In general, the bad outweigh the good. What he says he thinks of first and most is "seeing people . . . pulling in drownded people along the canal.

"One time here at four-mile-level brick house, a little girl died with scarlet fever. They carried her out—they just had overhalls on, they never dressed for the funeral—and put her in a spring wagon. Didn't have no casket, just a rough box. I helped to load her on the wagon. Their family lived back over the mountains. They lived in a tenant house. They worked for this farmer."

He remembers "a lot of breaks, a lot of drownings. Lots of

times it wasn't accidents, but you couldn't prove it. The oldtimers, they'd get these kids out of Washington, colored boys, and they'd take them for a month, and that's the last of them. You wouldn't see any more of them. That's the way it was. It was [dreadful], but it happened.

"A light boat's way up high, and that's where you get your worst falls. A loaded boat—with 100 or 115 ton of coal on—was down only about four foot above the water. You'd see women fall overboard, but mostly they'd try to stop and get them out. They'd get their family out, and they'd help to get the other ones; but, you know, a colored person in them days—.

"The worst tragedy I saw on the canal was down in the outlet lock going out in the bay at Washington. This man was drunk; I forget what his name was. He fell down between a loaded boat and the lock, and this boat killed him right there. Crushed him right there in the lock. I don't know what boat he was off. But there was three of us, three boats. I think I was boating for Mr. Jimmy Null that time. I think this guy was from Shepherdstown."

As Mr. Garrish remembers it, many accidents occurred because people had been "drinking and couldn't swim." He recalls a fair amount of drinking among boatmen. "Up in Cumberland we used to go over to Shantytown."

Shantytown was a section of Cumberland, a loading basin where coal was poured through chutes into holds of boats. One boatman remembers Wineow Street as a place of "old stores, half stories with shed roofs," and he remembers Bill Westbrook's tavern, Bill Colby's tavern, Mike Clark's saloon, and a saloon run by a woman whose name he can't recall. It was an area of what used to be called rough trade. The red light district was there, and saloons thick as hops; and anybody spoiling for a fight could simply go to Shantytown and be obliged without much shilly-shally.

Mr. Garrish remembers the Shantytown vividly for the fighting. "We'd go fighting all the time. You had to be pretty rough to be on the canal." He himself was in fights, "oh, many a time. We'd fight the colored boys. We didn't like them. It wasn't like it is now. In them days."

There was no need for provocation. Some boatmen fought blacks simply because they were blacks. "And they [the boatmen] fought amongst themselves. I just couldn't picture out [the cause] except that when you drink you're just two different people. Yes, you are.

"It was a rough place. Every time you'd go over there it was always a fight. Go over for meat, bacon, or coal oil. You had a bow lamp, and you had to use coal oil. I had a lantern, and course I had to use coal oil too. We didn't know what flashlights was in them days. Oh, yes, Shantytown was a rough place. And just think, I married a girl from up there!

"Every time you'd go over there, they'd say, 'Here comes a mule skinner. You can tell it; you can smell him.' Or they'd say, 'He's lousy.' And we *did* get lousy sometimes. But that started it. These were the people over there. The boatsmen went there and these town folks they'd make fun of them for the way they smelled, and the fight was on. Then we'd go over and get stuff at Jones's store, and, by God, there'd be a fight going on outside there too. And we'd get in it. Liked to fight, I guess. Made no difference [who you hit]. You got hit, you hit somebody."

260

The fighting seems to trouble Mr. Garrish as he looks back on it, but at the time he didn't mind. "I fought with the rest of them. Some of the fights were pretty bad.

"Sometimes you did [get enough rest], sometimes you didn't. You'd tie up at 10 o'clock or 10:30 at night, and if you didn't go to sleep right away. . . . Everybody's got nerves, and in them days you'd see something in the daytime. . . . If anything happened along the canal, say you'd seen somebody fall overboard and they was missing, why, you just couldn't go [to sleep]. It was preying on your mind.

"If you *knowed* a body was in the canal, somebody in that canal, drownded, you had to stop; you couldn't run over them. If somebody said somebody was drownded, you had to stop your mules and help find them. I've done that many a time—went and got clothes out of the middle cabin where I stayed, and put them on and dived down, eyes wide open, seeing them on the bottom and helping to bring them up. But you wasn't allowed to take them out of the water till the law got there. There was a fine. You had to leave the feet in the water. Some part of the body. I don't know why.

"Down at Georgetown level, a little boy and a girl—I imagine they was about 14 or 15 years old. There used to be a place down there below Swain's Lock, close to Seneca. Jess Swain used to rent canoes. This girl and boy, their canoe upset. We found the canoe and their pillows and the canoe paddles. We was the first boat, and Hebb's was the boat behind us. Course we had to tie up, and Hebb tied up behind us. I was younger and a right good swimmer; so Sam Apple's boy, Tom Apple, him and I dove down and got them. Both of them had drownded. We got them out. We had them laying on the towpath, and this cop come up on a horse. And, my Lord, I had to give my life's history.

"We found a straw hat. In them days the girls wore great big straw hats. There was a little straw basket. I don't know if it was a pocketbook or a basket; it was floating. Them's the kind of things that—I saw that little girl and that little boy for weeks.

"Then we used to haul fishing tackle down for people. And

Benjamin Garrish

261

we'd haul Boy Scouts. When a loaded boat come in to a lock, you was going down and maybe you'd get a bunch down here at Weverton and take them clear down to Seneca or maybe Georgetown level."

These visits could have broken the monotony for Mr. Garrish except that he didn't find the canal life monotonous, or, if so, not unpleasantly so. Reversing himself, as is his unalienable right, he says, "I enjoyed it. Same thing day in and day out, but I enjoyed it. I don't know why. Walking along, throwing stones in the canal, hearing the birds sing, . . . wildflowers . . . and deer up at the tunnel level."

He never felt lonely out on the towpath driving mules "because everything, I thought, was beautiful, everything around you, and you was out there. It was quiet and you was your own boss. Soon as you got on the boat, why, the captain took over. But you was boss as long as you was driving."

Going barefoot on the towpath was pretty rough on the feet, but Mr. Garrish felt that they all "got used to it, walking so much. But then when you'd get in port, like Cumberland or home or Washington, you put a pair of shoes on and your feet were swolled and you had one heck of a time. [Sometimes] you couldn't *get* your shoes on."

Worse, there was "what they called the cow itch. They called it [that]; I don't know why. It used to get so tender between your little toe and the one next to it; and we used to put corn starch in there, and iodine. We didn't have Mercurochrome then; we had iodine. We used to take a little bit of that stuff they used for the mules, that black stuff—WHEW!—they used for the sores. It healed, but HOO! Oh, man!"

Being outdoors was always a pleasure for Mr. Garrish. "Oh, Lord, yes." But his fondness for the towpath with its birdsong and its greenery was a daytime thing. "Soon as the sun would go down and it would get dark, why, it was different. It was lonely. I was half afraid on the towpath at night. All you could hear was the rustle of the harness and the mules, and you'd see that little bow lamp back 100 feet—the towline was 100 feet long. You were scared at night. Then it was another world."

Thinking back to the people he crewed with, Mr. Garrish had a decided preference in employers. "Christians. A Christian like Mrs. Shupp and Mr. Shupp. They were really church-going people. [On the boat] they read the Bible every morning. And they had prayers just the same as people nowadays go to church. Real Christians. Prayers every morning. Prayers going to bed. Grace.

"*Some* places you'd go, they'd just sit down and eat. Reach over or something, you'd get batted with a fork or a knife. Some of them was rough, rougher than others. You could tell if they liked you and you could tell if they disliked you. And some of them had a bad disposition. What I'd call a good disposition: not cussing you all the time. And all the mules had names, like George, Frank, Jerry, Fred, and Grace; but some of them wasn't

Swinging along the towpath below Lock 44 at Williamsport is 17-year-old Bennie Garrish. Mules pulling Captain James Null's boat No. 52 toward Cumberland are George and Frank, unless they're Jerry and Red. In background is Captain Henry Preston's No. 8; driver, John Williams. This picture appeared on post cards for years.

called that—they was called 'you son-of-a-hmm.' [Mr. Garrish can't bring himself to say the word.]

"Some boatsmen on the canal didn't think no more of a man than they did a mule, and they didn't think more of a mule than they did a man. Some of them old boatsmen, I mean them old ones—real tough. You'd be on the race plank, walking—you'd had to jump up on the hatches—and some would push you overboard just to see if you could swim. I got pushed over many a time. Older men, oldtimers, they tested you out."

Perhaps to ease the spookiness of the towpath at night or the contacts with crude and overbearing boatmen, Mr. Garrish made a friend of his little mouth organ. "For 15 or 20 cents. That's what I learned on. A Hohner. I made more mistakes than

When it became clear that the canal would not open in the spring of 1924, Mr. Garrish drew up the following list. It gives, as he remembered them, the names of the 45 captains and the numbers of their boats for the last boating season the canal knew.

Last on the Canal

Boat	Captain	Boat	Captain
1	Raleigh Bender	39	Pat Boyer
2	Weston Lizer	42	Charley Delaney
3	Harry Pryor	43	Tom McKelvey
4	Gus Hebb	45	Emmert Martin
8	Henry Preston	47	Lewis Snider
10	George Swangle	48	Newt Boyer
12	George Knight	49	George Byers
14	Bert Swain	50	Mack Knight
15	Clyde Stride	51	Owen Stickell
16	Foster Byers	52	James Null
18	Charley Byers	54	Frank Null
19	Will Colbert	55	Charley Huyett
20	Dick Haines	56	Orville Delaney
23	Rannie Mayhew	57	Albert Davis
24	Ben Hebb	59	Charley Pearl
25	Ed Rockwell	60	John Crampton
26	Ide Crampton	66	Lloyd Martin
28	Charley Eaton	69	Will Penner
31	Frank Zimmerman	70	Ed Renner
33	Hennin Twigg	74	Ruben Castle
35	Sam Atwell	78	Charley Brown
36	Jim McKelvey	89	Denton M. Shupp
		97	Robert Wright

enough, but I tried to master it. I think I played right good. [I still play] now and then. Mostly hymns now. I like to play hymns. My favorite is 'How Great Thou Art.' My mother loved that, and I will as long as I live. That's one of the oldest, I think, and the most beautiful hymns that ever was written."

Even with his mixed emotions about canal life—the haunting memories of many deaths, the hurt and resentment roused in him by the brutal treatment he saw inflicted on mules, the occasional feeling that he disliked canal work only less than going to school, the way he relished walking along in the sunlight with the mules—Mr. Garrish believes that most boatmen look back with fondness to their days on the canal. "I do [believe] they really enjoyed it. It was friendly. It was their living. It was home."

Benjamin Garrish

The Eleven Aqueducts of the C&O Canal*

Stream Crossed by Aqueduct	Length of Aqueduct	No. of Arches	Size of Arches	Materials	Construction
Seneca Creek	113'	3	33' each	Sandstone	Cut stone
Monocacy River	433'	7	54' each	Quartzite	Cut stone
Catoctin Creek	92'	3	20', 40', 20'	Mostly granite	Ranged rubble work below tops of piers. Above piers, beds and joints are cut and face left rough.
Antietam Creek	103'	3	28', 40', 28'	Limestone	
Conococheague Creek	196'	3	60' each	Limestone	Arches, skewbacks, ends of piers and abutments, water table and coping are cut; rest of face lines are hammerdressed and ranged.
Licking Creek	90'	1	90'	Limestone	Arches, skewbacks, water table, coping and inside of parapet are cut; rest of masonry is rubble work.
Big Tonoloway Creek	66'	1	66'	Limestone	
Sideling Hill Creek	66'	1	66'	Sandstone, Limestone	
Fifteen Mile Creek	50'	1	50'	A very hard sandstone	
Town Creek	60'	1	60'	Limestone	
Evitts Creek	70'	1	70'	Limestone	

*From "Report on the Present State of the Chesapeake & Ohio Canal. Estimated Cost of Completion to Cumberland." William H. Swift and Nathan Hale. Boston, 1846.

Glossary

Abutment: End support on which a bridge or aqueduct rests. Supports in intermediate positions are piers. Usually abutments and piers are masses of masonry going down to firm ground.

Aqueduct: Trough-like structure, usually of stone, as on the C&O, and often of striking beauty. The C&O's aqueducts were conduits that carried the canal over streams too large for culverts to deal with. The word comes from the Latin for "leading water."

Berm: Bank of the canal, opposite from towpath.

Culvert: Barrel-shaped structure that carried a stream under the canal.

Dam: Wall-like structure that impounded water by barricading the river and thus raising its level. Dams were placed where the canal level was lower than that of the river and water could be diverted by gravity.

Drop gate: A part of some lift locks. Located at the upper end of such a lock it dropped down to allow a boat to enter or leave the lock.

Fall board: A gangplank three to four feet wide. Over it, mules and people passed between boat and land. A long fall board, used on levels, would have one end placed on the boat and the other on the towpath. A short fall board, used at locks, would have one end on the boat and the other on the lock wall.

Feeder lock: Received water diverted from the river by a dam, and fed it into the canal to maintain the proper water level. Example: At Violette's Lock (a lift lock) there was also a feeder lock that conducted water, provided by Dam No. 2, into the canal to feed the portion of the waterway between Dam No. 2 and Lock 5.

Flume: A small channel, a component in the system that regulated the water level in the canal. Usually on the berm side of the lock, this offshoot of the canal proper bypassed water around the lock and then connected again with the canal at a lower level, thus feeding water from the level above the lock into the level below it. Each locktender was responsible for the level below his lock; a mark on the lock wall showed the height the water should reach.

Guard lock: This lock presented an obstacle to the river's flooding on the canal. Sometimes a guard lock's upper gates were twice as high as the lower. In combination with a dam, such a lock became a feeder lock.

Level: Flat stretch of the canal between locks.

Level walker: Inspector of an assigned length of the canal who scrutinized the banks for leaks. He made a round trip of 20 to 24 miles daily.

Lift lock: Moved boats from one level of the canal to the next. Water in a lift lock was raised to lift boats to a higher level of the canal, or lowered to pass boats to a lower level. An ascending boat entered the lock through the bottom or downstream gate, and this gate was then closed. Paddles in the lower parts of the upper gate were opened, allowing water in. When the lock's water level was raised to that of the higher reach of the canal, the top of the upstream gate was opened to allow the boat to pass out of the lock. In descending, the procedure was reversed, the water being drained off until the level in the lock corresponded with the level of the lower reach of the canal.

Light boat: A boat carrying no cargo.

Lock: A rectangular watertight chamber enclosable by gates at each end. Some locks lifted and lowered boats between levels of the canal; some connected the canal with the river. Some locks were multi-purpose structures. They were referred to as "grand," "feeder," "river," "inlet," and "outlet" locks in accordance with the uses to which they were being put.

Lock gates: A pair, one gate at each end of each lock. Each gate closed at a blunt angle that pointed toward the higher reach of the canal; this gave the gate strength to resist water pressure. When the ends of the gates met, they formed watertight mitered joints. Gates on the C&O were of wood. Their bases rested against wooden sills in the lock floors, and the sills too formed mitered watertight joints. When open, the gates fit into recesses in the lock walls.

Mole: A mound or massive work of masonry or large stones, often laid in the sea as a breakwater or in a harbor.

Overflow: The lowest spot on each level of the towpath. This allowed water, when it got a bit too high in the canal, to ease back into the river. Boatmen's colloquial term for these little depressions was "mule drinks," because their teams drank from them.

Race plank: A canal boat's approximately 12-inch-wide surround that narrowed as it bordered the cabin and the stable. Used as a walkway for boatmen.

Riprap: A foundation or sustaining wall of stones thrown together without order, as in deep water or on a soft bottom; also the stones so used. Also, to strengthen or support with riprap.

River lock: Passed boats back and forth between canal and river.

Slack water: An area of still water formed on a river above a dam. On the C&O, a dam produced behind it a body of water deep enough to accommodate canal boats, and along such a stretch the canal was discontinued and the boats went out into the river. They entered the slack water through a river lock, and the mules crossed a bridge over the lock to get to its land side. From there they walked alongside the river to tow the boats to the place where the slack water ended and the canal took up again. There they crossed another river lock to regain their customary position on the river side of the canal.

Snubbing post: A post on the towpath, generally at a lock, to which a boat could be tied overnight or long enough to change mule teams. Wrapping a heavy rope around the post helped to steady a boat as it entered a lock so that no damage by bumping would come to boat or masonry. This also helped to stop a boat before it could hit the gate at the far end of the lock.

Stop gate: Built opposite a dam and lowered when the river flooded. This blocked and sidetracked the direct assault of flood water, shunting much of it over to the countryside to disperse itself there.

Stop lock: Also and more aptly called a safety gate. It consisted primarily of two stone abutments, one on each side of the canal. Each abutment had a vertical slot running its full height. Thick wooden planks were dropped into these grooves when it was necessary to stop water from going through the canal. Placed at spots where the canal was especially vulnerable, this structure could separate the waterway into reaches isolated from one another so that, in the event of a break, the gate could be shut and the discharge of water confined.

Swing bridge: Sometimes called pivot bridge. Carried wagons across a lock. When boats went through the lock, this bridge was swung aside. There were swing bridges at Big Pool and Brunswick.

Towpath: Path parallel to the canal, usually on the river side, generally 7 feet wide in the 1900s (12 feet originally) but only 5 in the tunnel. Mules and drivers walked along this dirt path as mules pulled boats by towlines more than 100 feet long.

Wait house: Small frame building alongside the canal at a lock. The locktender kept his records in this "shanty" or "dog house," and sometimes spent nights in it to avoid disturbing the sleep of his family when boats locked through.

Waste weir: Slatted gate on the bank of each major level, with a primary function of removal from the canal of excess water that surged when locks were being emptied for the winter of inactivity or when repair work made drainage necessary.

Wide water: Basin that could be used as a turnaround for boats. The wide water 12 miles from Washington is a spot where an old channel of the river was incorporated into the canal as it was built, thus saving about four miles of blasting and digging of canal trunk. This particular wide water is around 500 feet wide and 40 deep.

Glossary

Works Consulted

Andrews, Matthew Page. *History of Maryland: Province and State.* Hatboro, Pa.: Tradition Press, 1965.

Bacon-Foster, Mrs. Corra. *Early Chapters in the Development of the Potomac Route to the West.* Washington, D.C.: Columbia Historical Society, 1912.

Baird, W. David. "Violence along the Chesapeake and Ohio Canal: 1839." *Maryland Historical Magazine* 66 (Summer 1971): 121–34.

Chesapeake and Ohio Canal Company. *Rules Adopted by the President and Directors of the Chesapeake and Ohio Canal Company for the Government of the Corps of Engineers. Together with a Distribution of the First Division of the Canal into Residencies, with the Engineers Allotted to Each. Also a List of Premiums, for Diligence and Fidelity.* Washington, D.C.: Gales & Seaton, 1828.

Chesapeake and Ohio Canal Company. *Twenty-First Annual Report of the President and Directors of the Chesapeake and Ohio Canal Company to the Stockholders.* Washington, D.C., 4 June 1849.

Chesapeake and Ohio Canal Company. *Twenty-Second Annual Report of the President and Directors of the Chesapeake and Ohio Canal Company to the Stockholders. Washington, D.C., 3 June 1850.*

Chesapeake and Ohio Canal Company. Twenty-Fifth Annual Report of the President and Directors of the Chesapeake and Ohio Canal Company to the Stockholders. Washington, D.C., 6 June 1853.

Coale, James M. *Report to the Stockholders on the Completion of the Chesapeake and Ohio Canal to Cumberland. With a Sketch of the Potomac Company and a General Outline of the History of the Canal Company from its Origin to February 1851.* Frederick, Md.: D. Schley and T. Haller, 1851.

Coit, Margaret L. *John C. Calhoun: An American Portrait.* Boston: Houghton Mifflin Company, 1950.

Cruger, Alfred. *Report of Alfred Cruger, Resident Engineer of the Chesapeake and Ohio Canal, on Certain Inquiries Submitted by the Representative of the Stockowners by the States of Maryland and Virginia, to the President and Directors of the Chesapeake and Ohio Canal*

Company, and by Them Referred to the Resident Engineer. Washington, D.C., 15 June 1832.

Dick, Oliver Lawson, ed. *Aubrey's Brief Lives.* Ann Arbor: University of Michigan Press, 1957.

Douglas, Henry Kyd. *I Rode with Stonewall: The War Experiences of the Youngest Member of Jackson's Staff.* 1889. Reprint. Chapel Hill: University of North Carolina Press, 1940.

Douglas, Paul H., and Jones, William K. "Sandstone, Canals, and the Smithsonian." *The Smithsonian Journal of History.* 3 (Spring 1968): 41–58.

Faulkner, Harold Underwood. *American Economic History.* 6th ed. New York: Harper & Brothers, 1949.

Flexner, James Thomas. *Washington: The Indispensable Man.* Boston and Toronto: Little, Brown and Company, 1969.

Gelb, Arthur and Barbara. *O'Neill.* London: Jonathan Cape, 1962.

Giedion, Sigfried. *Space, Time, and Architecture: The Growth of a New Tradition.* 5th ed., rev. and enlarged. Cambridge, Mass.: Harvard University Press, 1970.

Graham, Frank Jr. *Potomac: The Nation's River.* Philadelphia and New York: J.B. Lippincott, 1976.

Gutheim, Frederick A. *The Potomac.* New York: Rinehart & Company, Inc., 1949.

Hadas, Moses, and the editors of Time-Life books. *Imperial Rome.* Great Ages of Man: A History of the World's Culture. New York: Time, Inc., 1965.

Hadfield, Charles. *The Canal Age.* New York: Frederick A. Praeger, 1969.

Harwood, Herbert H., Jr. *Impossible Challenge: The Baltimore & Ohio Railroad in Maryland.* Baltimore: Barnard, Roberts and Company, Inc., 1979.

Hellman, Geoffrey T. *The Smithsonian: Octopus on the Mall.* New York: J.B. Lippincott & Company, 1966.

Hicks, John D. *A Short History of American Democracy.* Boston: Houghton Mifflin Company, 1943.

Janson, H.W. *History of Art: A Survey of the Major Visual Arts from the Dawn of History to the Present Day.* New York: Harry N. Abrams, Inc, 1977.

MacKendrick, Paul. *The Mute Stones Speak: The Story of Archaeology in Italy.* New York: St. Martin's Press, 1960.

Manakee, Harold R. *Maryland in the Civil War.* Baltimore: Maryland Historical Society, 1961.

O'Connor, Richard. *The Golden Summers.* New York: G.B. Putnam's Sons, 1974.

Philbrick, Francis S. *The Rise of the West 1754–1830.* New York: Harper & Row, 1965.

Pratt, Fletcher. *A Short History of the Civil War.* 1935. Reprint. New York: Pocket Books, 1948.

Radoff, Morris, ed. *The Old Line State: A History of Maryland.* Annapolis: Hall of Records Commission, 1971.

Sanderlin, Walter S. *The Great National Project: A History of the Chesapeake and Ohio Canal.* Baltimore: The Johns Hopkins Press, 1946.

Stewart, George R. *U.S. 40: Cross Section of the United States of America.* Boston: Houghton Mifflin Company, 1953.

Swift, William H., and Hale, Nathan. *Report on the Present State of the Chesapeake & Ohio Canal: Estimated Cost of Completion to Cumberland.* Boston, 1846.

Tebbel, John. *George Washington's America.* New York: E.P. Dutton and Company, Inc., 1954.

U.S. Bureau of Labor Statistics. *Union Wages and Hours in the Building Trades.* Washington, D.C.: 1981.
(Data are for 1980.)

Valentry, Duane. "The Worst of Halley's Comet." *Modern Maturity* 25 (April–May 1982): 69–71.

Walsh, Richard, and Fox, William Lloyd, eds. *Maryland: A History 1632–1974.* Baltimore: Maryland Historical Society, 1974.

Ward, George Washington. *Early Development of the Chesapeake and Ohio Canal Project.* Series 17, Johns Hopkins University Studies in Historical and Political Science. Vols. 9–11. Baltimore: Johns Hopkins Press, 1899.

Williams, Thomas J.C. *A History of Washington County, Maryland.* Hagerstown, Md., 1906. Reprint. Baltimore: Baltimore Regional Publishing Company, 1968.

Index

Mountain View Cemetery, 149
mules
　　use and abuse of, 25, 26, 38, 85–
　　　86, 135–36, 151–53, 168, 173–
　　　76, 200–01, 213–14, 252–53
muleskinner, 171n, 260
Myers, Catherine, 165
Myers, Charles G., 165
Myers, Christopher, 10
Myers, Columbus, 166
Myers, Commodore, 166
Myers, Emma, 165
Myers, Captain Frank, 187n, 188n,
　　209
Myers, Jacob, 156, 156n, 165–69,
　　177
Myers, Molly Shives, 165

N

narrows, 161
National Capital Parks System, 122
National Park Service, 58, 79, 122
National Road, 13, 14, 16n, 19
Navigation Acts, 6
Nelson Quarry, 76
Nemacolin, 16n
Netherlands, 6
New York (N.Y.), 42
Nicholson, George, 177, 183, 184,
　　185, 186, 209, 209n, 210, 211,
　　228–29, 237, 238, 239, 255, 256
Nimrod, 32
Nugent, Will, 236
Null, Jimmy, 259

O

O'Brian, Pat, 132
Occoquan (Va.), 221
Octagon soap, 191
Ohio Company, 8, 13, 16n
Ohio, 63
Ohio, 19
Ohio River, 18, 20, 61n
Ohio territory, 8, 13
Old Town (Md.), 72, 140, 218
Old Zack, 85
O'Neill, Eugene, Jr., 60n
Orleans (Md.), 49, 140, 171
O'Roucke, James, 227
overflow, **271**
overjets, 222

P

Paw Paw (Va.–W. Va.), 47, 250
Paw Paw Tunnel, 53–58, 129, 130,
　　135, 168
Payne's Falls, 10
Pearre, 140
Pennsylvania, 16n, 18, 19, 114
Pennsylvania Canal, 19
Pennyfield, Charlie, 233
Pennyfield, George P., 233
Pennyfield's Lock, 70, 142, 236
Peter, Bob, 234
Peter, Ed, 234
Philadelphia, 14
Pioneer, 32
Pittsburgh, 61n, 187
portland cement, 83n
Point of Rocks, 21, 36, 37, 37n, 38,
　　39, 40, 52, 86, 142, 179
pollution, 219
Potomac Acqueduct, 53, 257
Potomac Company, 5, 9, 10, 14, 18,
　　36, 37, 89
Potomac Edison Company, 211
Potomac Power and Light Compa-
　　ny, 211
Potomac River, 5, 7, 15, 52, 53
Potomac Valley, 31, 36, 41, 75, 90,
　　112
Powell's Bend, 205
Prather's Neck, 73
Prescott, Nippy, 234
Price, William, 62–63, 82n
prohibition, 40–41
Pryor, Frank, 247
Pryor, Genevieve, 247, 250, 256,
　　257
Pryor (Mary Ensminger), Mrs. Har-
　　ry, 255
Pryor, Captain Harry, 247, 248,
　　249, 256–57
Pryor, Hazel, 247, 250
Pullman Palace Car Company, 116
Purcell, Thomas F., 22n, 43, 72

R

race plank, **271**
rates, freight and toll, 87, 92, 105,
　　106, 108, 118
Reconstruction Finance Corpora-
　　tion, 121

Red Stone Creek, 13
Reddens Hill, 227
Reeves, Harry, 227
Reeves, Tom, 235, 236, 236n
Reindeer, 85
Renner, Alice (Mrs. Jake), 117
Renner, Charlie, 150
Renner, Ed, 150
Renner, Jacob, 150, 154, 170
Renner, Walter, 117
Riley, John C., 69, 226, 227, 229,
　　230, 231, 232, 235, 242, 246
Riley, Mrs. John C., 230, 231, 242
Riley, Katie, 230–31, 242
Riley, Raymond, 226–241
Riley, William, 227
Riley's Lock, 69, 70, 142, 226, 231
riots, 44–51
riprap, **271**
river lock, **271**
River Road, 132, 227, 231, 245
rivvels, 215–14
Roberts, Nathan S., 21, 22, 23
Robertson, Captain, 49
Roby Cemetery, 44
Rock Creek, 66, 142, 148, 155, 165,
　　237
Rockefeller, John D. Jr., 107
Rockefeller, John D. Sr., 107
Rough and Ready, 85
Rosslyn (Va.), 53
Route 40, 15n, 16n
Richards, Henry, 32, 35
Round Top Cement Mill, 158
Rumsey, James, 9, 10

S

Safford, Mrs. 194
Sager, Ran, 227
Sanderlin, Walter, 48
Sandy Hook (Md.), 37n, 141
Second Island, 238, 240n
Seneca, 236
Seneca (Md.), 10, 31, 35, 36, 69, 84,
　　122, 124, 142, 157, 180, 181
Seneca Creek, 226
Seneca Creek Acqueduct, 69, 70, 75,
　　161, 231, 231n
Seneca Falls, 10, 68
Seneca Quarry, 226
Seneca sandstone, 70, 82n

283

Y

Z

About the Author

Elizabeth Larisey Kytle was born in Charleston, South Carolina, and lived there until she was 12, when she and her parents moved to Valdosta, Georgia. A graduate of the Valdosta State Womans College (now Valdosta State College), she later lived in Atlanta, then Columbus, Ohio, and Washington, D.C. Since 1969 she and her husband, Calvin, have lived in Cabin John, Maryland, within easy walking distance of the C&O Canal. Her previous works include *Willie Mae,* a first-person biography of a Georgia black woman born around the turn of the century, and *Four Cats Make One Pride,* for which she also took the photographs.

Also available in the Series:

Library of Congress Cataloging-in-Publication Data

Kytle, Elizabeth.
  Home on the canal / Elizabeth Kytle.
      p.   cm.—(Maryland paperback bookshelf.)
  Originally published : Cabin John, Md. : Seven Locks Press, c1983.
  Includes bibliographical references.
  ISBN 0-8018-5328-1 (pbk.)
    1. Chesapeake and Ohio Canal (Md. and Washington, D.C.)—History.
I. Title. II. Series.
HE396.C5K95   1996
386'.48'09752—dc20   95-33629